Charleston to Phnom Penh

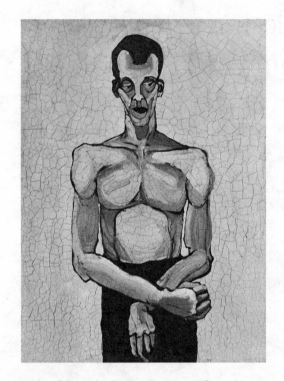

Portrait of the author by Margaret Katz; Athens, GA, 1977.

Charleston to Phnom Penh

A COOK'S JOURNAL

John Martin Taylor

THE UNIVERSITY OF
SOUTH CAROLINA PRESS

© 2022 by John Martin Taylor. All rights reserved.

Published by the University of South Carolina Press
Columbia, South Carolina 29208

www.uscpress.com

Manufactured in the United States of America

31 30 29 28 27 26 25 24 23 22
10 9 8 7 6 5 4 3 2 1

Library of Congress Cataloging-in-Publication Data
can be found at http://catalog.loc.gov/.

ISBN: 978-1-64336-350-9 (hardcover)
ISBN: 978-1-64336-351-6 (ebook)

The words "Hoppin' John's" and the portrayal of a chef
carrying a tray of books are the trademark of John Martin
Taylor. It is registered in the U.S. Patent and Trademark Office.

Frontispiece by Margaret Katz, courtesy of the author.
All illustrations by the author unless otherwise noted.

The author's royalties from this book will go into a trust
that will fund immersive foreign language study for
high school students.

This book is dedicated to the memory of these women:
Mama, Grandma, Mary Jervey, Addie Stewart, Una Belle Hoover, Sudie Bonnet, Mary Fanning, Keith Claussen, Brigitte Arndt, Alice Marks, Ruby Cornwell, Mary Ann Hodgson, Margaret Katz, Adele Maddry, Jane Grigson, Karen Hess, Madeleine Kamman, Libby Huger, Daphne Derven, Lucille Grant, and Dixie Lane.

Contents

Foreword

You are about to make a friend.

Meet John Martin Taylor, also known as Hoppin' John, also known as Bubba to a very select few among whom I number myself. In these pages he invites you to sit with him for a while. If you do, I can guarantee that he will dazzle you with his erudition, astonish you with knowledge garnered in his travels, and delight you with his sense of humor that will have you at times laughing out loud.

This book, a collection of essays, articles, snippets from books published and unpublished, recipes, musings, and more, is the work of a lifetime. In its pages you will meet Taylor's family and friends and the people who have influenced him: from his grandmother to food historian Karen Hess. You will discover the real origin of Charleston, SC, Huguenot tourte and unravel the food history of the field pea and rice dish that gave the author his sobriquet. You will do all of this, and you will also travel. . . . Oh how you'll travel!

Taylor has lived an astonishingly peripatetic life. He moved from Baton Rouge, the place of his birth; to South Carolina, that would claim him; and beyond to New York, Paris, and Genoa, to name but a few of the spots; before returning to Charleston, where he roosted for thirteen years and established a legendary culinary bookshop that catered to chefs in search of inspiration, fledgling food scholars, and anyone interested in going a bit deeper into the world of food.

He later added a cooking school and became one of the country's first purveyors of stone ground grits; one of the founding saints of the fresh, regional, and local movement; and a voice to be reckoned with in a world of southern food. Following his marriage to Mikel, he's taken off on another series of world adventures, living in Washington, DC; Eastern Europe; and most recently Asia, currently Cambodia.

Somewhere along the line, we met. I no longer remember the year or the circumstances, just that we rapidly became friends and coconspirators. We're both fiercely opinionated and thank goodness agree on the difficult questions that most matter. We've had enough adventures together to provide a companion piece to this volume; however, most of those are mercifully unrecounted. The tales that are told are an exuberant love letter to a life well-lived: a life that is savored daily—one seasoned with thought, simmered with humor, and served up with JOY. That's your new friend and my Bubba.

Jessica B. Harris, PhD

Introduction

My story begins twenty-five years before I moved to Charleston. I was born in Baton Rouge, Louisiana, where my parents, at barely thirty years old, were exploring their own passions of sports cars, food and wine, the arts, and the sciences. They were both scientists by training, and they were forever curious about the world. We moved to Orangeburg, South Carolina, when I was three, where we were among the first people "from off" to arrive. We must have been quite a sight with our cherry red Austin Healey sports car and our MG-TD roadster, my parents' wine collection, and the telephone pole in the yard holding my father's radio antenna. Daddy had a preternatural technological aptitude. He built a crystal radio from scratch as a child and went on to be an amateur radio operator ("ham") for most of his life. We were awakened early on many mornings to the clicking of Morse code and his scratchy verbal exchanges with fellow hams around the world. K4CUH—"Carolina's Ugliest Ham"—were his call letters. To many in town, he was known as Tom the Bomb—a nickname acquired when folks found out that he had worked on the Manhattan Project.

Mama was his intellectual match. She liked to think of herself as among the first of the animal behaviorists, but she chose to raise children and be a housewife instead. She was a unique cook whose personal book of recipes from the forties and early fifties is filled with international dishes unheard of in Orangeburg at the time. She was known by many as the best white cook in town.

Early on, I became visually oriented, possibly because Daddy was an avid photographer. His 8mm movies and color slides documented our holidays and travels as well as his interests: sports car races, fishing with Grandpa, the square trees and golden frogs in Panama, the flowers at Grandma's at Easter. My parents subscribed to dozens of magazines. I was riveted by the photographs in Life and *National Geographic*, fantasizing about travel, living abroad, and the photos I would take. To this day, my memory serves me best when the place or event was photographed. I was not much of an early reader, but I was always doodling and sketching houses. I thought that I would perhaps become an architect.

My parents' vision was worldly. They were both interested in "the big picture" more than the specifics—though they believed that if a job was worth doing, it was worth doing right, down to the finest detail. My father told me that he wasn't interested in science, per se, but in its implications and applications. Mama had studied zoology and often told me that science was more about the questions than the answers, that life was by nature forever changing. Daddy assembled intricate electronic components and did all the work on his cars and, later, his boats. My mother cooked elaborate meals, often venturing beyond the southern culinary borders within which she had been brought up. They both read voraciously. Daddy built the first stereo in town. Julie London shared the turntable with Les Sylphides. We were all encouraged to follow our bliss.

We lived not five hundred yards from the dark and sinuous Edisto River, the longest blackwater river in the world, where I swam with reckless abandon, ignoring the alligators and water moccasins. I knew what now seems like limitless freedom as a child. Our house rules were basically these: *Play outdoors. Don't slam the screen door.* (Later, when we got air conditioning, *Close the door—and don't slam the screen door.*) *Be home—on time—for supper.* If it was raining, we could come indoors, but we were never allowed to say we were bored: there were plenty of books and magazines to read, cards and board games to play, and music to listen to (or to play: there were musical instruments as well).

Supper was not extravagant, but it was exceptional: meat or seafood, vegetables, a salad, and a dessert, every night, homemade by Mama. There were no soft drinks except the occasional leftover from bridge club—or a ginger ale when we were sick. As we got older, we were allowed a taste of their wines. By the time I went away to college, I was familiar with not only the Lowcountry cooking of Carolina, but the Appalachian cooking of my paternal grandmother, the southern cooking of my maternal grandmother who lived in the western Tennessee River Valley, the Cajun and Creole cooking my mother had learned in Louisiana, and many international dishes that Mama had mastered in her determination to constantly expand her repertoire.

I was also deeply familiar with the Lowcountry itself. Though we were from off, we had all become real Sandlappers, as residents of the area are

My parents on
Daufuskie Island,
1964. Photo by
Page P. Robinson, Jr.

called. By the time my sisters went off to school, we were spending our
free time on our sailboat moored off Hilton Head. I shrimped, I crabbed,
I hunted marsh hens, I came to love rice with every meal, I beachcombed,
I birdwatched, and I danced.

Mother would peruse her *New Yorker* and *New York Times*, then go see
the new plays in the Big Apple with her bridge partners in the fall. When
we traveled as a family, we would visit the natural wonders of the world
such as Meteor Crater and the Grand Canyon as well as manmade marvels
such as the Empire State Building, the Seattle Space Needle, the Panama
Canal, and absurdly commercial establishments like the Las Vegas Strip
and Disneyland. By the time I was a teenager, I had eaten in the finest
restaurants of New York, New Orleans, and San Francisco. I think we visited every museum up and down the east coast, from Maine to Miami. On
one visit, I fell in love with painting and have pursued it as a hobby for fifty
years.

It's no wonder I was uninspired for much of my undergraduate life. Once
I picked up a camera, however, I was motivated. For the next fifteen years,

"Hide," 1976, mixed media. Photo by Robert Reeves, from his collection.

I was rarely without one. In 1974, I took a break from pursuing a master's in film and moved to Charleston. I had a degree in journalism, with a minor in French. The Recession was in full swing. I had a thankless job, though I managed to revel in my drawing, painting, and photography. In 1976, I quit the job and swore to myself that I would never again work where I had to wear a tie. I returned to grad school to finish my film degree.

In 1982, my mother died, and I inherited hundreds of cookbooks from her. I had helped my father care for her in her final months as she slipped away by river's edge in the Lowcountry, where I spent days on end reading through her library. I returned to Europe, where I had been living. The following year, in Paris, I applied for the job as Art Director of a hip new magazine. Jean-Sébastien Stehli, the editor, somehow picked up on my newfound culinary knowledge and hired me instead as the Food Editor. My life changed overnight. Painting and photography were thenceforth relegated to hobby and occasional freelance jobs.

We opened the New York offices of our stylish French-language magazine about the city in 1984. That year the University of South Carolina Press

In 1979, I freelanced in the Caribbean. This sketch in one of my journals shows the view from my apartment in Charlotte Amalie. Now part of the Special Collections of the College of Charleston.

released *The Virginia House-Wife by Mary Randolph: A facsimile of the first edition, 1824, along with additional material from the editions of 1825 and 1828, thus presenting a complete text, with Historical Notes and Commentaries by Karen Hess*. Jean-Sébastien and I interviewed Karen on the history of Thanksgiving for our November issue. Nowhere in the vast collection of cookery titles that I had inherited had I seen any sign of true scholarship, of original research, or even of the personal knowledge, gained through experience, that Karen's work exuded. Our conversation went on long past the sixty-minute cassette tape I had with me, wandering back and forth between French and English, touching on linguistics, horticulture, animal husbandry, the Middle Ages, European court life, and American politics. Food, through Karen's words, came alive in ways I had never considered.

Coincidentally, while visiting friends in Newport, Rhode Island, just prior to meeting Karen, I had quite literally stumbled upon a collection of recipes from some Lowcountry plantations that had once stood not an hour from where I had grown up. Someone had cleared out an old home and simply tossed its contents onto the street. Charlestonians have a long history of vacationing in Newport, so I was not surprised by the handmade book's presence there, but what amazed me was that I could barely recognize many, if not most, of the recipes. Dating the book was easy, because there were photos of the plantations from the early part of the twentieth century; further, I knew that most of those old houses had been flooded in the 1930s after a huge hydroelectric project was built. The unidentified author wrote in the Foreword, "An Epicure sighingly remarked that one of the serious calamities brought about by the surrender at Appomattox was the disappearance of Southern Cookery. Surely this is an exaggeration, but lest it should come true, shall we not endeavor to preserve the recipes which would otherwise soon be but a memory?"

I brought a photocopy of the book for Karen, and as she thumbed through it, dating many of the recipes to the Victorian era, she expounded on the provenance of ingredients and techniques the way an art historian might talk about contrapposto, chiaroscuro, or the arch, or how my history teachers would go on about battles and court cases won. Only this time, the history lessons came alive for me, reaffirming my belief in an inter-disciplinary approach to learning that I had fought for, unsuccessfully, in graduate school.

At that point, I had not read Karen's other work, but I had already decided, after a year in New York, to return to South Carolina and to open a culinary bookstore. Karen encouraged me to research the foodways of the Lowcountry. For the next twenty-three years, she and I worked in tandem on our historical research, calling each other with exciting finds, challenging each other's hypotheses, and bemoaning some dead-end we had encountered in our studies. I had, like Karen, cooked for my board in college. Neither of us had formal training in either history or cooking, but just before I had left for Europe, I convinced Thom Tillman, a demanding chef, to teach me all he could in nine months in exchange for my labor, rolling puff pastry dough, making *pâtes à génoise*, and washing dishes.

When I began my research, the field was new to me and most of the territory was uncharted. Karen had all but defined what the field could be, though there were no degrees being given, few books on the subject were being published, and there were no search engines available at our disposal. Most of my free time was spent poring over the fragile pages of manuscripts in the collections of the South Carolina Historical Society, the Charleston Museum, and the Caroliniana Collection of the University of South Carolina. There were some papers from illustrious Carolinians, such as Henry Laurens, that had been published by the University of

South Carolina Press, but even when they were filled with poignant culinary finds, such as his planting of eggplant twenty years before Jefferson mentioned them (Jefferson had, up until that point, been widely credited with single-handedly bringing them—and many other plants—to America), eggplant was not included in the indices because the serious study of food had not yet garnered the respect of academia.

As I trudged through the literature, such as it was, what I found was a dead cuisine. In Charleston in 1986, when I opened Hoppin' John's, my culinary bookstore, there was a handful of restaurants, the best of them French. A couple of places served "soul food" (their own moniker, not mine) and a couple of places served pasty versions of she-crab soup. But it was mostly a culinary wasteland, and almost nothing that was being served in restaurants resembled either the food of my youth or the glorious antebellum cuisine that was coming to life before my eyes. I couldn't find stone-ground, whole-grain grits anywhere. "Shrimp and grits" were on no menus anywhere that I knew of, except at Bill Neal's Crook's Corner in Chapel Hill, *North* Carolina. But even Bill's history was flawed, I knew. Like everyone before him, he quoted other food writers, few of whom knew historical methodology, or, if they were historians, it was all too apparent that they weren't cooks. Bill was the anomaly among them: a born-and-bred southerner who grew up eating fresh and local foods, but who had gone on to master classic cooking skills and techniques before beginning his crusade to revive traditional southern cooking. We became fast friends.

By 1992, when Karen and I both published books on the Lowcountry kitchen, I was entrenched as a culinary historian with a popular voice—the southern voice of a southern cook. In fact, it was in Europe that I had really learned to cook, shopping for each meal before planning. In Paris I would go to one merchant for cheese and another for cream. In Genoa, I shopped with an obstreperous peasant who resented coming into to town to sell her eggs, but I bought my chickens from one of her neighbors. I bought prosciutto from the handsome young man in the fanciest storefront in the tiny alleyway near my apartment in the *centro storico*—the old historic center of town—but I bought the remarkably delicate *salame di Sant-Olcese* from the back of an *ape*, the three-wheeled truck that came down from the *entroterra*, the inland reaches of Liguria high above the city, whose greens and herbs define so much of the local cooking there. Olive oil was replacing the butter that I used in the classical French cooking I had learned; that butter had previously replaced the bacon grease so revered in the South.

For years my battle cry in the kitchen has been fresh, local, and traditional, whether I am frying fish in South Carolina, pounding pesto in Liguria, or making spring rolls in Asia. I kept my culinary bookstore in Charleston for thirteen years. I added a cooking school in 1997 and invited local chefs in to share their knowledge as well. I championed stone-ground, whole, heirloom grains and convinced many chefs both in Charleston and around the country to offer grits dishes. I encouraged restaurateurs to seek out local purveyors. I convinced Lowcountry chefs to use local seafood and to keep the shrimp heads and crab shells to make stock. I have helped usher even humble dishes such as hoppin' john onto the menus of some of the gastronomic temples of the South. In the three decades since Hurricane Hugo in 1989, Charleston has seen an unabated culinary renaissance.

It is a different world now. Bourbon and barbecue may be king throughout the land, but Chinese spices season New England stews, upscale Greek and Lebanese restaurants are as popular as French bistros, and home cooks are following celebrity chefs as they traverse the globe, discovering new tastes. I, too, have changed. I began writing fiction and personal essays in 1998. The following year, I closed my shop, and my partner and I bought a house and got a dog, whom I sketched any time he would sit still. In 2004, we moved to Washington, DC, where I wrote food and travel articles for *The Washington Post,* as well as a controversial editorial, included herein. I started a blog in 2007. In 2010, I married Mikel—at the time we had been together for seventeen years. His work with the Peace Corps has taken us

Pantaloon
sleeping, 2004.

to Bulgaria, China, and, now, to Cambodia. I wrote four cookbooks while I had my shop, but for over thirty years I have been writing about all sorts of subjects, from rock and roll and film to civil rights and Transylvania. I have spoken at universities, museums, and symposia throughout the country on a wide range of subjects, including antiques and the creative process, as well as the culinary history of the South.

Before our most recent move overseas, I donated my culinary library to the state-of-the-art International Culinary Institute of Myrtle Beach and my "papers" to the College of Charleston Special Collections. There are handmade postcards from dozens of artist friends from around the globe. There are sketchbooks and photographs, and unpublished poems, short stories, and novels. There are notes taken while I researched the foodways of the Lowcountry. There are printed cheat sheets I used for my lectures. There are books given to me by their authors, and there are hard copies of many newspaper and magazine articles.

But they don't tell the whole story. Much of what I have written is simply gone. I did not own a desktop computer until I was halfway through my first book. Years of correspondence with Karen Hess were lost in one of my many moves. Not that those old, faded faxes would still be legible. And Hurricane Hugo took nearly everything I owned at the time. That's when I started over and bought my first computer. There have been at least a half-dozen computers since then. Articles on floppy disks. Interviews on clunky old VHS recordings and cassette tapes. Several different word processing programs. It's a wonder I had anything to offer the College.

I am often asked if losing so many of my possessions, including my visual artwork, was heartbreaking. It wasn't. I actually found it cathartic. It's probably a good thing that I was making my living in a different medium. And in the end, it's all just stuff. I'm sorry to have lost the daguerreotype of my great-grandfather, but I have no memory of him anyway. And, as Mama always said, life's not fair. And things happen for a reason. The hurricane kept me out of my home and business for a year, but that gave me time to fine-tune my first book, which is still in print, thirty years later.

My family and the South appear prominently in this collection of essays that includes scholarly articles, personal musings, travel pieces, and that *Washington Post* editorial. There are several recipes that have served me well over the years, though I wouldn't call this a cookbook. Nor is it a book about the South. This thirty-five-year anthology of my writing is presented chronologically to best illustrate the evolution of my peripatetic life and career, which have been joyous. The stories begin shortly after I opened Hoppin' John's in Charleston. There are datelines on the articles, but they often look back, sometimes decades, into the past. Because they were written at different times for different audiences, there are some repeated details. While I have chosen the ones that I think best tell my story, you needn't read them in any particular order.

John Martin Taylor
PHNOM PENH, 2022

The So-Called Huguenot Torte of Charleston

I first wrote about this dessert in William van Hettinga's irreverent Charleston monthly, Poor William's Omnibus. I was just beginning to make a name for myself as a culinary historian, and my sleuthing brought me both fame and disdain. Some Charlestonians, particularly the blue-haired ladies who had been serving the dish at the tea rooms that they ran during the spring and fall house tours, were furious that I would discredit its heritage. John Egerton, the illustrious journalist who wrote about the Civil Rights Movement and southern food, history, and culture, featured my finds in his nationally syndicated column. Book offers poured in for me from New York, but I was persona non grata to some in Charleston.

Charleston's most famous dessert is its poorly named "Huguenot Torte," an apple and nut cake which first appeared in print in *Charleston Receipts* (1950), and which by its author's admission was adapted from an Ozark Pudding recipe from the Mississippi River Delta. Evelyn Florance, who submitted the recipe for inclusion in the Junior League's cookbook (which has sold over 500,000 copies), used to make the dessert for the Huguenot Tavern in the heart of old Charleston in the 1940s. It was one of the last public dining places where you could eat Lowcountry food. I interviewed Mary Huguenin, one of the book's editors, and she put me in touch with Mrs. Florance, who was listed in the cookbook as Mrs. Cornelius Huguenin (Evelyn Anderson). She had since remarried and was living in an assisted living home.

The old recipe is neither a torte nor French. Leavened with 5 (five!) teaspoons of baking powder, it is a twentieth century conceit with no French antecedent. Pecans or walnuts are specified. I prefer a combination of two or even three nuts, because pecans weren't generally planted in the Carolina Lowcountry until the twentieth century, when the rice plantations finally folded, and black walnuts, the South's other native nut, are too unctuous, overpowering, and expensive by themselves—however delicious.

In my version, the baking powder, the salt, and the vanilla have been eliminated from the original recipe. All of the favorable and most familiar characteristics of this "modern classic" have been retained—that is, the lightness of a sponge playing off the richness of apples and nuts, the crunchy exterior, and the presentation with whipped cream. Researching the culinary history of the Lowcountry, I sometimes turn to professional cooks to help me develop recipes. My dear friend Joann Yaeger, quite simply the best cook I've ever known, was the chef/owner with her then-husband, Mickey, of Café Piccolo and The Primerose (pronounced "primrose") House. We worked on this torte until we had it right. It never ceases to please my guests. With no butter and the brilliant combination of nuts and apples, it's a year-round favorite that delights even those like me who don't have a particularly sweet tooth. Most folks are intrigued by the "gamey" flavor of black walnuts, so do include some in your nut mix.

Ozark pudding, the real antecedent of this dish, is one of those regional specialties that has gone the way of the Lowcountry's cooter pie and rice bread. It rarely appears in Arkansas cookbooks, though it seems to have originated in northwest Arkansas and southwest Missouri, according to John Egerton. The oldest recipe we have found is Mrs. S. R. Dull's "apple pudding" in her 1928 *Southern Cooking*. Ozark pudding was purportedly a favorite dish of President Truman. It was served to Winston Churchill when he visited the Trumans in Fulton, Missouri, and made his famous "Iron Curtain" speech.

Clementine Paddleford, hailing Mrs. Florance's Huguenot Torte in *The New York Herald Tribune* in the 1950s, might have recognized it as a dish fit for a president, but she did not know any more than we do about the reclusive inhabitants of the Ozarks. Recipes for the two dishes are identical. Mine is a real torte, though I suppose I should call it Huguenot Pudding after its two ancestors.

Apple Nut Torte

½ cup all-purpose flour plus flour for dusting the pan

1 cup pecans or a mix of pecans, walnuts, and black walnuts (see below), plus 8 perfect pecan halves

1 large, firm apple, peeled, cored, and cut up

3 eggs, at room temperature

⅞ cup sugar, plus 1 tablespoon more for the pecans

½ cup heavy cream

Bourbon or aged rum

Lightly grease a 9-inch round springform pan and lightly dust with flour.

Preheat the oven to 375°F and put a pan of water in the bottom of the oven. The water will help create the crusty top that is a defining characteristic of the pudding.

Finely grind the cup of nuts in a food processor, working in quick bursts so as not to render them oily. Remove the nuts from the work bowl and add the apple pieces. Chop by pulsing quickly until the apple is uniformly, finely chopped.

Warm the bowl of an electric mixer. This is an important step because the warmer the bowl, the more easily the eggs will increase in volume. I place a stainless steel mixer bowl in the sink, place the eggs in their shell in the bowl, and fill the bowl with hot tap water. When I'm ready to beat the eggs, I dry off the eggs and the bowl, and I also keep a small torch (otherwise used for caramelizing sugar, such as on *crème brulée*) handy to heat the bowl as it spins around.

Separate the yolk from one of the eggs and set the white aside. Break two of the eggs into the mixer bowl, add the yolk, and beat them on high speed until doubled in volume. It may take as long as 10 minutes if your mixer is an old hand-me-down like mine. Slowly add the ⅞ cup sugar and continue beating until tripled in volume. The eggs should be very thick and lightly colored.

Sift the flour over the egg mixture, sprinkle the ground nuts all around, then the apples. Fold the mixture together gently but rapidly, making sure that you get all the ingredients off the bottom of the bowl mixed thoroughly into the mixture. Pour the batter into the pan and bake in the middle of the oven for about 30 minutes, until the top is golden brown, and the sides have begun to pull away from the pan. Don't push on the meringuelike top or it may cave in. Place on a rack in a draft-free place and allow the cake to cool completely.

Lightly toast the perfect pecan halves in a skillet or oven, then, while they are hot, dip them in water then roll them in a tablespoon of sugar until lightly coated. Let them dry on a rack or paper towel. OR you may beat the reserved egg white until foamy throughout, add the cooled pecan halves to the whites and toss until well coated, drain them in a sieve, then roll the nuts one at a time in the reserved sugar. Let them dry on a rack or paper towel.

When the cake is perfectly cool, undo the clasp on the pan and place the torte on a serving platter. You can leave the torte on the bottom of the pan or remove it in which case you'll need to run a long thin blade such as an icing spreader under the cake to loosen it from the pan.

Whip the cream loosely stiff, adding a bit of bourbon or aged rum, if desired. Place 8 dollops of the cream around the cake. Garnish each dollop with a sugared nut and serve immediately with a shot glass of bourbon or aged rum neat.

Makes 8 servings.

NUT MIX

Mix two pounds of shelled pecans, walnuts, and black walnuts in whatever combination, but with no more than ⅓ pound of the black. My favorite combination is one pound pecans, ⅔ pound walnuts, and ⅓ pound black walnuts. Grind the nuts in small batches in a nut grinder or in the work bowl of a food processor fitted with the metal blade, working in quick bursts, until they are evenly ground. Do not blend them too long or they will become oily.

Ats Jaar Pickles

There is little doubt that when George Washington visited Hampton Plantation north of Charleston in 1791, he would have been served these mustard pickles, which had become popular in the Lowcountry and remained so well into the twentieth century. At the time, Harriott Pinckney Horry and her mother, Eliza Lucas Pinckney, both widowed, were living at Hampton. Washington stopped there for breakfast but stayed on for dinner. It is thought that he was there to honor the courageous roles that Harriott's two brothers had played in the war.

Recipes for *ats jaar* appear in Horry's personal collection of recipes which was published by the University of South Carolina Press in 1984 as *A Colonial Plantation Cookbook: The Receipt Book of Harriott Pinckney Horry, 1770, with historical notes by Richard J. Hooker.* Hooker, who died in 1986, was a historian who was neither a cook nor a linguist or he would have recognized the condiment as the achar/atzjar/achaar of South Asia. A bright ochre mixed pickle, the recipe is one of the world's oldest. I was able to trace its path backwards from South Carolina along the international spice and slave trade routes. The pickle appears in West Africa, whence came the enslaved to the South Carolina rice plantations; South Africa, where the Dutch had imported Malaysians as slaves (the double *a* is linguistic clue); Madagascar, where pickled mangoes were prized; and Java, where each district has its own version.

Throughout the subcontinent and Asia, *achar* is a generic term for both oil and brine pickles. They are served alongside breads as a first course in Indian restaurants even today. In colonial Carolina, these imported pickles were often highly valued for the novelty of their flavor; eventually, they were copied by Carolinians such as the Pinckneys and Horrys. The most popular of these were the mango pickles from Madagascar and India. Recipes for mock pickled mangoes abounded as early as 1699. All sorts of fruits were brined in imitation of that tropical pickle, to the extent that as late as the mid-19th century, Francis Holmes was describing mangoes on a vine (he meant muskmelons) in his marvelous *Southern Gardener and Market Farmer,* published in Charleston in 1842.

Only in the Carolina Lowcountry does the recipe appear in English-language cookbooks of the time. Horry's recipe contains garlic (rare in English cookery of the period), ginger, cabbage, long pepper, vinegar, mixed fruits and vegetables, and turmeric, which is native to Java and gives the pickle its distinctive color. The dish is typical of the traditional Lowcountry kitchen, and it accompanies the area's unique, elaborate rice dishes.

When I was growing up, before the FDA and SCDHEC (the South Carolina Department of Health and Environmental Control) had so many rules, the old Charleston restaurants set their tables with a tray of the bright ochre vegetables, cured in a bath of salt, turmeric, and vinegar, as a matter of course. I make the pickles today according to the ancient formula. All sorts of vegetables may be included in the pickle, including, but not limited to, green beans, asparagus, cauliflower, carrots, cabbage, radishes, and bell peppers. It is served as a condiment alongside complex rice dishes such as Country Captain, a popular dish also from the subcontinent and claimed by every old southern seaport.

Grandma and Grapes

The summer after my grandfather died, when I was twelve, I went to spend some time with my grandmother, who lived six hundred miles from the South Carolina Lowcountry, where we were living at the time. I learned more about food in those few weeks than I would learn in many years to come. It was Grandma's approach to living more than her recipes, however, that so influenced me, and I am forever grateful for that one time alone with a real homemaker and her garden. There was much solace for her in her daily chores, and I, too, learned to enjoy hanging clothes on the line, watching for cracks in the soil around the potato plants, and drying apples in the sun.

We removed all the window screens from her house, scrubbed and hosed them clean, and set them in the sun to dry. We then gathered green summer apples from the trees that bordered the garden, and she showed me how to pare, core, and slice them. We placed the slices on the screens which were stacked on concrete blocks in the sun. Every night we carried them into the garage, away from the dew, then back out into the sun each day until, after about a week, the apple slices were perfectly—and naturally—dried. But the real treat of the summer came when the grapes were ripe.

More species of *Vitis*, the grapevine, grow wild in the United States than in all the rest of the world combined. And second to apples, grapes are our most widely cultivated fruit. At Grandma's, there were both wild muscadines trailing up over the trees beyond her property, and cultivated

Part of this was published in my first book, *Hoppin' John's Lowcountry Cooking* (1992).

American concords, whose flavor is what most Americans think of as "grape," and wine connoisseurs as "foxy." The muscadines, which grow only in the South, are the sweetest of the American native varieties. They grow in bunches, not clusters, on vines which often climb into the highest reaches of hardwood forests.

On the border of the woods beyond my grandmother's garden, vines of wild purple muscadines and tawny scuppernongs—each a variety of native *Vitis rotundifolia*—could be found trailing up into the trees, entwined with reddish catawbas, a variety of *Vitis labrusca*, which probably escaped from 19th century cultivation. We would spread old sheets beneath the vines to catch falling grapes as we pulled vines down through the limbs. We didn't worry that the birds left us but a few grapes, because her concords were trained along the fence and on an arbor.

Making grape preserves that summer with my grandmother remains one of my favorite memories, and I look forward each year to the brief season, which varies from state to state, when I can buy these native American "slip-skin" grapes in farmers' markets and roadside stands. Basic to my grandmother's ideology was "waste not, want not." She would be proud that I know wonderful uses for those vines we would pull down, and for the grape leaves as well.

Early English accounts of the Carolina coast speak of vines so fragrant that they could be smelled from the ocean, days before the boats reached land. Nowadays, agricultural spraying that coincides with the vines' blooming often prevents the fruit from setting. Fortunately, both scuppernongs and muscadines have taken well to cultivation, and are widely available in the Deep South during the season in late August and early September. A delightful sweet muscadine wine is naturally fermented from the grape.

Greeks were among the earliest of the settlers in the Lowcountry, and many culinary traditions thought of as purely southern—such as watermelon rind preserves—have long histories in the Mediterranean, whence they came. Charleston's Greek Orthodox Ladies Philoptochos Society first published its excellent *Popular Greek Recipes* in 1957, including instructions for canning grapevine leaves. Leaves are best gathered in the spring and early summer, when they are large and bright green. The fruits mature in late summer. Then, in the fall, just as the leaves begin to drop, vines can be pulled down—while they are still somewhat green and flexible—and used in wreaths or cut into foot-long twigs for grilling. If there are hunters in your family, have them bring home some vines when they are out in the woods in the fall. The bright yellow and red leaves are unmistakable.

Charleston's English settlers embraced Indian chutneys and Southeast Asian pickling techniques; the French settlers were enamored of nutmeg, cloves, cinnamon, allspice, white pepper and ginger (ingredients in their "*quatre épices*"). Spiced grapes became a typical condiment in the Lowcountry. In India, the seeds of grapes are often ground into chutneys, but the seeds of our native slip-skin varieties are far too bitter for the American palate. If you do not live in the Lowcountry, look for any slip-skin variety available in your area. Concords are delicious as a substitute for scuppernongs in traditional southern recipes, but as they are sweeter than scuppernongs, you may wish to add a bit of lemon peel and juice when using them, and to use less sugar than the recipe calls for.

Boiled Peanuts
and a Sense
of Place

> I never eat boiled peanuts except when they are in season
> (July through September), because they are only good when
> made from freshly dug 'green' peanuts—and the small,
> red-skinned Valencias are the best.
>
> —*Hoppin' John's Lowcountry Cooking*, 1992

When I wrote my first book about the cooking of the South Carolina
coastal plain, I was trying to present as honest a survey of our traditional
foods as I could, without sacrificing the integrity of a single dish or ingredient. At the time, I would no more have eaten a boiled, previously
parched jumbo peanut from Virginia or North Carolina than I would have
eaten local oysters in July or peaches in February.

I was also trying to be as scholarly as possible, with solid historical doc-
umentation of what I was calling "traditional." But peanuts—particularly
boiled—still refuse to give up their roots.

I had always assumed that you could define the South as boiled peanut
territory, but in fact there are many southerners who have never even heard
of them. For those of us who know and love them, boiled peanuts have
probably always been a part of our lives. We do not recall a first tasting, but
the thought of boiled peanuts conjures profound memories of places and
people that we always associate with them. It has been suggested to me that
perhaps the appeal of boiled peanuts isn't really about taste but about those

A version of this was published in *Gastronomica* (Volume 1, Issue 4;
November 2001).

memories, but I don't think that that's true, either. I love them whether I'm eating them salty and warm on a brisk autumn day near the shore, or cold, right out of the refrigerator, as a leftover snack.

I've often said that the South is more emotion than nation—that describing the boundaries of the region is all but impossible. I've been asked to join "southern" organizations that include only the states of the Confederacy, but I know lots of folks from Kentucky, Arkansas, and Oklahoma who consider themselves southern. Few may think of northern Virginia as truly southern, though most West Virginians would be insulted if I called them anything else. Some writers have tried to define the South as where you are automatically served grits with breakfast, but there are pockets throughout the region where corn has never been ground to be used as a hot breakfast cereal. So grits aren't any more universally southern than boiled peanuts. But both of those southern foods do evoke profound memories. Memories like these may simply come as a response to the inevitable questions about boiled peanuts that arise these days at the outdoor events where peanuts are served. Invariably there is now someone who has moved here from elsewhere and who wants to know more about them.

I think of the late fifties, before interstate highways and air conditioning brought the hordes of people "from off" to the South Carolina Lowcountry where I was reared. When I was in the sixth grade, I would go water skiing with the Salleys. Their daughters, Walton, Ding, and Sam (D.D., their father, must have really wanted boys!) taught me how to ski. The family employed a Black cook who would boil up big batches of peanuts and put them in plastic Sunbeam bread loaf wrappers. We'd take them to Lake Murray, and D.D. would pick out a deserted island in the middle of the lake to use as a base for our day-long adventure. We'd take turns skiing until our arms and knees hurt. I remember trying to time our stops so that we'd land by one of the floating bags of peanuts. We'd just drop the rope and slowly sink down into the muddy water. The Salley girls could lean over and pick up a bag from their slaloms. I could barely get within ten feet of them. But no one loved the boiled peanuts more than I, and I always recall those floating bags of the warm, salty snacks whenever I eat them today.

Salley is an old Orangeburg County name. Settled by Germans and Swiss in 1730, the county is still largely populated by descendants of its original settlers, though by the time we moved there, it was seventy percent Black. (Salley, South Carolina, is in nearby Aiken County; it is home of the annual Chit'lin Strut Festival.) We weren't Old Orangeburg; we weren't even South Carolinians. We had moved there when I was three from the bayous of Louisiana, where my father worked in the chemical industry. He and Mother both were from Tennessee: she from the western part of the state—McNairy County, later of *Walking Tall* fame—and he from the hills around Knoxville.

Recently, I asked Daddy when he first remembered tasting boiled peanuts.

"Never heard of them till a trip to South Carolina in 1950. Everybody in Orangeburg ate them! In the Cajun country, everybody ate sausages—*rouge et blanc*—and tried to outdo each other with the intensity of the pepper."

My father and his wife have a summer house in the mountains of North Carolina now, so he's back near his childhood home. But he says he never saw boiled peanuts in the mountains when he first started going back up there about nine or ten years ago. "Now," he says, "all the roadside stands have them! We grew peanuts for our own consumption when I was a lad. Granny would soak them in brine, dry them, and then roast them in the oven. Salted in the shell. Of course, these were not green peanuts."

Green peanuts. That's the real key to understanding them. I used to eat them only in late summer, though these days I'm not as picky. There are many hybrids being grown now that taste pretty good—though I have never had a Virginia peanut (a variety known as "jumbo" in South Carolina) that tasted as good as the small ones—and that are available fresh ("green") from spring through fall. Of course, we never get green Virginias down here; they're always dried. The difference between fresh and dried is the same for all legumes, and a legume is, after all, what a peanut is.

Kathi Purvis, the food editor of the *Charlotte Observer,* says she comes from a family, Georgians all, of "boiled peanut fanatics":

"When I was a small child in eastern North Carolina, people treated my family like we were odd because we boiled our peanuts," she recently confided via email. "Parched and roasted peanuts are much more common in North Carolina and Virginia. I've long maintained (and had to, having spent much of my life in a non-boiled peanut state) that boiling peanuts makes much more sense than roasting them. They are, after all, a legume, and we would certainly never consider not boiling a kidney bean or a Great Northern."

The current trendiness of sushi bars throughout the country might help popularize boiled peanuts. Soybeans boiled in the shell—edamame—are becoming a very popular appetizer. I have a Japanese friend who visited

Charleston, where I live, one summer, and when I offered her boiled peanuts, she took to them immediately, saying, "These taste very much like edamame. We eat them with beer at the baseball games." Which is exactly where a lot of southerners eat them.

John T. Edge, the Director of the Southern Foodways Alliance at the Center for the Study of Southern Culture at the University of Mississippi, admits that they are, "bar none," his favorite snack. He admits to having "fond memories of going to the South Carolina State Farmer's Market in Columbia and buying them there. It always seemed that was the epicenter of boiled peanut culture for my family."

Columbia is about forty miles from Orangeburg. It's real peanut country. But when I went to college in Georgia, half the people I met, it seemed, came from south Georgia, where there are fifteen thousand peanut farmers. But not all southerners, much less Georgians, are fond of boiled peanuts. Some well-known authorities on southern cooking loathe them.

The *Atlanta Journal-Constitution*'s Jim Auchmutey, a native of the big city, "hate[s] them. I have tried to like them. Every year, when we're driving up to the mountains to see some leaves, my wife, Pam, a Savannah native, makes me stop beside a boiling cauldron to buy a bag. She eats a bunch of them—suck, swallow, spit—and then I try one to see if my tastebuds have changed in the past year, the way I suddenly liked cheese when I became a senior in high school. Boiled peanuts haven't happened for me yet. They always taste like those salt pills the coaches told you to take in track to keep from throwing up."

I prefer boiled peanuts that aren't all the same size, so that some of the smaller ones are cooked so soft that you can eat the shell as well as the peanuts. I asked Lucille Grant, one of Charleston's great cooks, whose grandparents were enslaved, if she had always eaten boiled peanuts.

"Oh, yes," she mused. "Boiled peanuts were one of my granddaddy's things. He really prided himself on his peanuts, and he would only grow those little Spanish ones. He'd come from the fields with some dug-up bushes and he'd boil them up and they were always so good! But you can hardly find those little peanuts any more, and they really do taste the best."

Peanuts are grown in nine states, but only about one percent of them are those little Valencias—and most of those are grown in New Mexico, far from boiled peanut territory. Nearly half of the peanuts grown in this country go into peanut butter.

Growing up in Orangeburg, I heard peanuts called ground-nuts, goobers, goober-peas, and pindars, but the dictionaries and usual sources haven't helped much with those words, either. Sir Hans Sloane published a natural history of Jamaica in 1707, in which he described the pindal, or Indian Earth-nut, but the first usage the *OED* cites for "goober" is from 1887. We know that the words "goober" and "pinda," like "okra," "gumbo," and "yam," are of West African origin. Food writers mostly avoid any mention of boiled peanuts, but Jessica Harris, the eminent scholar of the African diaspora, has found boiled peanuts in Ghana, whence the recipe probably made its way to South Carolina, and in Brazil, whence it arrived in Africa. In Ghana the peanuts were simply boiled and eaten as a snack—or with boiled ears of corn on the cob; in Brazil they were served as part of a Candomblé spiritual ceremony.

There are a lot of websites about peanuts, but I'm still at a loss to find much recorded history about boiled ones. Peanuts are still grown primarily in coastal southern states—Virginia, North Carolina, South Carolina, Georgia, Florida, Alabama, and Texas—as well as in Oklahoma and New Mexico. They require a long growing season and are very sensitive to frost. It's no wonder the recipe for boiled green peanuts didn't travel inland—the green peanuts didn't, either. I've found no mention of boiled peanuts in the many eighteenth- and nineteenth-century sources I've relied on for years in my research on the foods of the South, but I'm not surprised. There are also very few written recipes for some of the most basic dishes of the coastal South—especially for those for fish and vegetables. I do think it's telling that peanuts continue to be grown mostly in the coastal areas where West Africans were the majority prior to the Civil War. Nevertheless, culinary experts from New Orleans admit to knowing nothing about them. It's just not a Mississippi Delta thing.

It's apparently not a Virginia thing, either. Robert Waldrop is a Virginia writer whom I've known since our college days in Athens, Georgia. "First off," he told me, "Virginians abhor the thought of boiled peanuts. My mom, from Richmond, never heard of them till my family all started sharing an old beach cottage on Fernandina Beach, Florida, in the 1950s. I asked Shelby and Polly, neighbors of mine, if they had boiled peanuts growing up. All one of them said was a very direct, 'Lord, no, I'm from Richmond!' We got the old beach cottage each summer with my Uncle Hardy, Aunt Babs, and my cousins [who] lived in Blackshear, Georgia. I remember the peanuts getting boiled being a big occasion all by itself with the same mystique as crabs and shrimp. My mom says when she first saw Hardy eating them he was on the verandah in a rocking chair all by himself. She asked him what they were. He said, 'Sex food.' My mom said she asked to taste one, and Hardy said, 'No!' And he ate them right in front of her!"

Perfectly boiled southern-style peanuts are always salty, but not overly so. They should perfectly accompany a beer, iced tea, or soft drink, though lately I've seen people eating them with white wine. It's best to eat them outside where it doesn't matter if wet shells are tossed on the ground. I think most boiled peanuts are probably purchased from roadside stands, eaten while they're still hot in the car, the shells tossed out the window. Those stands may now be appearing in places where they never were before as southerners move to other parts of the country, but the popularity of boiled peanuts still seems very localized.

Fran McCullough, though, who edited my first two books on southern cooking, tells me that "there's a funny little urban gardenish place up in Harlem that often has a very excited sign saying something like 'We Got 'Em! Boiled Peanuts!' and I always think of you because I know you'd scream 'STOP!!!!' and run right in."

I know exactly which place she's talking about. It's the same place I'd go for my collards and butt's meat (smoked hog jowl) when I used to live in Manhattan. Some folks from South Carolina drive a truck up to New York once a week during the late summer and fall, full of old-time southern specialties that simply aren't available elsewhere, like just-picked okra without a hint of black on it, and thin Porto Rico sweet potatoes, no more than two inches in diameter and pointed at both ends. They get green peanuts, the little Valencias, before they dry up and lose that fresh beany flavor. They boil them in salted water for a couple of hours, then let them soak in the water until they've reached the right degree of saltiness, just like back home. They usually sell out, right from the kettle, before they cool off.

I was at a dinner party recently with some friends from Alabama. He's from Mobile—Old Mobile—and she's from Opelika, near the Georgia border. He never ate them when he was growing up, and wasn't introduced to them in college, either (he went to Washington and Lee, in Virginia). She knew them well, from summers spent in the Florida panhandle—about as deep in the South as you can get. They are both fond of them now, and try to offer them amidst the pistachios and almonds that they serve in their home in the Hollywood Hills (if for, I know, no other reason than to assert their southernness).

A new southerner standing near us at the bar overheard our conversation and screwed up her face in disgust.

"I just don't see how you can eat those things," she said. "I can't stand the texture."

She proceeded to eat olives and a black bean dip with gusto, and I just smiled and said, "Fine, that means more for us."

I knew that if she had liked them, she would have used the plural "y'all."

Purdue

My mother was on odd bird, at once very private and very social. Though she cooked three meals a day and did all of our voluminous laundry and housecleaning herself, she managed to play bridge often (at one point, seven times a week!) and to attend church, garden club, circle, and PTA meetings regularly. She somehow managed to travel as well—to the shore on the weekends, to New York with her girlfriends in the fall, sailing in the Caribbean with my father, and on a big family trip each summer. We always spent the holidays together, either at home in South Carolina or visiting relatives in Tennessee. One year, I was the first to arrive home from college at Christmas. I found my mother playing hymns and carols on the console piano in the living room. It was the first and last time that any of us heard her play.

My parents were young when my mother died. Daddy had retired early so that they could spend their lives together aboard their sailboat. He was ill-prepared for her demise. He started dating fairly soon after Mama's death; the women were much younger than he was. He wanted an energetic companion who could be his first mate, the way my mother had been. Before long, Lila, a young woman just a little older than his eldest child, moved aboard with him. They seemed genuinely happy, though I've never seen two people more different.

Both of my parents were scientists by training, but Mother agreed to raise children while my father pursued his career. From the beginning of their marriage, she developed an almost fanatical interest in cooking. Though firmly rooted in her rural southern upbringing, her repertoire came to include Spanish paellas, Viennese desserts, and French stews. Her

Mama sailing in Calibogue Sound, 1979.

adventurous palate was enhanced by both her reading and her travels. (When fairy rings of agaric mushrooms appeared in our yard, for example, she harvested them, sautéed them, and added them to omelets.) Her first handwritten collection of some of her favorite recipes—a book we all called "Purdue" because it was recorded in an old chemistry department notebook from the university where my father had attended graduate school—was a source of both recipes and pride. Invariably, my siblings and I would call Daddy at Christmas, desperate for a cookie recipe, for while Mother had been an exceptional cook, she never really taught us how.

Daddy had always shared Mother's enthusiasm for good food. When we traveled, we ate in the Duncan Hines—and *New York Times*—recommended restaurants. We even had wine in a small town in South Carolina in the fifties! And while he always did the grilling at home, Mother had always been the cook. When she became ill, he took to cooking the way he had to sailing. He became quite a home chef. I had just begun my career as a food writer, and he and I read through the literature of food together. We shared kitchen tips and tested each other's theories and recipes.

When he sold his house and moved aboard the boat, Lila joined him. I got Mother's collection of cookbooks—hundreds of them—but Dad kept a few gems, most importantly, Purdue. After a couple of years, he and Lila got married; their pre-nuptial arrangement was a division of labor: he'd do the shopping and cooking, and she'd do the cleaning—an arrangement they've stuck with through the years. Eventually, when handling the boat became more work than fun, they bought a simple house on a canal in Florida. Dad continued to cook elaborate meals, which Lila and their friends enjoyed, but Lila admitted that her major culinary interests were good chocolate and even better coffee.

We all felt even more honored and surprised, therefore, when, one land-locked Christmas, she and Daddy presented each of us—there are four kids—with the most thoughtful gift I've ever received. At age seventy-two, my father had bought himself a computer, taught himself how to type, and painstakingly copied the fragile yellow pages of Purdue, recipe by recipe, page by page, omitting some of the possible substitutions such as marga-rine, but remaining true to Mother's originals. By then, he had been the cook at home for over ten years, and he was used to testing recipes for me.

Mama's perfect recipe for asparagus, from Purdue.

Purdue is a wonderful collection. In a concise forward, Daddy wrote, "These recipes were collected and recorded . . . beginning in 1942 and continuing for about ten years. . . . They were by no means her repertoire but rather, I suspect, those not in cookbooks and those not committed to memory . . ." While he transcribed, Lila baked. For Christmas that year we each received not only a copy of the marvelous recipes, but also tins of cookies, a dozen each of a dozen varieties, each labeled with the recipe title and page number in the book.

I continue to find wonderful ideas among the recipes. There are deli-cious "Pecan Shells"—buttery, nutty crusts that you drape while still warm over custard cups to hold your favorite ice cream, mousse, or pudding. There are hot cheese tarts enlivened with country ham. There is a recipe for the Indian bread chapati, as well as a classic pizza, with a slow-rise yeast dough, tomatoes, mozzarella, anchovies, Parmesan, and oregano. Mother's deviled crab, I found, has a roux made with cream. No wonder it tasted so good! Her gumbo included shrimp, ham, and crabmeat. There are reci-pes from Lindy's and The Four Seasons. Her Bourbon Balls are made with homemade shortbread instead of the more pedestrian store-bought vanilla wafers.

Purdue also contains her lengthy and precise directions for making Danish pastry from scratch, which we always had first thing on Christmas morning, before we went outside for oysters and Champagne—before the ham biscuits, the quail, the ambrosia, the cookies, and the eggnog. Now that I've got the recipes, I still don't see how she managed it all.

Pesto

Having lived in Genoa, Italy, the home of *pesto*, I feel a sort of proprietary right to the dish. I was, if I'm not mistaken, the first *New York Times* food writer to write for the paper about the food of Liguria, the northwestern panhandle of Italy of which Genoa is the capital, back in the 1980s. I have seen pesto made, both in Italy and in the States, in innumerable ways. There are as many "authentic" versions among Genoese cooks as there are real gumbo recipes among Cajuns. I own a dozen Ligurian cookbooks in Italian and another half dozen in English. The recipes vary widely. Even Fred Plotkin, whose work I greatly admire, offers seventeen pages of recipes in his marvelous *Recipes from Paradise* (Little, Brown, 1997), and they differ from the version he offered in his equally brilliant *The Authentic Pasta Book* (Simon & Schuster, 1985).

Every home cook I met in Liguria, and all the authorities I've met on the cooking of the area, agree on five basic pesto principles, no matter how widely varied their recipes:

1. The basil should be Genoese basil, freshly picked, with all suggestions of stems removed. In Liguria, basil is grown in stony soil, sharing beds with garlic. The local basil, a small, round-leaved variety, is grown most often in greenhouses on steep slopes above the coast. The slanted roofs of the greenhouses open during the day to catch the warm sea breezes and are closed at night. The basil has a rounder flavor as well, much more delicate than most basil grown in the States—or in Italy, for that matter. When I lived in Italy in the early 1980s, there was an unwritten rule that if a restaurant (even in Rome) offered *Pesto alla*

Genovese, then the basil used must indeed be Ligurian, not just the recipe. Obviously, you aren't going to find fresh authentic Genoese basil in the States, and even if you have brought back seeds from Genoa, they won't produce an herb with the delicate aroma and flavor of Genoese basil grown there. (That's what *terroir* is, after all: why California Chardonnay never tastes the same as Chablis.) Nevertheless, I encourage you to grow your own (even on your Manhattan windowsill, as I have done) and choose the mildest-tasting leaves from your plants. At the end of the summer, I pluck leaves from the spindly, the robust, the flowering, and the drooping. I choose the smallest leaves and taste them. I use the most delicate tasting. A *manciata* is what most of the Ligurian recipes I have call for. That's a handful, about fifty leaves, which is enough to make pesto for four people.

2. You must use a mortar and pestle. Pesto means made with a mortar and pestle. *Pestare* means "to crush," but in the sense of grinding by pressing against the sides of the mortar, not in a mill. A friend eating pesto at my house recently asked, "How do you get the basil so fine?" It's easy. As Fred Plotkin says, "Using a wooden pestle, crush the leaves and salt gently and firmly against the bottom and sides of the mortar so that the leaves gradually come apart." My favorite recipe in Italian says to press the leaves until they melt, without pounding. However, one person I knew when I lived there, an antique dealer in Nervi, lived in an ancient olive mill high above the city. He made his pesto by constantly, but gently, pounding the pestle up and down, continually crushing the basil and garlic paste until it was creamy, even before the addition of cheese. Pesto made in a blender is always called *Pesto al Frullatore*, and, while it can be delicious, it is not the same thing as pesto.

3. Ligurian olive oil, made only from *taggiasca* olives, is the only traditional oil to use. If you don't have Ligurian oil, use a mild oil such as one from Provence or Andalucía.

4. Only one tablespoon of sauce is used per person.

5. Pesto is never cooked.

Rules stated, there are myriad variations: the order that the ingredients are placed in the mortar, the quantities of those ingredients, the type of cheese(s), and whether or not to use nuts. In Genoa, it is traditional to dilute the pesto just before serving with a tablespoon or two of the hot pasta water, though pesto is never cooked. I have also seen a little cream or butter swirled into the sauce throughout the region. Probably the biggest variation is in the amount of oil added to the sauce. One "classic" version I have calls for a glass and a half of oil (!), though I learned to add merely a few tablespoons, until the sauce begins to glisten.

According to most historical sources, *pecorino sardo* (a hard sheep's milk *grana*, or grating cheese, from Sardinia, often called just *sardo*), is traditional, though many sources now list both *pecorino romano* and *parmigiano-reggiano* as traditional as well. Whatever *grana* you use, buy a chunk fresh and grate it just before using. In Genoa it's also traditional to serve pesto with *trenette*, a flat pasta similar to linguine, but more like wooden matches in thickness. Finally, a little boiled potato and green beans are tossed in with the pasta and sauce upon serving. In this case, I add neither pine nuts nor walnuts, which all of my Ligurian cookbooks say are "modern" or "more recent" additions, though my Genoese friend Gianni Martini says they are "fondamentale"! The following is a traditional recipe for *pesto alla genovese*.

. . . .

Pesto alla Genovese

50 small, round, mildly flavored basil leaves

2 cloves garlic, not too big, with green shoots removed

1 big pinch of salt

3 tablespoons freshly and finely grated pecorino sardo, pecorino romano, or parmigiano-reggiano

3 to 4 tablespoons delicate olive oil, preferably from Liguria, more or less

8 ounces peeled, cubed, and cooked potato, preferably the waxy kind

(CONTINUED)

Place the basil, the garlic, and the salt in a large mortar. Using a wooden pestle, crush the basil and garlic against the sides and bottom of the mortar until the mixture is uniform and the basil has begun to melt.

Add the cheese and continue to grind the mixture together until the cheese is uniformly incorporated.

Add the oil gradually in a stream, continually blending with the pestle, until the mixture begins to glisten with oil; 3 or 4 tablespoons should be enough.

Cook the pasta al dente, and, just before draining, add 1 or 2 tablespoons of the cooking water to the pesto, stirring it well to dilute it.

8 ounces cooked green
   beans
1 pound pasta of your
   choice

Drain the pasta and return it to the cooking pot. Add the potato cubes, the green beans, and the pesto, stir it all together and serve in pasta bowls with crusty bread.

Serves 4.

Note. To keep batches in the refrigerator, use a glass jar and pour a good, thick layer of oil over the surface of the pesto. When you go to serve it, scoop down into the jar with a spoon, then be sure to pour another good layer of oil over the pesto again before returning to the refrigerator. I have a friend who freezes his pesto in ice cube trays, using one cube per person throughout the winter, but I've never tried it.

Old-Fashioned Sweet Potato Pie

This old-fashioned sliced sweet potato pie is one of my favorites. No milk, no eggs, no cream, no custard—just beautiful sweet potatoes, a little sugar and butter, and my favorite pie crust made with lard and butter.

The pie is one of two traditional sweet potato pies that were popular not only in America but also in England long before printed recipes for them appeared. It's unfathomable that the custard pie became so popular while this simpler, more elegant pie didn't. If you are a lover of sweet potatoes, as I am, then this is the pie for you! If you are avoiding dairy products, other than butter, this pie fits the bill. And if you are in the mood for a seasonal, not-too-sweet dessert, try this lovely creation that cookbook authors have been presenting for nearly two hundred years, though I think the recipe has disappeared for periods of time only because it was misunderstood, since many of the older recipes called for potatoes, when sweet potatoes were meant.

George Washington Carver offered a recipe for "Sliced Potato Pie" in a 1936 article he wrote for the Tuskegee Institute, but he added cream to the traditional recipe:

> Line a deep baking dish with a rich sheet of pastry. Parboil the number of potatoes desired. When two thirds done, remove the skins, slice lengthwise, very thin, cover the dish to a depth of 2 inches, sprinkle with ground allspice and a dash of ginger, cloves, and nutmeg. To a pie sufficient for six people, scatter around the top in small pieces a lump of butter the size of a hen's egg; add one teacupful of sugar and ½ teacupful of molasses. Add ½ pint of cream, dust a little flour over the top sparingly;

cover with hot water, put on upper crust, crimp edges and bake in a moderate oven until done. Serve hot, with or without sauce.

A hundred years earlier, *The Kentucky Housewife* offered the following "Sliced Potato Pie," a much more elegant recipe:

> Boil your potatoes in a very little water till half done, then peel and slice them thin. Line a deep patty-pan that is well-buttered, with a tolerably thick sheet of standing paste, put in a layer of the sliced potatoes, disseminate over them some grated nutmeg, powdered cinnamon, grated lemon, a small portion of butter, rolled in flour, and broken up, and a small handful of brown sugar; put in a second layer of the potatoes, and then the seasonings, stratifying them till the pan is full; pour in a glass of water, one of white wine, cover it with a sheet of paste, trim it smoothly round the edge, and bake it in a moderate oven. Grate sugar over it, and eat it warm.

Curiously, a nearly identical recipe appeared the same year (1839) in *The Southern Gardener and Receipt Book* by the Camden, South Carolina, shopkeeper Phineas Thornton. A mere eight years later and just down the road in Charleston, the author of *The Carolina Housewife* included two sweet potato pones and a pudding, but no sliced potato pie like these. The recipe seems to have drifted in and out of popularity. By 1870, Mrs. Hill, writing in Atlanta, is advising her readers to bake the sweet potatoes ("yams are best") instead of boiling them, layering the slices with spices, thin slices of butter, and a sprinkling of flour, and mixing together "equal quantities of wine and water, lemon juice and water, or vinegar and water" and pouring in enough to half fill the pie. A decade later, the *Boston Cooking School Cook Book* noted that baked sweet potatoes "are better," and "much richer when twice cooked." The yams Mrs. Hill refers to are not really yams (a different plant family, and tropical to boot), but since New World potatoes, sweet potatoes, and yams all entered European kitchens at the same time, the common names of the plants have forever been confused. Most likely, Mrs. Hill was referring to a favored variety of sweet potato, such as the Dooley Yam and Pumpkin Yam that George Washington Carver would recommend decades later.

In 1919, the Eighteenth Amendment was passed, outlawing the manufacture, sale, and transportation of alcoholic beverages (the language actually reads "intoxicating liquors"). *Mrs. Dull's Southern Cooking* appeared in 1928, also in Atlanta. Her Sliced Sweet Potato Pie sees the potatoes being boiled again, and for flavor, she suggests "¼ cup spiced vinegar or spices, to taste, and grape juice." "Season highly," she writes. "There should be plenty of juice on the inside so when served this juice is a rich brown sauce to serve with the seasoned potatoes, pastry, and hard crust. This pie tastes something like a mince pie and an apple could be added along with the potatoes. A few pieces of dried apple which have been soaked would answer. Use cloves sparingly." Poor woman! She sounds deprived of alcohol to me, trying to make her sweet potato pie taste right during Prohibition!

As for the version I use, I'll be damned if my crust is hard, and since I so love the flavor of sweet potatoes, I advise you *not* to season highly. And lover of alcohol that I am, I don't include any. Modern-day recipes often advise the cook to add a tablespoon of "pumpkin pie spice," but I try to buy my spices in very small quantities and grind and blend them myself. After my travels in Sri Lanka earlier this year, I got spoiled by real Ceylon cinnamon (you can buy it in Latin American markets; most cinnamon sold elsewhere comes from an entirely different plant), dried ginger, and fresh nutmeg (all of which I grind at the last minute). No cloves. No allspice. Just a little freshly ground cinnamon, ginger, and nutmeg with a bit of lemon.

When I'm buying sweet potatoes to roast and eat alone, I usually look for the oldest ones that are, as George Washington Carver says, "cured" of excess moisture. One of my favorite varieties is the Porto Rico, which is small (never more than 2 inches in diameter), pointed at both ends, and with dark orange flesh. For this recipe, however, I find it best to use the larger, hard sweet potatoes you can find in most supermarkets, because they will not have been cured and so will cook evenly. I peel them and cut them into uniform bite-size pieces and gently poach them until they just barely give to the tip of a sharp knife.

....

Sliced Sweet Potato Pie

1 pound all-purpose flour, preferably a soft southern flour, about 4 cups, plus more for dusting and filling

salt

1 tablespoon sugar, plus more for dusting pie

(CONTINUED)

For the crust: Sift the flour with a pinch of salt and 1 tablespoon of the sugar into a large mixing bowl. Add a few ice cubes to ½ cup of the water and set aside. Cut the lard and 4 ounces of the butter into the flour with a pastry blender, a large fork, or two knives, until the mixture is uniform and, as the old cookbooks say, it resembles small peas. Do not touch the dough with your hands. Place

1½ cup water, divided, plus ice cubes

4 ounces chilled lard, cut into pieces

4 ounces (1 stick) cold unsalted butter, cut into pieces, plus one tablespoon for the filling

salt

2½ to 3 pounds sweet potatoes, peeled and cut up, about 6 cups

½ cup lightly packed brown sugar

Grated zest of a lemon

2 tablespoons lemon juice

Freshly ground ginger, nutmeg, and cinnamon to taste

1 egg white

Milk or half-and-half

a wet towel under the bowl so that it will not slide around on the counter. Working deftly, scoop up large spoonfuls of the mixture from the bottom of the bowl with a metal slotted spoon while sprinkling water into the mixture a little at a time. Work quickly as you "lift in" the water, stopping before all the water is in. You should stop the second you feel the dough will hold together without more water. Now grab the entire mass of dough up in your hands and push it all together into a ball. Divide the ball in half and, if your filling is ready, wrap the dough halves in some wax paper or plastic wrap and put them in the freezer for 10 minutes; otherwise put the wrapped dough in the refrigerator to chill while you prepare the filling.

For the filling: Add a healthy pinch of salt to the remaining cup of water in a saucepan that has a lid. Add the sweet potato pieces, bring to a boil, reduce to a simmer, and cook, covered, until the sweet potato pieces just barely give to the tip of sharp knife, about 5 minutes. Drain the sweet potatoes, rinsing them gently with cold water to cool them off. When completely cool and drained, put them in a bowl and toss with the brown sugar, 1 tablespoon flour, lemon zest, lemon juice, and spices.

For final assembly and cooking: Preheat the oven to 425°F Remove the pastry dough from the freezer or refrigerator and place one half on a large, lightly floured surface. Try not to touch it with your hands. Roll the dough out into a circle about 12-inches in diameter. It should be evenly thick, about 1/8 inch. Place a 9- or 10-inch pie plate that has a lip on top of the dough and, with a sharp knife, cut the dough around the pie plate so that an area large enough to fill the pie plate is marked off as one large piece. Set the pie plate off to the side. Place the rolling pin on one edge of this large piece of dough, and gently roll it up off the surface and onto the pin. Lay the dough down in the pie plate, allowing it to roll off the pin, and always avoiding handling the dough. Press it lightly into place, allowing any excess dough to hang over the sides.

Lightly beat the egg white and paint the inside of the crust with it. Fill the crust with the sweet potato mixture. Dot the mixture with the extra tablespoon of butter, cut up into small pieces.

Roll out the second half of the pastry dough so that it's big enough to fit over the entire pie. Gently roll it up onto the rolling pin and unroll it onto the top of the pie. Run a sharp knife blade at an angle around the rim of the pie plate, trimming excess dough off. Crimp the edges of the pie crust layers together on the lip of the pie plate with a large fork. Brush the top of the pie crust lightly with milk or half-and-half, then sprinkle the pie lightly all over with a little sugar.

Place in the middle of the preheated oven and bake for ten minutes, lower the heat to 350°F and bake until the crust is nicely browned all over, anywhere from thirty minutes to an hour. Be sure to bake the pie well so that the crust will not be soggy. If you have clear glass pie plates, you can leave the pie in until the bottom has begun to brown. Don't worry about the timing. All ovens and batches of flour bake differently. Bake the pie until it is a rich golden brown and it will be delicious.

Allow the pie to cool for at least an hour before serving, in spite of what *The Kentucky Housewife* said.

Peaches Aswim
in Rose Petals

When Mikel and I got together, neither of us had ever grown roses. We always liked having fresh flowers in the house, but we were always disappointed in the perfectly-shaped florists' roses that had no scent whatsoever. And so we dug into rose gardening with a passion, even in the tiny patch of land that was our dooryard in DC. Back in hot and humid South Carolina, it was a constant struggle against black spot, but in DC we didn't have anywhere near the problems that we had had down south. Even when it was hot, the cool nights saw bloom after bloom after bloom appear on our handful of bushes. The varieties we have grown are all fragrant roses, among them Abraham Darby (a cross between a climber and a floribunda, one of David Austin's modern roses that looks and smells like an old-fashioned pink English cabbage rose), Mister Lincoln (a deep red, fragrant hybrid tea rose, long an American favorite), and, our hands-down favorite, Papa Meilland, which is supposedly a clone of Mister Lincoln, though some sources say that it was introduced in 1963, a year before the Lincoln. They're both glorious roses, but I dare anyone to show me another rose that is more fragrant than the Meilland. Mister Lincoln is the standard-bearer of long-stemmed, fragrant, deep red roses in the United States.

One year, our friends Elizabeth and Seth were coming to have dinner with us on a Saturday night. Elizabeth Schneider is a world-renowned food writer, and she has one of the most sophisticated palates—and senses of smell—that I have ever known. She walked into our house and immediately upon entering the front door said, "What's that lovely fragrance?" What she smelled was a single Papa Meilland rose in a vase at the back of the house—on the other side of the kitchen, where I had been cooking an intensely aromatic dinner of shrimp gumbo!

For dessert, we had one of those stunning culinary experiences: a dish whose flavors were so ethereal and elegant that for many years I never even tried to reproduce it. I have made this elegant dish several times since, and so can you, if you can get your hands on fresh peaches and fragrant roses.

We had driven to South Carolina for a funeral and had stopped at a produce stand to buy peaches to bring home. Though neighboring Georgia calls itself "the peach state," South Carolina grows more, and tastier, peaches. I had planned to simply serve sliced peaches for dessert but picked up the cookbook on Fruits from the excellent *Time-Life Good Cook* series, which was edited by the late, great food writer, Richard Olney. The book fell open to a recipe called "Peaches Aswim in Rose Petals," which, coincidentally, came from Judith Olney's *Summer Food*. (Judith was the sister-in-law of Richard, whose work I already knew and admired.) I had never cooked from Judith Olney's books before, but the recipe spoke for itself: highly scented rose petals poached in a simple sugar syrup, peeled peach halves added along with the almond-like kernel from inside the peach pit, and the cooled fruit served with a raspberry puree. I knew that both Elizabeth and I would love the dish. Neither of us are true fans of sweets, but we love fruit and nuts. I simply *had* to try the recipe.

As it turned out, the recipe also called for a scented geranium leaf, which I didn't have; however, I did have a lemon verbena plant growing under Mister Lincoln, so I added leaves from it to the infusion. And the raspberries I bought were flavorless, so I decided not to serve the puree. I also did not refrigerate the dish but plated the poached peaches and left them at room temperature before serving. I can't think of a more delicious way to end a meal.

If you grow fragrant roses, and don't spray them, I cannot steer you towards a lovelier dish for peach season. It's amazing how the sugar syrup tastes exactly the way the roses smell. I used our beloved Papa Meilland red roses for the syrup and the spicy-sweet pink Abraham Darby petals for the garnish.

Here's my version of the twice-Olneyed dish:

6 highly scented red roses

1 rose geranium leaf or several small lemon verbena leaves

¾ cup sugar

1½ cups water

2 tablespoons fresh lemon juice

6 large, ripe, fragrant peaches, peeled, halved, and pitted, with the pits reserved

2 highly scented pink roses

Remove the petals from the red roses and tie them and the rose geranium or lemon verbena leaves loosely in a cheesecloth bag. Bring the sugar and water to a boil in a saucepan, add the petal bag, and simmer for 5 minutes. Remove from the heat, add the lemon juice, and allow to steep, covered, for ten minutes. Remove the bag and press to extract all the flavor and color possible.

Crack the reserved peach pits and remove the almond-like kernels. (This is a tricky job that I do outside, on concrete, with a hammer, while wearing goggles. If you have a heavy-duty nutcracker, you may be able to do this indoors.) Add the peach halves and the kernels to the syrup and simmer until the peaches are tender. I use a large sauté pan that will hold all of the peaches in one layer, and carefully turn the fruits halfway through the poaching. Allow the peaches to cool in the syrup.

When the peaches have cooled, transfer them to dessert bowls, giving each diner two peach halves. Remove the kernels with a slotted spoon, skin them, and chop them coarsely. Pour the syrup over the peaches, then top with the chopped kernels. Allow the dish to sit at room temperature until serving.

Just before serving, remove the petals from the pink roses, cut off the white part from the base, and scatter the rose petals over the peaches.

Serves 6.

Shrimp and Grits

Shrimp and Grits is probably the dish that I get the most requests for. I've published at least a dozen different recipes. This is an Italian-influenced version. Imagine my surprise the first time I was served *Gamberetti con Polenta* on the Riviera in the early 1980s! This recipe is my nod to those Mediterranean cooks from whom I learned so much.

Polenta, grits, and cornmeal are all, even at their finest, nothing more than ground corn. The best are whole-grain, stone-ground heirloom varieties, whether you are in northern Italy or the American South. The industrially-produced grits and polenta you buy in grocery stores have been degerminated—that is, robbed of the germ, where the precious flavor-carrying oil is stored. They last forever on unrefrigerated shelves, but they taste like the paper they're packaged in. Ground between steel rollers that actually heat up and cook the corn, they are also ground too finely. The best have nothing added to or taken away from them. I tried products from thirty mills before I found millers who used the right corn, grown in mountain hollers and allowed to dry in the fields, then ground between blue granite stones, with nothing added to or taken away from the corn.

In Italy, the traditional corn for polenta is hard flint corn, often yellow. It is ground much more finely than American cornmeal. In Appalachia, where my millers live, dent corn has been grown since before Columbus's discovery of America, so I like to think of this as the original mountain corn. You can use whole-grain American grits (the coarser grind) or cornmeal ground from dent corn in polenta recipes, and they'll be much more flavorful.

Gianni Martini and his father gathering hay before a storm at their farmhouse in Rossiglione, high above Genoa in the entroterra.

It is said that the cooking of Genoa, where I lived in Italy, is green—of herbs and forests, not of the sea. The story goes that because it was a major seaport, sailors returning home wanted fresh vegetables from the *entroterra*, the inland reaches of land up above the city, where chestnuts, porcini, and wild herbs thrive. For centuries, the peasants of this rugged land used ground chestnuts, often smoked, as the flour in both their pasta and their polenta. There are several famous Ligurian dishes that are still based on chestnut flour.

After the arrival of Europeans in America, however, corn came to the valleys above the Ligurian coast, where the terrain is remarkably similar to the Appalachian hollers where my father grew up. By the time I went away to college, though, nearly every mill in eastern Tennessee had closed, and most folks I knew were eating Quaker or Jim Dandy grits. Nasty stuff. No fat. No flavor. No wonder Yankees hated it. But I knew better, as do the grandmothers from the entroterra, and, as in the States, there is a movement to preserve the old folkways and dishes that have all but disappeared. Farmers are growing tasty heirloom varieties of corn, and mills are grinding the whole grains. You've got to look for these products online, in gourmet shops, and at farmers' markets, and you've got to keep them in the freezer or the oils will go rancid, but the taste is infinitely superior. I'm proud to have been a part of this movement and to have restored Shrimp and Grits to menus in Charleston, where, before my arrival there in the late 1980s, not a single restaurant that I know of was offering it.

. . . .

Gamberetti con Polenta
(Shrimp and Grits)

When I lived in Charleston, I helped reestablish this "national" dish of South Carolina. This is my version of a classic that is both Charleston and Liguria. You can use grits, cornmeal, or polenta in this recipe, but if you use the finer grinds, you'll have to carefully and slowly add the meal to the pot of boiling water, or it may clump. I prefer more coarsely ground grits of dent corn because it is softer, less gritty, and more flavorful than Italian polenta, which is closer to cornmeal in grind.

Italian cookbooks often tell you that you must stir polenta relentlessly, and that's true if you are using degerminated flint corn polenta. Whole-grain, heirloom dent corn is full of fat and won't stick to the pot, and cooks up perfectly in about a half-hour, though you can cook it for an hour or more. The longer you cook it, the more it falls apart and the creamier it becomes. Allow ½ cup grits for four people if the grits are a simple side dish; double the amount for a plate of grits topped with sauce as the main course. As the liquid cooks out of the grits, add water or stock (or whatever you have on hand to keep the pot from drying out). Some chefs like to add milk or cream, but when making shrimp and grits, I use only water in the grits so that the corn flavor is an earthen counterpoint to the intense shellfish sauce finished off with a little butter. Butter is not traditional in much of Ligurian cooking, but in the hinterlands closer to the Lombard plains, and on the Riviera di Ponente, close to France, sauces, even pesto, are often finished with a bit of butter swirled in. I also put a little in with the grits as they are cooking.

As a nod to the polenta cooks of Liguira, I season the grits with a bay leaf as they cook. You can also cook them in a slow cooker set on low for about eight to ten hours. You can also cook them in a rice steamer, using only three parts liquid to one part grits.

For the shrimp and stock:

1 pound fresh head-on shrimp

Freshly squeezed juice of one lemon

Sea salt and cayenne pepper

1 celery rib, broken into pieces

1 small carrot, broken into pieces

1 small onion, unpeeled, and quartered

A handful of fresh herbs such as thyme, parsley, oregano, and basil

6 cups water

Remove the head and shells from the shrimp, dropping them into an enameled or stainless steel stockpot. If you are planning to serve the dish within a couple of hours, sprinkle the shrimp bodies with the lemon juice and salt and cayenne to taste, cover, and refrigerate. If waiting till later, put the shrimp on ice and wait to season them until about an hour before you plan to eat.

Add the celery, carrot, the onion, and the herbs to the pot and cover with the water. Cook, uncovered, at a low boil until the onion is transparent, the carrots are soft, and the stock is pleasantly infused with the shrimp flavor—about 45 minutes. The liquid should be reduced by a third. Strain out the solids and discard. Cool, then freeze what you don't plan to use immediately.

For the polenta:

4 to 6 cups water

1 bay leaf

2 tablespoons salted butter, or 2 tablespoons unsalted plus 1 teaspoon salt

1 cup stone–ground, whole-grain corn grits

While the stock is cooking, bring 4 cups of the water to boil in a heavy stockpot that has a lid. Drop in the bay leaf, the butter, and the salt. Stir in the grits, return to a boil, and reduce the heat, allowing the grits to cook on a low boil for 10 minutes or so, until the grits are very thick and have absorbed most of the water, stirring the pot occasionally to prevent the grits from sticking. Add about ½ cup more of water to the pot, cover, and turn down the heat, allowing the grits to simmer another 10 minutes or so. As the liquid cooks off or is absorbed, add more water, cooking the grits until the desired consistency is reached, a total cooking time of about an hour. The grits should be piping hot when served, slightly soupy but full-bodied enough that they do not run on the plate.

Remove and discard the bay leaf before serving. The grits will remain hot for long after you have turned off the heat, so go ahead and divide the portions into the serving dishes while you are finishing the sauce.

For the gamberetti:

3 tablespoons olive oil

2 shallots or ½ small onion, peeled and chopped, about ½ cup

1 cup dry white wine or Vermouth

1 large ripe tomato, peeled, seeded, and chopped

1 ½ cups hot shrimp stock

3 tablespoons unsalted butter

Reserved shrimp

Heat the olive oil in a skillet over medium-high heat and sauté the shallots until they are soft and translucent, about five minutes. Add the wine, raise the heat, and cook until the liquid has disappeared and the oil begins to sputter. Add the tomato, stirring, and continue to cook over fairly high heat until almost all the liquid has evaporated. Add the shrimp stock and reduce until just shy of serving consistency, then whisk in the butter and the reserved shrimp. Keep stirring, tossing the shrimp around in the buttery sauce until they are just barely done and the sauce is shiny and silken, about 2 to 3 minutes. Serve immediately over the grits.

Makes 8 appetizers or 4 mains.

Cheese Straws

> When Rickey was upset, he almost always made cheese
> straws. They were one of the few things he had ever learned
> to cook, and making them seemed to comfort him.
>
> —from *Liquor: A Novel*, by Poppy Z. Brite[1]

Of the many foods that I have made and served to my guests over the years,
there is none that folks seem to love more than the old southern cocktail party standby, cheese straws. Since cheese has always been imported
into the hot and humid South, cooking it in cracker form has long been a
southern way of "preserving" the cheese, or at least the cheese flavor. There
are some relatively new artisan and farmstead cheesemakers in the area
today, but they are the exception, not the rule.

Outside the South, cheese straws just don't seem to be a part of the vernacular. You find them here and there, but only in the South do they seem
so firmly entrenched as truly regional fare, like boiled peanuts or grits.
The late Bill Neal, my dear friend who spearheaded the revival of traditional southern cooking, wrote that cheese straws came from England, but
my research doesn't exactly bear that out.[2] The British *have* adopted them,
and they occasionally appear with cocktails in the English-speaking islands
of the Caribbean, but I'm reasonably sure that they are a fairly recent—
meaning not much more than a century old—American culinary phenome-
non, even if the first printed recipe I have found is in a British cookbook

A version of this ran in *Gastronomica* (Volume 8, Issue 4, November 2008).

(by the notoriously plagiarizing Mrs. Beeton). If they are truly British, why do my friends in London ask me to bring them with me when I visit?

It's true that Queen Mary (Queen Consort, that is, wife of George V), enjoyed a cheese biscuit made with parmesan and no cayenne, according to her chef, Gabriel Tschumi, but his memoirs weren't published until 1954, at the end of her reign.[3] The Brits' use of parmesan is telling. Bill Neal wrote that in England cheese straws were often made solely from parmesan, "despite the superb true cheddar."[4]

I would attribute the use of imported cheese to snobbery, yet another way of separating one from the lower classes. In 1970, Elizabeth David, the great English food writer, quoted a recipe for "Thick Parmesan Biscuits" from *The Cookery Book of Lady Clark of Tillypronie*, published in 1909, nine years after Clark's death. A dozen biscuits call for ¼ pound of flour, 2 ounces each of butter and grated Parmesan, the yolk of one egg, salt, and cayenne. Rolled to ½-inch thickness and cut into 1-inch diameter rounds, the biscuits' thickness are their distinguishing characteristic. David tells us, "The Parmesan is also essential. English cheese will not do."[5] Ironically, David also says that cayenne adds "an important zest to . . . the beloved English cheese straws," but offers no recipe, not even in her comprehensive *English Bread and Yeast Cookery* (1977).[6]

The year prior to David's claim that cheddar wouldn't do, Adrian Bailey wrote *The Cooking of the British Isles* for the influential *Time-Life Foods of the World* series. His cheese straws, which he identifies as "cheese-flavored pastry sticks," are typical of English recipes, with a bit of unnecessary ice water, which indeed makes them more like pie dough. But at least they include sharp cheddar.[7] Neither Jane Garmey nor Jane Grigson, who wrote extensively about British cooking in the 1980s, offer recipes for what I would think of as cheese straws, unless I am to seriously consider Garmey's version, which is one inch thick,[8] or Grigson's cheese and oatmeal biscuit from northeastern England, which calls for "a hard, dried-out piece of cheese, Cheddar or a mixture of Cheddar and Parmesan in the proportions of 3:1."[9]

I don't pretend to have culled every cookbook looking for recipes, though I own hundreds and have pretty much devoured my own collection as well as several yards of shelves of the Library of Congress, where, incidentally, 2,500 cheese straws were served at the Library's sesquicentennial celebration in 1950. But I am reasonably sure that cheese straws first appeared in the late nineteenth century, and on this side of the Atlantic.

In my research, I look for recipes for cheese crackers, biscuits, or wafers. A straw, after all, is just a cracker (or biscuit or wafer, depending on where it's made). Though named, presumably, because of their shape, cheese straws might be round, according to hundreds of recipes I've found in cookbooks and on the web. Horticulturists complain about how difficult common nomenclature is, but I think we culinary historians have it worse, since, other than Escoffier, hardly anyone has bothered to codify recipes, and it's nearly impossible to recognize some of today's versions of the French classics as having been based on the originals. Mayonnaise comes to mind. And biscuits are as varied as cookies.

An English dictionary will tell you that a biscuit, "a crisp dry bread," is so called because it is "twice-cooked" (from the Latin *biscotum*, like Italian *biscotti*). The word, variously spelled, appeared in fourteenth- and fifteenth-century works, but from the sixteenth through the eighteenth centuries, *bisket* was the regular form. *The Oxford English Dictionary* sounds downright disdainful: "The current biscuit is a senseless adoption of the modern French spelling, without the French pronunciation," it proclaims, while citing its earliest appearance as "besquite" in 1330.[10] My *Petit Robert*, an abridged French dictionary, gives "bescuit" in 1175 as the first French use.[11] It's all Latin to me.

Of course, American biscuits are another thing entirely, more like scones. And what we call English muffins are really crumpets. And what the English call biscuits are more like crackers, though they're often sweet— what we would call cookies. And the same is true in France. "Cracker" is an American word for "a thin, hard biscuit," used as early as 1739 in New England, according to the *OED*.[12] But *cheese crackers* are harder to trace. One of the earliest published references to cheese straws was in the Victorian magazine *Young Ladies Journal* in 1874, according to the *OED*, which makes a distinction between cheese *fingers*, "puff paste on which cheese is spread, the paste being then folded over, cut into strips, and browned," and cheese *straws*, "grated cheese and flour, or other material, made into a paste, cut into thin strips, and baked crisp."[13]

I was so glad to find those distinctions in print, because if there's one thing I can't stand, it's puff pastry sprinkled with cheese masquerading as cheese straws. Don't get me wrong: the imposters are perfectly delicious. The Italians call them *salatini al formaggio*, and I can think of nothing better to nibble with a glass of *prosecco*. And the French make cheese crackers, *brins de paille*, which have some added milk. Always served hot, they beg for claret, as do those made by Eastern Europeans, who add sour cream or yogurt.[14] But none are my idea of cheese straws, which are bold with hot pepper, and beg for stronger libations. I'm reminded of Vertamae Grosvenor's "Name Calling" chapter from her *Vibration Cooking or the Travel Notes of a Geechee Girl* (1970):

> If you are wondering how come I say so-called okra, it is because the African name of okra is gombo. Just like so-called Negroes. We are Africans. Negroes only started when they got here. I am a black woman. I am tired of people calling me out of my name. Okra must be sick of that mess too.[15]

There aren't any cheese straws—or biscuits, crackers, or wafers (another culinary term that can mean waffles, crackers, or cookies)—in any of the major English or American cookbooks published in the eighteenth century or the first half of the nineteenth. I've looked through the work of Hannah Glasse, Eliza Acton, Susannah Carter, Amelia Simmons, Eliza Smith, Eliza Leslie, and Lydia Child, as well as in *The Virginia House-Wife* (1824), *The Kentucky Housewife* (1839), and *The Carolina Housewife* (1847). Cookbooks are conspicuous in their absence in both the North and the South during the war years that followed.

The first published recipe that I've found is in *The Book of Household Management*, printed for Isabella Beeton in London in 1861. Most scholars believe that most of Beeton's 2,100 recipes were lifted from other sources: "She bore four children and died at the age of twenty-eight. It seems doubtful that she had time even to try the recipes."[16] Nevertheless, her "Cayenne Cheeses," with a half-pound of butter, a half-pound of cheese, and a half-pound of flour seasoned with cayenne and salt are approaching our modern straws, and I have yet to find an earlier printed recipe.[17]

Six years later, *Mrs. Hill's New Cookbook* was first published in New York, on the heels of the Civil War. It's a wonder that there was any cheese at all in the American South during the war and Reconstruction, which lasted another ten years after Hill's book appeared. But Atlanta, where the author lived, was the transportation center of the entire South, and the new economy was intertwined with the railroads. Agribusiness, coincidentally, was just beginning; refrigerated railroad cars weren't far behind. Cheese from Philadelphia or New York or England arrived in the South unspoiled. Mrs. Hill's recipe for a cheese biscuit is a classic European-style biscuit, never mind what the historical notes for the University of South Carolina's facsimile of the 1872 edition say.[18] Mrs. Hill was the wife of a once-prominent judge and politician; she was sophisticated and worldly.

Her cheese biscuits, rolled thin, "with very little handling, like puff paste," also approach my idea of cheese straws, but still aren't quite there.[19]

The White House Cookbook (1887) includes the first recipe I've found for a cheese straw per se. "Cayenne Cheese Straws" call for a cup of flour, three tablespoons of butter, two tablespoons of grated parmesan cheese, a pinch of salt, and a few grains of cayenne pepper (though the quantities of flour, butter, and cheese vary in different editions of the book).

> Mix into a paste with the yolk of an egg. Roll out to the thickness of a silver quarter, about four or five inches long; cut into strips about a third of an inch wide, twist them as you would a paper spill and lay them on a baking-sheet slightly floured. Bake in a moderate oven until crisp, but they must not be the least brown. If put away in a tin these cheese straws will keep a long time. Serve cold, piled tastefully on a glass dish. You can make the straws of remnants of puff pastry, rolling in the grated cheese.[20]

But Lord knows where the recipe came from. The publishers highly praised one of the book's two authors, Hugo Ziemann, Steward of the White House, as the "preeminent . . . one time caterer for that Prince Napoleon who was killed while fighting the Zulus in Africa. He was afterwards steward of the famous Hotel Splendide in Paris. Later he conducted the celebrated Brunswick Café in New York, and still later he gave to the Hotel Richelieu, in Chicago, a cuisine which won the applause of even the gourmets of foreign lands."[21]

The New Dixie Cook-Book was a popular updated edition of an earlier book first published in Atlanta in 1879. Its index does not include Cheese Straws, but there is a recipe. The authors suggested serving them with salad, "piled on a plate, crossing them in pairs and tying with ribbon of different colors; or, bake in eight-inch lengths and serve in log-cabin style." An illustration of crossed, tied pairs of straws accompanied the recipes.[22]

The following year, the Ladies' Aid Society of the First Presbyterian Church in Marion, Ohio, north of Columbus, published a recipe for "Cheese Sticks" with no allusions to puff pastry:

> One cup of grated cheese, one cup of flour, a small pinch of cayenne pepper, butter same as for pastry; roll thin; cut in narrow strips. Bake a light brown in a quick oven. Serve with salads.[23]

A recipe for Cheese Straws, contributed by Mrs. Fred Schaeffer, followed:

One cup of flour, two cups of grated cheese, one teaspoon of salt, one teaspoon of baking powder, and water to roll out like pie dough; roll thin, and cut with pastry wheel in long, narrow strips. Bake in hot oven.[24]

Cheese straws were obviously popular by the turn of the nineteenth century, and they often appear alongside recipes for dozens of homemade cordials, wines, and drinks. The remarkable *Picayune Creole Cook Book*, published in New Orleans in 1901, includes recipes for nearly one hundred spirited beverages, as well as for cheese straws, which the editors also give their Creole name, "*pailles de fromage.*" The recipe includes the requisite "salt and cayenne to taste," although it also includes an egg yolk—typically New Orleans rich, but not necessary. "This is a very dainty dish," the book says.[25]

I empathized with Rickey, one of the protagonists in Poppy Brite's foodie novel, quoted above. He and his partners constantly struggle in their efforts to open a restaurant with a menu based entirely on booze. A dainty treat, so easy to make, must have truly comforted him in the alcoholic madness that Brite conjures as post-Katrina New Orleans.

I think that cheese straws became so wildly popular in the South because they would keep (most southern homes didn't have air conditioners until the late 1960s), because they're good, and, possibly most importantly, because they're so good with drinks. And drink we do! How could we not in this godawful heat?! That would also explain their recent popularity in the Caribbean, though few recipes featuring any cheese at all appear in cookbooks from the islands prior to the 1980s. Perhaps the recipe went to Barbados with southerners vacationing there in the twentieth century; more than likely, it arrived with cruise ships. Perhaps it traveled to England with British vacationers on Barbados. However they arrived there, by 2005, cheese straws were being proclaimed the "King of Canapés" in a poll of forty top chefs, food experts and critics conducted by Waitrose Foods, the upscale British supermarket. It scored nine out of ten in a survey that judged cocktail fare by social rating, taste, and "wow factor":

> Maligned by some as dull, the cheese straw is, in fact, and quite correctly, pre-eminent among canapés. Its glowing, golden complexion can entice and it brings with it a message of comfort and wholeness. It rises above the one-bite rule and can be waved around and drive home important conversational points. It's solid enough to provide a good foil to alcohol,

and its only drawback is its threat of crumbs falling to the carpet. But hey, as long as it's not your house, who cares?[26]

There is also a prevailing nostalgia for the foods that our mothers and grandmothers made, even if it's Kool-Aid.[27] Nowadays when we talk about the "old days," though, we usually mean *post*-World War II, not *pre*-. The late forties, the fifties, and the sixties were times of great prosperity (and cocktail parties!) in America. Recipes for canapés flourished in the old port cities of New Orleans, Charleston, Mobile, and Savannah, each well-known as drinking towns from their beginnings.

The Junior League of Charleston's *Charleston Receipts*, first published in 1950, is the oldest continuously-published fundraiser cookbook in America. It includes, in its second chapter, "Canapés," a perfectly acceptable recipe (though I usually add some red pepper flakes as well as the finely ground cayenne called for). Like *The Picayune Creole Cook Book*, *Charleston Receipts* includes an entire "Beverages" chapter—the first!—composed mostly of highly potent punches to serve dozens.[28]

I'm sure that cheese straws were already a tradition in the Lowcountry prior to *Charleston Receipts*, although they don't appear in *Two Hundred Years of Charleston Cooking*, published in 1930, which was assembled under the watchful eye of some visiting Yankees who certainly knew from cocktail parties, as they say. I remind myself, however, as the late scholar Karen Hess often proclaimed, that "the lag between practice and printed word is one of the most frustrating aspects of work in the discipline of culinary history."[29] And so I keep looking. Since beginning this article, in fact, I have found recipes nearly identical to the one in *Charleston Receipts* in several fundraiser cookbooks published in South Carolina in 1948, as well as in *The Savannah Cookbook*, from 1933.[30]

I have published some very good recipes for cheese straws that will cook up perfectly every time, but, truth be told, I like to tinker with cheese straws more than just about anything that I cook. Sometimes I use that egg yolk and sometimes I don't. I've tried flavoring them with anchovies, red pepper paste (that I buy in a squeeze tube), *tuong ot toi* (Vietnamese chile paste with garlic), and a variety of cheeses. I used to insist on unbleached flour and very sharp, authentic cheddar. I also used to mix the dough by hand, and roll them out once. Because there's no liquid in the dough, though, I've found that the more it is worked—that is, the more times it is folded over itself, like pastry dough—the flakier the cheese straws will be. But you *should* use a soft southern flour such as White Lily if you can find it, because it has less gluten (the tough molecules that stretch and hold the air in yeast breads, giving them substance): you want your straws to be flaky and light. The thinner you roll them, the flakier, as well.

I assembled ten typical recipes from a variety of sources both old and new, then figured the average ingredients: 3 cups of grated cheese, 1½ to 2 cups of flour, 7 tablespoons of butter, 1 egg yolk, and salt and cayenne to taste (from ⅛ to 1 teaspoon of each). When all is said and done, recipes vary little.

One thing's for sure: the more flavorful the cheese and seasoning, the better the straws. Shirley King (1931-2005), the great chef and food writer, spiced hers with anchovies and advised, "If you like a sharp-tasting cheese straw, use Gruyère."[31] Lately I've been making them with blue cheese, to much praise. The crackers will have a slightly bluish tint to them. Put them out with the beverage of your choice and watch them disappear!

. . . .

Blue Cheese Straws

Use a fairly dry blue cheese, not a creamy one, in this recipe. There are some flavorful ones made in America these days. You can even use the already crumbled blue cheese found in every grocer's dairy case. Believe me, I've used it at friends' beach houses and folks have raved.

2 ounces (½ stick) unsalted butter
½ teaspoon salt, plus more for garnish
½ pound blue cheese, crumbled (see headnote)
¼ teaspoon cayenne, plus more for garnish
1 cup all purpose (preferably soft southern) flour, plus more for dusting
1 egg yolk (optional)

Preheat the oven to 350°F.

Put all of the ingredients except the egg yolk in the work bowl of a food processor and blend with the steel blade until the mixture comes together in a ball. If the cheese is very dry, you may need to add the egg yolk to make the mixture form a ball. But let the processor do its thing. It will probably make the ball without the yolk.

Divide the dough in half, dust a counter and rolling pin with flour, and roll the first half of the dough out to ¼-inch thickness, in a rectangular shape. Keep folding the dough over and rolling it out until you have a perfect rectangle, about 5 by 9 inches. Place any trimmings with the remaining half of dough. Using a long knife, score the rectangle into twenty crackers, each about ½-inch wide and 4½-inches long. Carefully lift the straws up, using a metal spatula if necessary, and place them close together, but not touching, on a heavy baking sheet. Roll out the remaining dough and cut similarly. Sprinkle with salt and/or cayenne, if desired. Bake the straws for 20 to 25 minutes, or until they just begin to brown. Lift them up onto racks to cool. When perfectly cool, remove them to airtight tins to store. They may be frozen for later use.

Makes 3 to 4 dozen.

NOTES

1. Poppy Z. Brite, *Liquor: A Novel* (New York: Three Rivers Press, 2004), 61.
2. Bill Neal, *Biscuits, Spoonbread, and Sweet Potato Pie* (New York: Alfred A. Knopf, 1991), 54.
3. Gabriel Tschumi, *Royal Chef; recollections of life in royal households from Queen Victoria to Queen Mary* (London: W. Kimber, 1954), 194–226.
4. Neal, 54.
5. Elizabeth David, *Spices, Salt and Aromatics in the English Kitchen* (Harmondsworth, Middlesex, England: Penguin Books, 1970), 230–31.
6. Ibid, 25.
7. Adrian Bailey, *Recipes: The Cooking of the British Isles* (New York: Time-Life Books, 1969), 15.
8. Jane Garmey, *Great British Cooking: A Well-Kept Secret* (New York: Harper Perennial, 1981, 1992), 162.
9. Jane Grigson, *Jane Grigson's British Cookery*, 1st American ed. (New York: Atheneum Publishers, 1985), 132.
10. *The Oxford English Dictionary* (Oxford: Oxford University Press, 1971), 877.
11. *Le Petit Robert* (Paris: Société du Nouveau Littré, 1978), 187.
12. *OED*, Supplement, 246.
13. Ibid, 183.
14. *Cookies and Crackers* (Alexandria, VA: Time-Life Books, 1982), 162.
15. Verta Grosvenor, *Vibration Cooking or The Travel Notes of a Geechee Girl* (Garden City, NY: Doubleday, 1970), 74–75.
16. John L. Hess and Karen Hess, *The Taste of America* (New York: Grossman Publishers, 1977), 134.
17. Mrs. (Isabella Mary) Beeton, *The Book of Household Management* (London: S. O. Beeton, 1861), 817–18.
18. Annabella P. Hill, *Mrs. Hill's Southern Practical Cookery and Receipt Book: A facsimile of Mrs. Hill's New Cook Book, 1872 edition,* with Historical Commentary by Damon L. Fowler (Columbia: University of South Carolina Press, 1995), 430.

19. Mrs. A. P. Hill, *Mrs. Hill's New Cook Book* (New York: Carleton, Publisher, Madison Square, 1872), 232.

20. F. L. Gillette and Hugo Ziemann, *White House Cook Book* (New York: Gillette Publishing Company, 1887), 254.

21. Ibid, iii.

22. *The New Dixie Cook-Book and Practical Housekeeper* (Atlanta: L.A. Clarkson & Co., 1889), 189–90.

23. Marion, Ohio, First Presbyterian Church. Ladies Aid Society, *Recipes Tried and True* (Marion, OH: Press of Kelley Mount, 1894), 84.

24. Ibid.

25. *The Picayune Creole Cook Book*: An unbabridged republication of the second edition, as published by *The Picayune* in 1901 (New York: Dover Publications, Inc., 1971), 199.

26. *Waitrose Food Illustrated*, November 2005, as quoted on the grocery giant's website at www.waitrose.com/food/celebritiesandarticles/foodissues/0511038 .aspx.

27. John L. Hess and Karen Hess, *The Taste of America*: a reprint edition with new comments by the authors. (Champaign: University of Illinois Press, 2000), xi.

28. The Junior League of Charleston, *Charleston Receipts* (Charleston, South Carolina: Walker, Evans & Cogswell, 1950).

29. Karen Hess, *The Carolina Rice Kitchen: The African Connection* (Columbia: University of South Carolina Press, 1992), 44.

30. *Orangeburg's Choice Recipes*, sponsored by Orangeburg's P.T.A. (Orangeburg, SC: Walter D. Berry Printing, 1948) 81; *Mt. Pleasant's Famous Recipes* compiled by Mt. Pleasant P.T.A. (n.p., 1948), 74; Harriet Ross Colquitt, *The Savannah Cook Book* (Charleston: Walker, Evans & Cogswell Co., 1933), 18.

31. Shirley King, *Saucing the Fish* (New York: Simon and Schuster, 1986), 82.

Mikel's Mother's Chocolate Chip Cookies

For years, I tried to get the recipe from Dixie, my mother-in-law, who swore to me time and time again that she simply followed the Toll House cookie recipe on the package of Nestlé Semi-Sweet Morsels.

I've been a chocolate snob since my father first brought us rich dark candies from Switzerland, Belgium, and Germany in the early sixties. I've never cared for milk chocolate, which has always tasted to me the way powdered milk smells. And until the vast improvements in the 1990s, I always found the waxy quality and insipid taste of American chocolates inferior. I never liked Nestlé's chocolate chips. But I made "America's Favorite Cookie Recipe," as it's called on the package, several times, hoping to capture the elusive qualities of Dixie's. Though I followed the recipe precisely, they never tasted like hers. I finally decided that it was simply because they were Dixie's that her cookies were better. I couldn't really know, though, since I had never eaten more than one or two of them.

We were living in South Carolina then and would often go to her farm in the Pee Dee region of the state for relaxation—and for Mikel to get his fill of cookies. I began tasting them with a cook's discerning palate. Though I knew she included a cup of pecans in the recipe, and I could taste them, I could barely perceive their physical presence. I asked her if she ground them finely in a food processor, even though I had once witnessed her chopping them by hand with a knife. "I chop them as finely as I feel like it at the moment," she told me. "The finer, the better, but sometimes I give out sooner than others." She lives near the world's largest seller of pecans, so I bought some freshly shelled jumbo halves while visiting her and made the recipe, chopping them by hand until they were fine, but not so fine as a food processor would do.

They still weren't right.

A couple of years went by. The recipe on the package calls for "packed brown sugar." Light or dark?

Dixie swore it didn't matter. "Whichever I have on hand."

I tried half-and-half. No go.

She sent some to Mikel for Christmas one year, in an old Christmas tin. There's a piece of masking tape on the top of it that says, "Better if frozen."

The cookies were delicious, very finely grained and delicate. Aha! I thought. She uses soft southern flour, like White Lily. So I rushed out and bought some, and made a new batch, and put them in the old Christmas tin with Dixie's handwriting on it. We had guests coming for the weekend, and as I watched Mikel take his first bite of the imposters, I asked him how they were. "Not bad," was all I got.

"Well, don't eat all of them, we've got guests coming."

He closed the tin and put it back in the freezer.

"How did they taste?"

They tasted fine, I knew, but, after several days, I got him to explain to me that it was the fact that his mother's freezer is always filled with them, and that he can eat as many as he wants, whenever he wants, that makes them so special. There really is something deeply maternal going on here, I thought, and, no matter what, mine will never be Dixie's cookies. I even convinced myself that the tins themselves were what made the difference. At Dixie's they are all old Tetley tea tins from the fifties. So I went online to try to find some, but it was Christmastime, and folks were asking fifty to a hundred dollars apiece for the tins, obviously capitalizing on the nostalgia factor during the holidays! I had my limits.

At some point last winter, I was chatting with Dixie on the phone and asked her point-blank: Are you *sure* you are telling me everything? Do you use a special flour?

"No, I just use SwansDown, the same I always have."

I could have killed her! All these years I've been trying to duplicate a cookie whose formula is a world-renowned, often-published recipe that appears on every bag of Nestlé's chocolate chips. Except one little thing: she uses cake flour!

About the same time, Mikel's birthday was approaching, so I went back online to see if I could find Tetley tea tins, and, eBay be thanked, I found two for ten dollars, including shipping! I couldn't find SwansDown, but I did find Pillsbury's Softasilk.

I made the cookies, put them in the Tetley tins, and tucked them into the freezer. I let him find them there himself, and even let him think that his mother had sent them. I wasn't about to tell him that the supply was limited. And he tasted them and smiled. But we both knew: they weren't Dixie's. I've read the recipe a hundred times. I follow it to a tee. I'm not going to print it here, because you can find it online very easily, or on the Nestlé package.

I do know that Dixie's are more delicate than mine. Maybe it's the flour. Maybe it's the hand-chopping of the nuts, which I let the food processor do, which I know renders them oilier. But I also know that the recipe says to use rounded tablespoons and Dixie's are more like rounded teaspoons.

And since mine will never be Dixie's, I've also given up the Nestlé for better chocolate chips. The richer chips are creamier and darker and maintain a molten core, even when they're frozen. I like them, and Mikel tolerates them. They just aren't his mother's.

French Fries

When I lived in Paris, there was a bistro a block from my apartment that served the best *pommes frites* I've ever eaten. It was a neighborhood hangout, full of working-class men, gallery owners, students, and an occasional tourist. I remember it as always being open, though I often arrived too late for the roast chicken, the house specialty, which was always simply prepared with the finest *poulet de Bresse*. The chicken, like the steak, was served with fries.

The bistro was really not much more than a café, and it was run by a husband-and-wife team; they both cooked and worked in the front of the house. Though I never knew her name, "Madame" let me into her kitchen to watch her fry potatoes. Like the English, Madame used to use rendered beef fat for frying. The last time I saw her, they had stopped frying altogether and had simplified their menu to mostly sandwiches. One of the art dealers in the neighborhood had hopes of maintaining the café after Madame and Monsieur retired, but I feared then that I would never have fries like those again.

In an ironic twist of fate, however, there has been a great resurgence in traditional fare on the other side of the Atlantic, and I recently discovered that the space was taken over in 2005 by the Michelin-starred chef Alain Ducasse. He is playing on its history and maintaining classic bistro fare, though it is fancier now. I now know that the restaurant was in the same family for three generations. Their name was Petit. The bistro, Benoit, is located at 20, rue St Martin, in the fourth arrondisement. Just a few blocks from the Pompidou Center.

My fries are pretty damn close to the Petits'. I use lard, but you can use peanut oil as well. The potatoes are fried twice, once at a lower temperature, then quickly again in hotter fat. Beef fat or lard will begin to smoke if it goes above 375°F; you must put the fries in the second that it reaches that temperature. Madame fried all of her potatoes for the day ahead of time, then set her fryer at the higher temperature and flash-fried them to order. Her fryer had a basket that allowed excess oil to drain off; she did not pat them dry, but simply dumped them out onto the plates and served them piping hot.

. . . .

3 pounds (4 Idaho or russet) baking potatoes

Lard or peanut oil for frying

Salt

At least 30 minutes and up to 2 hours before serving, peel the potatoes and cut them into ¼-inch batons. Lay the potatoes out on a towel and fold it up around them so that they don't darken while you heat the lard or oil. Line a large colander with crumpled paper towels and set aside.

Put lard or oil in a deep pot to a depth of 3 inches. Heat over medium heat to 350°F. Fry the potatoes in five or six batches, about 1 cup at a time. As each batch is lightly browned, after about 7 minutes, remove the potatoes from the oil with a wire mesh strainer, allowing any excess oil to drain back in the pot before placing them in the colander. Place more crumpled paper towels on top of the batch before adding the next. Fry all of the potatoes, then remove them from the colander to a baking sheet, discarding the paper towels and patting the potatoes dry of all grease. Place them in a dry place such as an unheated oven. Turn off the heat under the fat until ready to finish frying.

When ready to fry, reheat the fat to 375°F. Be very careful if you are using lard and do not let it go any higher. Remove the fries from the baking sheet to another container. Place a wire rack on the baking sheet. Fry the potatoes in batches again, keeping the oil right at 375°. Fry until golden brown, between 1 and 2 minutes. Remove immediately to the prepared baking sheet to drain and finish the frying. Do not salt them until serving; better yet, let each diner salt his own so that they don't get soggy.

Serve with homemade mayonnaise, not the blender variety (recipe follows).

Serves 6.

MAYONNAISE

This is so much easier if someone helps. It only takes a couple of minutes to make and you'll wonder why you ever bought that weird white stuff at the store made from all sorts of things like soy oil and sugar! Mayonnaise was originally made with only olive oil, as it still is in Liguria, where I learned to make it in a mortar with a pestle. Most Americans and Europeans today are used to mayonnaise made with lighter tasting oils, and often gussied up with mustard and other flavorings. Do yourself a favor and omit the mustard this time and be sure to include at least 25% of the olive oil of your choice (if you like a bold mayo, go ahead and use a bolder oil such as a Tuscan blend). You won't be disappointed.

All ingredients must be at room temperature. Take your time. If the mayo is too thin, add some more oil. If it's too thick, add some more lemon juice. If it separates, warm it in a hot water bath, begin with a teaspoon of prepared mustard, and start whisking in the broken sauce just as you would the oil.

2 large egg yolks
freshly squeezed lemon juice
¾ cup lightly flavored oil such as grapeseed or peanut combined with ¼ cup lightly flavored extra virgin olive oil, such as a Spanish oil made from arbequina olives or a Ligurian oil made from taggiasca olives
salt and cayenne to taste

Place the egg yolks in a heavy bowl or mortar or place the bowl on a damp towel so that it won't move around on the counter. Whisk the eggs lightly and add about a teaspoon of the lemon juice, beating the mixture until it is foamy.

Now, beating constantly, slowly add the oil, drop by drop at first, until you have added about ¼ cup. (This is where the extra set of hands comes in handy: one to add the oil, the other to beat.) When the mayo begins to thicken, you can start adding the oil in a stream, whisking constantly and adding only so much oil at a time as you can whisk in at once.

Continue adding the oil until it is all incorporated.

Season to taste with salt, cayenne, and more lemon juice, if desired. Whisk thoroughly and serve immediately or store covered in the refrigerator for no more than a couple of days.

Makes about 1 cup.

Minestrone

··

Genoa, Italy, is said to be the home of minestrone, but the soup appears there in as many forms as it does in the States. The most common Genoese form, *menestron* in dialect, does not resemble the "big soups" that we know from the Italian-American tradition—that is, a vegetable soup chock full of fully recognizable ingredients. Throughout Liguria, and in Genoa in particular, minestrone is more likely to be a thick soup of beans and vegetables cooked down until they have totally fallen apart and melded together. Sometimes bolstered with pasta, and often seasoned with a parmesan rind, the minestra might also be finished off with a swirl of fresh pesto just before serving.

Recipes might include one or more types of beans, both shelled and fresh green; cauliflower; pumpkin, or winter squash; potatoes; carrots, celery, leeks and/or onions; tomatoes; zucchini; peas; eggplant; mushrooms (usually dried); cabbage (*cavolo cappucio*, our common cabbage) as well as other greens such as kale or chard; and herbs. Most versions contain neither meat nor broth. In one book from 1867, the author says that the soup is a summer specialty of Genoa, but that it can be made in other seasons if you can find sun-dried vegetables, canned tomatoes, and dried beans to substitute for the fresh.

One of my Genoese cookbooks provides only two traditional recipes, one seasoned with soffrito (aromatic vegetables cooked in oil) and another with pesto. The latter calls specifically for *fagioli lumé*, also known as Fagioli di Lamon della Vallata Bellunese, which we know as either cannellini (white) or borlotti (cranberry) beans, from north of Venice. The recipe also specifies "a little cabbage called in Genovese *gaggetta*," of which I've never heard, though "half of a Savoy cabbage" can be substituted. I love winter soups made with dried white cannellini beans and greens. Sometimes I add sausage, and sometimes I use stock. I've never really used a recipe.

In looking through my Genoese cookbooks, I found several variations, generally defined as follows:

Minestrone con Soffrito. Aromatic vegetables cooked in oil (the soffrito). This summer version is made with fresh beans.

Minestrone con Pesto. Also called Minestrone alla Genovese, according to David Downie, who writes that "for inexplicable reasons, in this case the pesto does not contain pine nuts and sometimes does not contain cheese."

Minestrone con Corsetti, a coin-like fresh pasta that is stamped in a mold.

Minestrone al Pesto con Brichetti, a type of pasta made specifically to be used in soups (De Cecco makes them).

Minestrone di Riso, made with rice in the summer, with fresh beans and tomatoes.

Minestrone Alla Sudista

This southern ("sudista") minestrone, is made with collards, which take much longer to cook than the normal cabbages and chards of Italian versions. Being a southerner, I'm used to making these winter soups with animal fats (bacon and duck fat, for example) or with sausages, country ham, or meats to bolster them. Ligurians are right to distinguish between summer and winter versions of minestrone, for it's hard to get the bright flavors of a summer soup in a vegetarian winter broth. That's why they often swirl in a bit of pesto just before serving. I've been known to add hot pepper vinegar, soy sauce, Asian fish sauce, anchovies, lemon juice, and chopped herbs to vegetable soups in winter to boost the flavors. I also don't throw away any of the tough rinds from grana—Italian grating cheeses—such as parmesan and pecorino; they add complexity and flavor to soups such as these. If ever "season to taste" means just that, it's in soup making!

You don't have to soak the beans overnight. There's a popular quick method of soaking beans in hot salted water for an hour, but I find that it loosens the skins and dulls the flavor. In a pinch, you could use canned. But I usually soak them overnight, as I've done here.

¾ cup dried cannellini
   beans
2 cloves garlic, unpeeled
1 sprig fresh thyme
Sea salt
Extra virgin olive oil
1 cup chopped celery,
   3 to 4 ribs
1 cup chopped carrots,
   about 2
2 cups chopped onions,
   about 2
1 pound collards, 1 to 2
   dozen leaves, stems and
   tough ribs removed, cut
   into strips
Hot red pepper flakes
   (optional)
2 large, ripe plum
   tomatoes, peeled and
   chopped
2 average red potatoes,
   peeled and diced
8 cups chicken or
   vegetable stock
1 tablespoon red wine
   vinegar
1 tablespoon hot pepper
   vinegar (optional)
Parmesan rinds (optional)
3 ounces (about ¾ cup)
   dried, short tubular
   pasta such as ditalini
Butter, optional
3 tablespoons fresh
   chopped parsley, basil,
   and/or marjoram
Freshly ground black
   pepper and other
   seasonings to taste
Freshly grated Parmesan

The night before, soak the beans in water that covers them by at least an inch. Drain, rinse, then place in a saucepan with 5 cups of water, the garlic, and the thyme. Bring to boil, reduce the heat, and allow to cook until tender, but slightly al dente. It will take anywhere from 1¼ to 2 hours, depending on the age of the beans and how slowly you cook them. I boil them hard for a few minutes, then turn them down low and let them cook very slowly. I find that by the time they are done, the water is nearly all gone. When they are almost done, discard the thyme, remove the garlic and set aside, salt the beans lightly, then cover the pot, and set aside.

Cover the bottom of a large, heavy pot, such as an enameled cast-iron Dutch oven (I use my 7 quart Le Creuset pot), with a film of olive oil, slip the garlic from the bean pot out of its papery skin and add it, then, over medium-high heat, add the celery, carrots, and onions, sautéing the soffrito until the vegetables are limp. Work quickly, stirring constantly, but don't allow the vegetables to brown. Grab handfuls of the collards and add them to the pot, continuing to sauté over medium-high heat. Add the water that clings to the collards as well as you stir-fry the vegetables until the collards wilt. Continue adding handfuls of collards and stirring, adding more olive oil and a pinch of salt with each handful, if desired. If you want your soup spicy, you can add some hot red pepper flakes along with the collards (or you can add hot pepper vinegar later).

When all of the collards are wilted and glistening with oil, add the tomatoes and potatoes and stir well, then add the stock. Bring the mixture to a boil, reduce the heat, add the reserved beans, vinegars, and optional cheese rinds, and simmer until the potatoes and collards are done to your liking. In the meantime, cook the pasta until it is al dente, drain, and toss with a little butter or olive oil and the chopped herbs.

Add the pasta to the soup and stir well, then correct the seasoning with salt, pepper, and whatever else you want.

Serve hot with crusty bread and freshly grated Parmesan.

Makes 8 servings.

Why I Don't Make
Wedding Cakes

In 1993, I had just met my partner Mikel, and life was good. The press was raving about my first book, even a year after its debut, and I was at work on my exciting second project, which took me all over the South. My best friend was thinking about moving to Charleston, my sister was running my shop for me, and I had offers from a dozen publishers wanting a book from me. Charleston had recovered from Hurricane Hugo, and business was hoppin'. Another one of my dearest friends, Mary Edna Fraser, the batik artist, had fallen in love with her children's pediatrician. She asked me to make their wedding cake.

I am a decent baker, but I don't do "pretty." My desserts tend to be on the homey side—cobblers, simple layer cakes, ice creams and custards, and poached fruits. I know a perfect cake recipe that I vary a dozen ways, but I wouldn't put any of them in a bakery display case, however delicious they may be. I told Mary Edna that I would make her cake as long as she didn't care what it looked like. I promised her it would be delicious.

The wedding was planned for August. There would be fifty guests at the reception. Casual. Outdoors. At Mary Edna's home on the marsh.

No problem! I'll make a cake to feed eighty!

Charleston's master confectioner Mark Gray and I had just spent a week candying figs, an ancient, and nearly impossible, task. I had a tin full of them, four or five dozen. A wedding cake seemed easy by comparison.

I made the cake layers the night before the wedding and tucked them into the refrigerator to chill, to make them easier to slice into even thinner layers. As I wrote in *The New Southern Cook*, which I was working on at the time, I had no fear of cake baking. Here's what I wrote then:

. . . .

Cakes

It is bewildering to me why people—even good cooks—shy away from cake baking. Everyone seems to have a fear of the cake falling or being too dry, or of what is perceived as strict scientific method. I seldom refer to a recipe when I bake cakes, because I know one good, basic formula that is infinitely variable. It's a variation on a European sponge cake, and it relies on no artificial leavening, just air beaten into eggs.

Different flours, cocoa, bread or cake crumbs, or ground nuts can be used in this basic cake recipe. The coconut cake and Huguenot torte in my first book are both butterless variations of this recipe, the one full of fresh coconut, and the other of chopped apples, pecans, and walnuts [see Nut Mix for Apple Nut Torte, p. 4]. The cake keeps as well as a classic génoise, can be drenched in fruit syrups or liqueurs, and is simplicity itself to make.

Basic Cake Recipe

13 eggs at room temperature

2 cups sugar, divided

½ cup unsalted butter, melted but not hot

1 tablespoon vanilla

2 cups sifted soft southern flour or cake flour

Pinch of salt

Grease three 9-inch cake pans, line with parchment or wax paper, and grease the paper. Dust the insides of the pans lightly with flour. Preheat the oven to 350°F and set the oven rack in the lower third of the oven.

Separate the eggs, putting the yolks in a wide stainless steel bowl that will fit snugly over a saucepan. Add 1 cup of the sugar to the yolks and beat well with a whisk, then place the pan over simmering water and continue beating until the yolks are thick and light-colored, about 5 to 7 minutes. Add the butter a little at a time and continue beating until the mixture is very thick and has doubled in volume. Stir in the vanilla, turn off the heat, and proceed with the recipe, occasionally beating the yolk mixture to keep it fluffy and to prevent a skin from forming.

In the large bowl of an electric mixer, beat the egg whites until they are very foamy, then gradually add the remaining cup of sugar and continue beating until they have formed soft peaks. Remove the yolk mixture from the heat and fold in the beaten whites, using the wire whisk. Sift the flour and salt over the mixture and fold in swiftly, but gently, until just mixed. Scoop big batches of the batter up from the bottom of the bowl and pull the whisk straight up, allowing the flour to sift through the wires. You do not want to knock the air out of the mixture.

Divide the batter between the three cake pans and bake in the preheated oven for about 25 minutes or until the cakes just begin to pull away from the pans and a toothpick stuck in the center of the cakes comes out clean. Remove to racks to cool in the pans. As soon as they are cool enough to handle, remove the cakes from the pans, remove the paper lining, and set them to finish cooling on the racks before assembling the cake with fillings and icings.

FILLINGS AND ICINGS

The above cake can be drenched in your favorite liquor or liqueur, covered with jam, and iced with buttercream. I once made a friend's wedding cake by stacking six large layers of this cake, shaved slightly so as to form a large cone. The layers were drenched in the sugar syrup from preserved figs. Between the layers, a layer of those preserves was topped with buttercream sweetened with the fig syrup. The entire cake was wrapped in rolled fondant then covered with crystallized golden figs. It was the most delicious cake I have ever eaten, and the eighty servings were devoured by the fifty guests in a matter of minutes. But the easiest icing, made with whipped cream, is also one of the most delicious. Bolstered with egg whites, it will hold up a little longer than plain whipped cream.

. . . .

I can't believe how nonchalantly I told the story in *New Southern*. The day was a near disaster! A few years ago I saw a book entitled *Don't Try This at Home: Culinary Catastrophes from the World's Greatest Chefs*. I remember thinking, they should have asked me (though I am NOT a chef)!

On the morning of the wedding, I awakened to discover, to my horror, that the air conditioning unit that had somehow survived the hurricane had indeed finally succumbed to the salt water that had drenched it. It was close to a hundred degrees already, and the wedding was in the middle of the day. For some idiotic reason, I decided to make fondant icing. Fondant is one of the trickiest of sugar concoctions. I had never made it before. What was I thinking?!

Fondant icing is made by softening the coating over gentle heat and diluting it carefully so that it remains the right consistency to encase pastries with a shiny, pure white layer. I had read the instructions in several different pastry books and made notes that I had stuck to the oven hood. One of them I wrote in block letters: NEVER LET IT GO ABOVE 100°!! I looked at the thermometer on the wall: it was 102 degrees in my closet of a kitchen!

Emboldened by my fig work with Mark, I marched on, the fondant rolling off the edge of the counter and never setting up. The wedding was in less than two hours. I panicked!

I drenched the cake layers in fig syrup and slathered fig preserves between them. I made buttercream icing, using fig syrup instead of sugar, and added that between the layers as well. I tried coating the cake with fondant, but it rolled off the sides. I had to start anew with the icing. Again I stupidly tried to make fondant (the first batch was filled with cake crumbs). I called my friend Paula, who is a great home cook, but who, I doubt, had any experience with professional baking, much less a wedding cake to feed fifty. Her husband, Tommy, a friend of mine since graduate school, answered the phone. Paula was out of town. He would be right over. Having known me so long, I'm sure he had never heard such despair in my voice.

I called Mary Edna. The wedding was in an hour.

"Do you remember what I told you when I agreed to make your wedding cake?"

A short pause, but she, too, could sense the panic in my voice. "Yes."

"What did I say?!" I all but screamed at her. An hour before she was to wed.

"You said that you couldn't promise what it would look like, but that it would be delicious."

"Okay, as long as you remember. My air conditioner's broken and it's a hundred degrees in my kitchen and I'm having a real problem with the icing."

"I'm sure it will be fine. See you soon!"

I had to shave the cake layers down because the first batch of fondant had taken the edges with it as it oozed down the sides of the cake. I rolled the new batch of stiffer fondant out and somehow managed to get it wrapped around the cone-shaped cake, but no sooner had the fondant covered the cake than it started to slide down the sides again. I stepped outside, where it was actually cooler, and placed the cake down inside a chest freezer I had on the covered patio just outside the door. I felt like a fool.

Tommy arrived. The wedding was in less than an hour. "What's wrong?"

"Mary Edna's wedding cake! My A.C. is broken and the icing won't set." I was nearly in tears. I opened the freezer and showed him my mess of a cake.

"Oh, my," he said. "Do you have any vodka?"

"Yes, in the freezer inside. Why?"

He opened the freezer, poured two juice glasses full and toasted Mary Edna and John, her soon-to-be husband. "Drink this. We'll just have to decorate it with some greenery and flowers."

I drank up, despondent. It was August, and there were no flowers or edible greenery, I knew, anywhere near my house. Charleston was at its hottest, its muggiest, its worst season. Nothing was blooming. But the vodka felt good.

Tommy was sifting through the refrigerator, through cabinets, drawers, and canisters. "Go take a shower. We'll fix it."

I showered and got dressed but was soaking wet from sweat within a matter of minutes. Tommy was standing in the living room, with the vodka bottle in one hand, refilling our glasses. In the other, he held my figs. My precious figs. "How many people is the cake supposed to feed?" he asked, handing me another glass of vodka.

"Fifty, why?"

"Perfect. You have exactly fifty of these. I ate one. They're delicious. Didn't you say the cake is filled with figs?" His mind was racing. I needed to leave for the church. "Do you have any toothpicks?"

My heart sank, not only because of my culinary disaster, but also because I saw that Tommy was going to offer up all fifty of my figs—a week's worth of work—for Mary Edna and John's wedding cake.

"Go," he said. "I'll put the figs on the cake and put it back in the freezer. Swing by again after the wedding and pick up the cake. I'll wait for you."

I had to go pick up our friend Kate. I had nothing on my stomach but two juice glasses of vodka. But I was no longer worried. I kept saying to myself, over and over, "Remember she doesn't care what it looks like." I knew it would be delicious, as I had promised. I was dying for a piece of it right then!

The wedding was a hoot. Though it took place in the Second Presbyterian Church in downtown Charleston, on the highest point in the peninsula, there was nothing "high Presbyterian" about it. "I'm in Love with a Big Blue Frog" was used instead of the Wedding March, to give you a clue.

Mary Edna upon first seeing her wedding cake I had made. Photo by Kate Bennett.

Mary Edna and John live on a high bluff overlooking Ellis Creek on James Island. As the crow flies, it's just a mile or two from downtown. After the church service, Kate and I rushed by my house to find a note from Tommy. "Tell Mary Edna I said hello. It's too hot over here."

We opened the freezer and found the cake, studded with all fifty of my candied figs. One for each of the wedding guests. Kate managed to get a snap of Mary Edna the second she saw the cake. I had made her turn her back and repeat what she had told me—that it didn't matter what it looked like—before I let her see it. As it turned out, some folks were mesmerized by it: they had never seen candied figs. Given that it was the cake for a frog wedding, it does seem fitting.

And, as I wrote in *New Southern*, it was delicious, and all eighty pieces were devoured by the fifty guests in a matter of minutes.

But never again will I agree to make a wedding cake!

Watermelon

➤ WASHINGTON, DC, 2009 ···

Charleston watermelon market, *Frank Leslie's Illustrated Newspaper,* **1866.**

I didn't realize that people actually paid for watermelon until I went away to college. In the Lowcountry of South Carolina where I grew up, there were melon fields all over the place, and while the growers certainly shipped their melons to markets and grocers across the country, some of them even operating roadside stands near their fields, there were also often pyramids of the heavy fruits stacked near the road for people to take what they wanted. Down on Edisto Island, we would often have huge meals in the middle of the day, with two meats—say, fried chicken and ham—and a plethora of the local produce from the neighboring truck farms: squash and okra, field peas and tomatoes, corn, butterbeans, cucumbers, and, for dessert, watermelons. Mrs. McGee always had a cake, pie, or cobbler as well, and we would all gorge ourselves on the bounty, napping and playing cards and board games for an hour after lunch before we could head back into the surf. We would often take long slices of watermelon—they were nearly always the Charleston Gray variety, the long, striped preferred melon of the Lowcountry—with us into the water, where we would swim out beyond the breakers, allowing the slices to float amongst the swells, salted by the splashing foam.

Since childhood, I have loved my melons salted. Peppered, too. So I was not surprised when my chef friend Philip Bardin of the Old Post Office on Edisto called me in the early nineties and told me that I must come try his latest concoction—watermelon with Clemson Blue Cheese. What a perfect idea!

Clemson University maintains the Cooperative Extension in all of the state's forty-six counties, as well as five Research and Education Centers. Their developments in agriculture, horticulture, animal husbandry, pest control, food safety, nutrition, forestry, and dairy farming have been exemplary and world-renowned. They have helped restore important heirloom crops to the state, such as the famous Carolina Gold Rice, on which Charleston's fortunes were amassed. I can't tell you how many times I called someone at one of the extension offices when I was researching the culinary history of the Lowcountry, and when I was a backyard gardener in South Carolina.

Out of curiosity, I searched watermelons on the Clemson site, to see which variety they recommended for the area. Not surprisingly, it was the Charleston Gray.

The melon is a large one, twenty-five to forty pounds. We grew them in a community garden we were involved with in Washington, DC. The flesh is deep red, crisp, fibreless, and delicious. When I'm shopping for melons, I pick them up to see if they feel full of water. I thump them to see if they have a resounding hollow report. I ask where they were grown. Melons need warm soil; a long, hot growing season; a lot of room; a lot of water; calcium-rich soil; and to be grown on rotation basis. If your melons are from Florida, they will probably be good, as long as they are ripe.

Nowadays I see it copied everywhere on the internet and on other restaurant menus, but when Philip called me to tell me about his new salad in the 1990s, I had never heard of it. In his 2004 cookbook (with Jane and Michael Stern), he called it a "redneck version of melon and prosciutto. It's a weird dish . . . but it works." In the published recipe, he added country ham.

I emailed Philip to ask about the recipe, and in his reply, he wrote, "I came up with that one in the '90s—maybe 1992. Cubed and topped with Clemson Blue Cheese (I now use buttermilk blue). Sometimes chopped mint and a grilled piece of country ham. . . . BTW—it has to be watermelon and real sweet. The textures are strange with other melons and do not work to my taste."

. . . .

Watermelon with Blue Cheese and Mint

There's really no recipe here.

Just cut up some melon and some blue cheese however you choose, in whatever proportions you choose; toss them together, or arrange them in salad plates or bowls; and add a few fresh mint leaves, if desired. It's a lovely beginning to a meal.

Deconstructing
My Namesake

In 1985, I was apprenticing with Nach Waxman at his Kitchen Arts & Letters in New York, preparing to open my own culinary bookstore in Charleston, South Carolina. I hadn't decided on a name yet, but I was leaning toward the Educated Palate, which was roundly rebuffed by nearly everyone I knew. On New Year's Day I attended a party at another southern friend's apartment. I agreed to bring the hoppin' john, the celebratory southern dish made with rice and cowpeas (dried field peas). When I arrived with the dish, my friends began calling me "Hoppin' John," and the name stuck. There was no doubt what my business would be called.

I was born in Baton Rouge, Louisiana, but moved to the very similar terrain of the South Carolina coastal plain when I was three years old. I have eaten Creole cooking all my life. The first written recipe that I know of for hoppin' john, the "national" dish of the Lowcountry, appeared in *The Carolina Housewife* in 1847. Writing anonymously, as was the custom for Charleston women prior to the Nineteenth Amendment, Sarah Rutledge was the "Lady of Charleston" who penned this early American cookbook that established Lowcountry cooking as a creole cookery separate from the other cuisines emerging throughout the South. She was the daughter of Edward Rutledge, a signer of the Declaration of Independence, and niece of Arthur Middleton, another signer. Her version, calling for bacon, "red peas," and rice, is a Charleston "PER lō," as we say—a pilau or pilaf, a sort

The following article appeared in the Winter 2011 issue of *Gastronomica* (Volume 11, Issue 4), and is based on a lecture I gave at the first Beans + Rice conference at the Historic New Orleans Collection in 2010.

At the shop, late 1980s.
Photo by Gerald Wilkie.

Hoppin' John's° logo.
Batik by Mary Edna Fraser.

of bean and rice jambalaya. Miss Rutledge suggested adding, "*if liked*, a sprig of green mint." [Italics mine.][1] The Lowcountry classic, served on New Year's Day for good luck, is a very dry version of the dish, but it is served with greens (for financial success throughout the year) with their juices, as well as a side dish of more cowpeas and pot likker. Most folks today use black-eyed peas, which are one of many types of cowpeas.[2]

There have been many conjectures about the name, hoppin' john. My dear friend and colleague, the late, great culinary historian Karen Hess,[3] was convinced, and attempted to prove through assiduous research, that the name comes from the old Persian *bahatta kachang*, meaning cooked rice and beans, from Hindi and Malay origins. Her sources are historical, etymological, and sociological.[4] It makes sense, but I'm not convinced, though it's certainly more compelling than the folk etymologies surrounding the dish, for example, that it was hawked on the streets of Charleston by a crippled man known as Hoppin' John; that the name is a corruption of "pois à pigeon" (pigeon peas), another legume brought to the New World from Africa; or that children were required to hop around the table before the dish was served. Historians call these apocryphal tales "fakelore" because they are based on neither fact nor historical record; Karen added that "most of the proposed origins are demeaning to African Americans."[5]

The dish certainly came from West Africa, whence came both cowpeas and the enslaved who were great growers and cookers of rice. Wherever rice is grown in the world, you find dishes of rice and legumes, whose synergy is legend. The white men who owned the vast rice plantations in early Carolina, on which the fortunes of Charleston were built, probably knew little about rice prior to their arrival in the New World, where they found themselves the owners of not only land, but humans as well. It is to the ancestors of today's Black Americans that I raise my glass on New Year's, with our meal of hoppin' john, collards, sweet potatoes, and roast pork. For it is they, the enslaved people from the West African Rice Coast, who knew the systems of wetland rice cultivation; it was they who cleared the land, built the embankments, cultivated the floodplains, sowed the seeds, maintained the weeding, harvested the crop, hoed the stubble, burned the remains, threshed the sheaves, winnowed with baskets of their own making, milled with mortars and pestles of their own making, and, finally, cooked the rice.[6] As I have written many times before, neither the French nor the English who owned the rice plantations in Carolina knew much of anything about rice cookery; I dare say they still don't.

Hess speculated in her seminal work, *The Carolina Rice Kitchen: The African Connection,* that there is a Provençal connection to the pilaus of Carolina. In Charleston you might hear "pĭ LŌ" or "PER lŏ" or "per LOO" or several other pronunciations of the word, but I always say "PER lŏ" no matter how it's spelled. Hess wrote, "Pilau is the most characteristic dish of the Carolina rice kitchen. . . . Word and dish come from Persia. . . . The classic pilau is not so much a receipt as a culinary concept." Twenty pages later, as she traces the pilau by following Islam through Turkey and Spain to Paris as early as 1300, and to Provençal cookbooks of the nineteenth century, she hypothesized that "the pilau was brought to Carolina by Huguenots fleeing persecution." Hess asked me to read the manuscript twice before publication, and twice I protested. But she countered in the book, "It has been objected that most Huguenots in Carolina did not come from Provence, or even the Midi. Considering that some of the most important strongholds were in the Midi, particularly in the Cévennes, adjacent to Provence, it seems reasonable to suppose that there must at least have been a few. Nor does the objection take into account the compelling presence of rice in South Carolina." Her supposition that since the rest of the French and English settlers would have known nothing about rice cookery, but "even a single family from Provence could very nearly have introduced such a concept into the new rice lands" diminishes the strength of the major thesis of her work, which she calls the "skill of the African-American cooks who had long known rice cookery, almost surely including certain versions of pilau."[7]

Culinary history is fascinating, but these days I'm far more interested in both the "big picture" and the cultural aspects of food. Hoppin' john is, simply, a bean and rice pilau which has traveled from the Lowcountry plantations to wherever both black and white southerners have settled. The dish may have originated in West Africa, but this delicious, nutritious favorite of the enslaved Africans must have quickly moved from slave cabin to the "Big House," and from there to the tables of Charleston merchants and freedmen, European Americans, Jews, Christians, cooks and eaters both rich and poor alike who left the Lowcountry and settled across America, taking a love of hoppin' john with them.

Before Miss Rutledge provided us with a recipe, Caroline Howard Gilman wrote in her *Recollections of a Southern Matron* in 1838:

> Lo! there stood before papa a pig on his four feet, with a lemon between his teeth, and a string of sausages round his neck. His grin was horrible.
>
> Before me, though at the head of many delicacies provided by papa, was an immense field of hopping John; a good dish, to be sure, but no more presentable to strangers at the South than baked beans and pork in New-England. I had not self-possession to joke about the unsightly dish, nor courage to offer it. I glanced at papa.
>
> "What is that mountain before you, my daughter?" said papa, looking comically over his pig.[8]

Caroline Howard was a proper Bostonian who married Samuel Gilman, a Harvard graduate who became the minister of the Archdale Unitarian Church in Charleston in 1819, a position he kept for nearly forty years. She was neither southern nor the plantation mistress she purported to be in her recollections. She published under her own name, which was unheard-of for a woman in Carolina society (before the passage of the Nineteenth Amendment, a Charleston lady's name appeared in print only upon birth, marriage, and death). She did own house servants, and most historians agree that her observations of daily life are poignant and relevant, however fictional. Her scene of hoppin' john's appearance at the table (which she felt necessary to footnote and explain as "bacon and rice") is perhaps the first of many to follow in southern writing.[9]

In 1946, Carson McCullers wrote in *The Member of the Wedding*:

> They stopped off for a few minutes to get on with the dinner. F. Jasmine sat with her elbows on the table and her bare heels hooked on the rungs of the chair. She and Bernice sat opposite each other, and John Henry faced the window. Now hopping John was F. Jasmine's very favorite food. She had always wanted them to wave a plate of rice and peas before her nose when she was in her coffin, to make sure there was no mistake, for if a breath of life was left in her, she would sit up and eat, but if she smelled the hopping-John and did not stir, then they could just nail down the coffin and be certain she was truly dead. Now Bernice had chosen for her death-test a piece of fried fresh-water trout, and for John Henry it was divinity fudge. But though Jasmine loved the hopping-John the very best, the others also liked it well enough, and all three of them enjoyed the dinner that day: the ham knuckle, the hopping-John, cornbread, hot baked sweet potatoes, and the buttermilk.[10]

The Member of the Wedding is fiction, but it is said to be the most autobiographical of her works, and the character Frankie, who is the F. Jasmine of the cited passage, is *the one* of all of her many characters "who seemed to her family and friends most like the author herself," according to the author's sister Margarita Smith.[11] Set in a small southern town in the 1940s, the book is a brilliant window into adolescence, but it truly illuminates the culture as well. Just before hoppin' john makes its appearance, we read:

> "Don't call me Frankie!" she said. "I don't wish to have to remind you any more."
>
> It was the time of the early afternoon when in the old days a sweet band would be playing. Now with the radio turned off, the kitchen was solemn and silent and there were sounds from far away. A colored voice called from the sidewalk, calling the names of vegetables in a dark, slurred tone, a long, unwinding hollering in which there were no words. Somewhere, near in the neighborhood, there was the sound of a hammer, and each stroke left a round echo.[12]

McCullers could simultaneously draw broad strokes and pinpoints of light. Hoppin' john was part of her world.

It was also part of Tennessee Williams's. Southern food and drink are often major characters in his plays, and in *Cat on a Hot Tin Roof*, Big Mama knows how to satisfy Big Daddy:

> BIG MAMA: Did you all notice the food he ate at the table? Did you all notice the supper he put away? Why, he ate like a hawss! . . . Why, that man—ate a huge piece of cawn-bread with molasses on it! Helped himself twice to hoppin' John.
>
> MARGARET: Big Daddy loves hoppin' john.—We had a real country dinner.
>
> BIG MAMA: Yair, he simply adores it! An' candied yams? That man put away enough food at that table to stuff a . . . field-hand!
>
> GOOPER: I hope he don't have to pay for it later on . . .
>
> BIG MAMA: Why should Big Daddy suffer for satisfying a normal appetite? [13]

Much has been written about the rice plantations of South Carolina and the knowledge system that came with the enslaved from West Africa.[14] Until my gentleman planter friend Dick Schulze reintroduced Carolina Gold to the Lowcountry in the 1980s,[15] there had been virtually no rice grown in the area in sixty years. The Civil War had taken away the slave labor; the grain had been introduced into Arkansas, Louisiana, and Texas, where the new machinery, which was too heavy for the soft Lowcountry soil, made competition impossible for the Lowcountry rice planters, whose aging plantations were battered by a series of storms, freshets, and silting caused by upriver cotton farming.[16]

Interestingly, though, people still ate rice at nearly every meal. And many Sandlappers, as residents of the Lowcountry are apt to call themselves, continue to do so. When Fritz Hollings was elected Governor of South Carolina in 1958, he learned that its largely rural population was suffering from malnutrition, even though they were eating the same foods they had eaten since the end of the Civil War. He funded a study of the diets of the malnourished and found that all of the rice being eaten in the state was also imported. Stripped of its nutrients in the milling process, it was filling bellies, but not sustaining life. He rushed a bill through the state legislature requiring that all rice sold in the state be fortified with the vitamins and minerals stripped off in the milling process; further, directions must instruct the cook *not* to wash the rice before cooking, which would rinse away those restored nutrients. The law is still on the books.[17]

I grew up eating hoppin' john in the land of cowpeas—those "red peas" that Sarah Rutledge called for in that earliest of written recipes for the dish. Many food writers seem to think that boiled peanuts and grits are the defining foods of the South, but I sell stone-ground, whole-grain, heirloom corn grits to folks in every state, and many of my customers are chefs in restaurants. Very few of them are, in fact, southerners. And the Lee Bros. have popularized boiled peanuts in New York City, though I do think that the popularity of edamame (the boiled green soybeans of sushi bars, similar in texture and flavor), has also helped boiled peanuts' visibility. Everyone has heard of black-eyed peas, perhaps the best known of the cowpeas, but no one would call them "red." And there's even an heirloom *California* black-eye. But few Americans outside the Deep South grow or eat the myriad other varieties of *Vigna unguiculata*. The nomenclature, both scientific and common, can be maddening. Even the botanists can't agree on the pronunciations, and subspecies continued to be isolated. All peas and beans, including *Vigna*—the cowpeas, *Pisum*—green peas, *Glycine*—soybeans, *Cajanus*—pigeon peas, and *Phaseolus*—the common beans such as lima beans, black beans, Navy beans and green beans, belong to the legume family, *Fabaceae*, which means Fava-like. That is, they resemble Old World beans. There are both subtle and dramatic culinary differences among the peas and beans. New Orleans red beans and rice, for example, does not taste like hoppin' john, but cowpeas in the pod can be eaten unripe, like common green beans. At the turn of the last century, Sturtevant classified cowpeas with pigeon peas, but today cowpeas are recognized as a separate genus.[18] They are neither peas (as in green peas) nor beans (as in green beans or favas), but you may hear them called either. If you hear a southerner talking about shelling peas, he means cowpeas, which are also known as crowders, field peas, and, tellingly, southernpeas. Crowders are so called, some say, because the beans are crammed together in the pod, squaring off the shoulders of the peas,[19] but William Woys Weaver, the food historian and master gardener, has written that as poor whites began to eat them in the eighteenth century, they began to call "them crowder peas, from the Scotch-Irish word crowdy, a porridge."[20] Tom Fitzmorris, New Orleans's venerable restaurant sleuth, says the name comes from the practice of planting them in cotton fields "where they would crowd (and fertilize) the rows."[21]

Yet another shelling bean of the South is the butterbean, or sieva bean, but those lima types are, well, an entirely different bag of beans, as are yard-long beans, which resemble green beans, but which are a subspecies of *Vigna unguiculata*, which may have originated in Africa but have been in Asia for thousands of years[22] and are not directly related to the New World beans. Because of the confusion, I urge food writers to use scientific nomenclature, and not worry about how it's pronounced.

Cowpeas are as varied as grapes or apples, and southerners tend to crave the type that was grown in their neck of the woods. I'm partial to cream peas and some of the lesser-known black-eyed types, such as whip-poorwills, but, in truth, I love them all.

Thomas Jefferson wrote in 1798 that the cowpea is "very productive, excellent food for man and beast." He praised the plants' ability to improve the "tilth and fertility" of the soil, and he sowed them in the South Orchard at Monticello between 1806 and 1810.[23] Perhaps the cowpea's reputation as both fodder and a soil enhancer has kept it off tables, because the season is *not* too long for many American climates. Indeed, Weaver grows several varieties in his awe-inspiring garden in Devon, Pennsylvania. Mine matured as quickly as my tomatoes and squash, and before my corn and melons, in my Washington, DC, community garden. And that's how it should be. Native Americans knew all about the companion planting that the rest of us are learning about now that gardening has become one of the country's most popular pastimes. "The Three Sisters" are the trinity of corn, beans, and squash planted together. The corn provides a pole for the beans to climb; the beans restore the nitrogen that corn demands back into the soil; the squash rambles on the ground, providing shade to lock in moisture and to block out the sun's rays on which weeds thrive. Further, the prickly stems of the squash plants deter insects.[24]

Jesus quoted the Torah when he said that man does not live by bread alone, imploring his flock to cultivate spiritual health as well. I choose to believe that the ancient texts were based on far more practical homilies. That is, grains do not provide us with all we need to live. Neither wheat nor corn nor rice alone can sustain life. They lack certain amino acids to form complete proteins. When grains are combined with pulses, however, complete proteins become accessible to humans. The enslaved West Africans who arrived in Carolina had for centuries grown cowpeas and pigeon peas to complement their rice, as well as root vegetables, greens, and other grains such as millet and sorghum, most of which quickly became established, or were replaced with similar plants, in the New World. Many of the enslaved were also excellent herdsmen who understood free-ranging cattle long before and much better than their European masters. As Judith

Carney explained in *Black Rice*, in the vast wetlands of the Inland Niger Delta, following rice harvests, cattle entered the fields to graze on the stubble, "their manure fertilizing the soil. This seasonal rotation between rice cultivation and pastoralism embraces a clever land-use strategy that satisfies both cereal and protein . . . needs while improving crop yields through the addition of animal manure. Rice farmers [farther] south . . . in the absence of cattle . . . rely upon other techniques to maintain soil fertility, such as rotating fields with nitrogen-fixing legumes and intercropping plants that add crucial nutrients to the soil."[25] In her latest book, Dr. Carney and Richard Rosomoff point out that "the practice of leaving cattle to graze on the plants' [leavings] . . . is likely responsible for the plant's alternative names in English (cowpea), Portuguese (*ervilha de vaca*) and Spanish (*chícaro de vaca*)."[26]

It's too bad that future southerners didn't pay more attention to the successful and sophisticated Native American and African farming techniques. Monoculture, as we know, has continued to destroy even the smallest farmers of the South, who have gone from one ill-fated crop, such as cotton, to another, such as the Christmas trees that replaced heirloom corn and bean patches throughout Appalachia and now are dying from root rot and acid rain.[27]

In Carolina, the taste has never died for the cowpeas and rice and sorghum and greens and sesame seeds that came there early on with the slave trade from West Africa. By 1708, there was a black majority in South Carolina. When I was growing up, there were three hundred varieties of cowpeas being grown on traditional, small truck farms throughout the Lowcountry. In the forty years that followed, however, most had all but disappeared until the interest in heirloom plants took off a few years ago. Now, through the efforts of dedicated farmers, seed-savers, universities, and non-profit organizations such as Monticello, the Carolina Gold Rice Foundation, and Southern Exposure Seed Exchange, and thanks to the work of scholars such Will Weaver and Steven Facciola, I can type the name of just about any heirloom cowpea variety into my browser and probably find someone with seeds to sell.[28]

In Washington, I've grown Mississippi Silvers, razorbacks, purple hulls, and clay cowpeas—a rare old favorite of Confederate soldiers who both added them to their rations and planted them alongside battlefield stations.[29] One of the great beauties of growing them is that you can eat them fresh (I simply boil a piece of smoked ham hock or neck bones in water until it's seasoned, then add the peas and cook on a low boil for about half an hour) or save the dried beans for winter use, though let me advise you to freeze them first to kill any critters. There's nothing more disheartening than opening your precious stash of whippoorwills on New Year's Day to find them riddled with bugs. Sometimes I can harvest both green and dried cowpeas on the same day from the same plants. Cowpeas will grow right up until first frost, and then you simply leave the plants in the ground to provide nutrients for next year's corn.

Cowpeas are favored all over the world now. And wherever you find them, you are likely to also find rice. And wherever you find rice, you're likely to find some form of rice and beans. In a recent Facebook exchange, I followed several well-known southern cookbook authors' discussion of what they thought was southern and what wasn't. "I draw the line at Saigon Hoppin' john," wrote one. "I don't care how many Vietnamese live down south now." I couldn't resist butting in and telling her that we've known for several years now that cowpeas got to Asia several thousand years before they got to America.[30] In Vietnam, rice and black-eyed peas are cooked just like hoppin' john, though the street vendors who sell it often have a stalk of lemongrass garnishing it in lieu of Miss Rutledge's mint.[31]

It's no wonder that the black-eyed type became the defining cowpea of the dish as it spread across the country in what I call the Southern Diaspora. Mature at sixty-five to seventy days, it doesn't require the eighty-five to ninety or more days that many of the other more delicate lady peas, cream peas, and white acres do. The common names are as confusing as the scientific nomenclature, and, like barbecue and jambalaya, the way you like your hoppin' john probably has more to do with where you grew up than with actual taste. Hoppin' john has managed to keep its name, but even the same varieties of cowpeas seem to change names as you cross county lines. You can grow them anywhere you have full sun and warm, well-drained soil. Their ability to grow in poor soil is legendary, but they still remain a mostly southern vegetable. Like many African plants, they are extremely versatile, though few people today use these old foodways: the green seeds can be roasted like peanuts, the leaves may be used as a potherb, and, in hard times, you can dark-roast the seeds as a coffee substitute.[32]

Weaver claims that their "close association with African Americans and the New England perception of the peas as a fodder crop for slaves" kept them not only out of non-southern gardens, but also out of the books. But not out of the literature, so to speak, for Thomas Jefferson described raising a black-eyed pea he referred to as French, though many varieties are now thought to have come to America via the Caribbean or Brazil rather than directly from Africa. That would certainly make sense in Carolina, which was granted to some Barbadian planters who restored Charles II to the throne. Nevertheless, Weaver writes, "cowpeas are not generally considered among the vegetables fit for the kitchen garden . . . Because cowpeas require considerable space, they have always been treated as field crops. On the other hand, they are no more troublesome in this respect than sweet potatoes, and the bush varieties can be raised like bush beans. If there is a drawback, it is only that cowpeas cannot be grown in much of the country due to their need for a long, warm growing season. For this reason their culture is most closely associated with the South."[33]

In 1879, Marion Cabell Tyree edited the remarkable *Housekeeping in Old Virginia containing Contributions from Two Hundred and Fifty of Virginia's Noted Housewives, Distinguished for Their Skill in the Culinary Art and Other Branches of Domestic Economy*. In it there appears, attributed to Mozis Addums, a "Resipee for Cukin Kon-Feel Pees,"[34] complete with condescending eye dialect, which is the spelling device used by writers to disparage a speaking character's non-standard pronunciation and grammar. Such spellings can be effective in fiction, but they usually are intended to make the writer appear superior by making the speaker seem uncouth and illiterate.[35] There was no Moses Adams. It was one of several pseudonyms for the blowhard racist, George William Bagby, author of *The Old Virginia Gentleman*, in which I read the most disturbingly bigoted diatribes I've ever encountered. Field peas were so dear to Bagby's heart, however, that he argued that Virginians were the greatest people on earth simply because they lived where "cornfield peas" grew. In spite of his hysterical, racist ranting, Bagby does demonstrate one truism: in the South, the white man came to love the black man's food.[36]

Two more recipes appear in Tyree's book: One, for Cornfield or Black Eye Peas, "submitted" by a Mrs. S. T. (who is in fact Tyree herself), reads, "Shell early in the morning, throw into water till an hour before dinner, then put into boiling water, covering close while cooking. Add a little salt, just before taking from the fire. Drain and serve with a large spoonful fresh butter, or put in a pan with a slice of fat meat, and simmer a few minutes. Dried peas must be soaked overnight, and cooked twice as long as fresh."[37]

Mrs. Tyree's advice to salt only just before serving shows what black South Carolinians would call "an old hand," referring to the wisdom of experience that makes good cooks.[38] Salt toughens peas and beans, so it's prudent to avoid salting them while they cook.

Mary Randolph's *The Virginia House-Wife* of 1824 had long before waxed poetic about field peas: "There are many varieties of these peas," she wrote, "the smaller kind are the most delicate.—Have them young and newly gathered, shell and boil them tender, pour them in a colander to drain; put some lard in a frying-pan, when it boils, mash the peas and fry them in a cake of a light brown; put it in the dish with the crust upper-most, garnish with thin bits of fried bacon."[39] So much for California chef Jeremiah Tower's laughable claim to have invented the bean cake in the 1980s![40]

Many cookbook authors would add their own tips through the years. Lettice Bryan advised in *The Kentucky Housewife* in 1839 to harvest the peas "when full grown, and the pods just beginning to turn yellow; then they have their full flavor, and are perfectly tender, and may be shelled without difficulty."[41]

But in just as many southern cookbooks, recipes for vegetables and fish are conspicuous in their absence. I am convinced that the cooks assumed that you would know the most important thing about both: don't overcook them. Prior to the twentieth century, when rice *is* mentioned, it's mostly in Carolina and Georgia cookbooks, or the recipes clearly have a Caro-lina provenance. I like to think that Miss Rutledge published her version of hoppin' john, like many Charlestonians after her, as an attempt to get the old slave recipes down on paper before those days were over. Surely hoppin' john had long been a favorite on the master's table by the time her recipe appeared. We culinary historians generally agree that written recipes lag many years behind common usage.[42] Rutledge and Randolph were both from aristocratic families. When Randolph wrote about rice, though she was a Virginian, she was writing about Carolina rice cookery. But she didn't mention hoppin' john, and it's rarely mentioned outside the rice-growing Lowcountry until much later.

Immediately after the Civil War, *Mrs. Hill's Southern Practical Cook-ery and Receipt Book* appeared in Atlanta. Fish and vegetables are finally given their due. For asparagus, she warns: "Take them up as soon as done; too much cooking injures the color and flavor." "Vegetables intended for dinner," she wrote, "should be gathered early in the morning. A few only can be kept twelve hours without detriment. . . . They lose their good ap-pearance and flavor if cooked too long." Her devilled crabs are made with "fresh olive oil"; frogs' legs are broiled or fried, "their meat is beautifully white; the taste delicious."[43]

She also included her version of "Hopping John: Pick out the defective ones from a quart of dried peas; soak them several hours in tepid water; boil them with a chicken or piece of pickled pork until the peas are thoroughly done. In a separate stew-pan boil half as much rice dry; take the peas from the meat, mix them with the rice, fry a few minutes until dry. Season with salt and pepper."[44]

After the Civil War, however, much of the South was weakened and impoverished. Many formerly wealthy landowners struggled on small plots of land, just like their Black neighbors. Coincidentally, industrialization and the modern railway system brought cheap canned and dried foods to areas where everyone had once eaten fresh, local produce. It was mostly *after* the war that simpler foods began to be embraced by the former gentry, when overcooked canned vegetables became the norm, and when the South came to be defined as the land of hog meat and hoe cake.

In summary, this is what we know: Field peas and rice came to Carolina from West Africa, along with Africans who knew how to cook both, and together. The dish spread throughout the South. Favored varieties of peas were saved. New varieties appeared through selective breeding. Dishes of rice and beans are served throughout rice-growing lands as a sort of good-luck dish, associated with the harvest of both grain and pulse. In the antebellum Lowcountry rice fields, the New Year marked the ancient celebration of days becoming longer, and of the one time of year when field hands could take a break from the backbreaking work of rice cultivation.[45] As descendants of those enslaved moved inland, and southerners, both black and white, spread throughout the land, the dish, and custom, traveled with them. I honestly don't care what you call hoppin' john, but you better serve it to me on New Year's. I don't think I've ever not had it, and I seem to have had pretty damn good luck.

NOTES

1. [Sarah Rutledge], *The Carolina Housewife, or House and Home: By A Lady of Charleston* (Charleston, 1847. In facsimile, with Introduction by Anna Wells Rutledge. Columbia: University of South Carolina Press, 1979), 83.
2. Stephen Facciola, *Cornucopia II: A Source Book of Edible Plants* (Vista, CA: Kampong Publications, 1998), 113, 350–51.
3. John Martin Taylor, "Karen and Me," *Gastronomica* 7, no. 4 (Fall 2007).
4. Karen Hess, *The Carolina Rice Kitchen: The African Connection. Featuring in Facsimile: Carolina Rice Cook Book* (Columbia: University of South Carolina Press, 1992), 97–100.

5. Hess, 98.

6. See Hess. Also, Judith A. Carney, *Black Rice: The African Origins of Rice Cultivation in the Americas* (Cambridge, MA: Harvard University Press, 2001).

7. Hess, 36–64.

8. Caroline Howard Gilman, *Recollections of a Southern Matron* (New York: Harper & Brothers, 1838), 142.

9. http://www25.uua.org/uuhs/duub/articles/carolinegilman.html

10. Carson McCullers, *The Member of the Wedding* (New York: Houghton Mifflin Company, 1946, 2004), 81.

11. http://www.houghtonmifflinbooks.com/readers_guides/mccullers_member.shtml.

12. McCullers, 77.

13. Tennessee Williams, *Cat on a Hot Tin Roof* (Sewanee, TN: University of the South, 1986), 63.

14. See, especially, Carney, *Black Rice*.

15. John Martin Taylor, "Carolina Gold: A Rare Harvest," *The New York Times* (December 28, 1988). Also Richard Schulze, *Carolina Gold Rice: The Ebb and Flow History of a Lowcountry Cash Crop* (Charleston and London: History Press, 2005).

16. John Martin Taylor, *Hoppin' John's Lowcountry Cooking: Recipes and Ruminations from Charleston and the Carolina Coastal Plain* (New York: Bantam Books, 1992), 13.

17. John Martin Taylor, "Lowcountry Gold Rush," *Oxford American* 49 (Spring 2005).

18. U. P. Hedrick, Ed. *Sturtevant's Edible Plants of the World* (New York: Dover Publications, Inc., 1972), 597. One of the best of the modern horticultural dictionaries is *Hortus Third* by the Staff of the L. H. Bailey Hortorium at Cornell Unversity (New York: Macmillan General Reference, 1976).

19. See, for example, Elizabeth Schneider, *Vegetables from Amaranth to Zucchini: The Essential Reference* (New York: William Morrow, 2001), 62.

20. William Woys Weaver, *Heirloom Vegetable Gardening: A Master Gardener's Guide to Planting, Growing, Seed Saving, and Cultural History* (New York: Henry Holt and Company, 1997), 151.

21. http://www.nomenu.com/subscriber/MD051210.html.

22. Schneider, 718.

23. Quoted in *Thomas Jefferson's Garden Book*, Edited by Edwin Morris Betts (Thomas Jefferson Memorial Foundation, Inc., 1999), 262.

24. Native American companion planting methods are well documented. For practical instructions, see Sally Jean Cunningham, *Great Garden Companions* (Emmaus, PA: Rodale Press, Inc., 1998).

25. Carney, *Black Rice*, 47.

26. Judith A. Carney and Richard Nicholas Rosomoff, *In the Shadow of Slavery:*

Africa's Botanical Legacy in the Atlantic World (Berkeley: University of California Press, 2009), 149.

27. From conversations with Cecilia Holland, my miller, who lives near Blairsville, Georgia; 2003–2005. Also see various articles at www.appalachianvoices.org, e.g., April 2001. Also see http://www.forestpests.org/southern/whitepineroot .html and http://www.forestbiotech.org/pdf/fraserfir.pdf.

28. Dr. Merle Shepard at the Clemson Coastal Research and Education Center near Charleston is a fount of information about the heirloom plants of the Lowcountry. He is a board member of the Carolina Gold Rice Foundation, whose mission is to "advance the sustainable restoration and preservation of Carolina Gold Rice and other heirloom grains and raise public awareness of the importance of historic ricelands and heirloom agriculture." See http:// www.carolinagoldricefoundation.org/, http://www.monticello.org/chp/index .html, http://www.southernexposure.com/index.html, Weaver, and Facciola.

29. See http://davesgarden.com/guides/articles/view/86/.

30. Carney, *In the Shadow of Slavery*, 33.

31. Hess, *xv*, and in conversation and correspondence, with accompanying photograph taken of the dish in Saigon, 1990.

32. See Carney, *In the Shadow*, 149; and Facciola, 113.

33. Weaver, 150-151.

34. Marion Cabell Tyree, *Housekeeping in Old Virginia* (Louisville, KY: John P. Morton and Company, 1879), 253–54.

35. Wikipedia has an excellent entry on eye dialect at http://en.wikipedia.org/wiki /Eye_dialect.

36. George William Bagby, "The Old Virginia Gentleman," *The Old Virginia Gentleman and Other Sketches*, ed. Thomas Nelson Page (New York: Charles Scribner's Sons, 1910).

37. Tyree, 254.

38. Many old expressions such as this one are common in Charleston and the surrounding Lowcountry. They are often based on Gullah, the creole language of descendants of enslaved Africans in the area, or on the original West African idioms.

39. Mary Randolph, *The Virginia House-Wife. A Facsimile of the first edition, 1824, along with additional material from the editions of 1825 and 1828, thus presenting a complete text*, ed. Karen Hess (Columbia: University of South Carolina Press, 1984), 135–36.

40. Jeremiah Tower, *New American Classics* (New York: Harper & Row, 1987), 175.

41. Lettice Bryan, *The Kentucky Housewife*. With a new introduction by Bill Neal (Columbia: University of South Carolina Press, 1991), 211–12.

42. See Hess in Randolph, xv.

43. Annabella P. Hill, *Mrs. Hill's Southern Practical Cookery and Receipt Book*,

facsimile ed. Damon L. Fowler (Columbia: University of South Carolina Press, 1995), 179.

44. Hill, 196.
45. See, in particular, Charles Joyner, *Down By the Riverside: A South Carolina Slave Community* (Champaign: University of Illinois Press, 1984), 101–02.

Oysters Mournful

This editorial was written for the Washington Post *at their request.
I was working on an article for the paper on oyster farming at the time,
but the Deep Horizon Oil Spill in the Gulf of Mexico was on everyone's
mind. The paper ran the article in the food section, which caused an
outcry among some readers who thought—rightfully so—that it should
have gone on the Opinions page. Because I was known as a food writer,
not an editorialist, I refused payment for the piece so that I, not my editor, could take the blame.*

The festive mood of Friday lunch at Galatoire's did not seem changed since
the first time I ate at the 105-year-old New Orleans institution in the late
1950s: the ladies resplendent in their hats and finery, the gents in their seer-
sucker suits, the gin and bourbon flowing like water. The merriment belied
the tragic reality of the day's headline: P&J, the city's 134-year-old oyster
company, had stopped shucking that morning.

I was in New Orleans to speak at a culinary conference, and of course
we ate well, including a three-hour lunch of pig dishes at Cochon. I had a
crabmeat omelet at Galatoire's, which has issued a public statement about
the oil-spill disaster in the gulf: "Nearly 80 percent of Louisiana's seafood
comes from thousands of miles of coastline west of the Mississippi River,
hundreds of miles away from the currently affected areas of the Gulf of
Mexico. Galatoire's has taken steps to support our seafood producers and
ensure that the freshest, highest quality fish, shrimp, crawfish and crabs are
available without interruption."

Maricel Presilla and Jessica Harris at Bourbon House.

Oysters are conspicuous in their absence from the statement. As Brett Anderson reported in the *Times-Picayune* on June 13, the dwindling supply of local oysters in the wake of the oil spill forced Galatoire's executive chef, Brian Landry, to scour the restaurant's decades of menus, looking for traditional dishes to replace those featuring the local bivalves. Chicken livers en brochette, however, just don't appeal to me as much as oysters prepared the same way.

As food writers, we were already lamenting this latest devastating blow to the vibrant cuisine. At the end of the conference and before the speakers' dinner, I slipped away in a merciful rain shower with culinary scholar Jessica Harris and Latin chefs Maricel Presilla and Patricia Wilson (all three PhDs) to Dickie Brennan's nearby Bourbon House, renowned for the quality of its oysters. We were reassured that the oysters were all from Area 9 in Plaquemines, west of the Mississippi River. It's one of two areas that have been reopened temporarily as the Louisiana Department of Health and Hospitals tests gulf oysters and oyster waters. It was Saturday afternoon, about 5 o'clock. Bourbon House sits squarely on the corner of Iberville and boisterous Bourbon Street, in the heart of the French Quarter.

The Beans + Rice conference (where we had lectured), the Creole Tomato Festival, and the Louisiana Seafood Festival were going on simultaneously in the Quarter, so there were even more foodies than normal in

New Orleans, if that's imaginable. But Bourbon House wasn't half-full—at happy hour on Saturday—and several lesser-known oyster bars we passed were empty.

I'm the first to admit that I prefer the brinier East Coast oysters of the R months, if for no other reason than that's what I grew up with. But, as Presilla noted, the plump, meaty oysters from Plaquemines that we ate on Saturday "beg to be cooked and sauced." We ordered several dozen, both cooked and raw, tossing them back with Champagne. (The best I had were the wood-fired ones at Cochon.) Wistfully, we snapped cellphone photos of what might well be among the last Gulf Coast oysters for a while. We walked back to the hotel in the rain.

I don't get to the Gulf Coast often, but no food writer can ignore the bountiful cornucopia of the New Orleans table. There's no place else in the world quite like the Crescent City, with its Creole and Cajun cultures, its sultry weather, its magnificent architecture, its self-proclaimed decadence. Mardi Gras, Jazz Fest, and Friday at Galatoire's are no more excessive than an ordinary meal in New Orleans. Mounds of beans and rice, sweetbreads, vegetables swimming in hollandaise, and oysters Rockefeller are mere side dishes or appetizers. Courses that follow are stuffed with crabmeat, garnished with crawfish, and invariably sauced, followed by gumbo, jambalaya, or fried soft-shell crabs with sauce Choron.

For as long as I can remember, I have eaten oysters, frogs' legs, shrimp, crawfish and drum. That's because I was born a stone's throw from the

Sketch for an oyster roast in Athens, Georgia, 1978. Collection of Betty Alice Fowler.

Mississippi, in Baton Rouge. When I was three, we moved to the very similar terrain of South Carolina. I have lived through several hurricanes, including Hugo, which put me out of house and business for a year.

When I was growing up, my mother would send me out in our sailboat's dinghy to catch lunch. In autumn, I would cast our old circular shrimp net into the brackish waters of the salt marsh, pulling in several pounds of shrimp. At low tide in winter, I would gather oysters and clams from the then-pristine waters, my mother tossing back into the creek any oysters under ten inches long. In spring, the crab trap offered up not only those luscious blue crabs, but flounder and eel as well.

My older sister Nancy returned to Louisiana to attend LSU. On the rare occasion that she was home, she gloated about her meals at Galatoire's: turtle soup, shrimp remoulade, crabmeat omelet, crawfish etouffée, and, of course, those oysters. Shortly after Nancy went away to school, we began spending a lot of time on our sailboat down on the estuaries behind Hilton Head Island. For years ours was one of a handful of pleasure craft docked or moored there. We envied her restaurant meals in Louisiana, but we had a wealth of seafood a cast or trap away.

These days, I drive a car, use air conditioning, and leave all sorts of appliances and electronic equipment plugged in, their digital clocks constantly draining electricity and increasing our demand for cheap fuel. No matter what I think about BP, I know that I, too, am partly to blame for the oil spill, because I add to that demand.

We are all incensed about the ecological damage to the gulf, but multinational oil companies have spilled many millions of gallons in the Niger Delta over the years, polluting the air, water, and soil of millions of Nigerians who depend on fish from the rivers simply to sustain their lives. I can give you a ballpark estimate of how many turtles and dolphins have washed up dead in the oily mess in the gulf, but I cannot tell you the name of a single one of the people who lost their lives in the rig fire.

I am embarrassed by my own myopia and greed.

I am livid about the gulf oil spill, and I worry about the seafood industry, but I also know that many of the thousands of jobs affected by the spill are for manual laborers who will never set foot in the temples of Creole cuisine about which I, with my bourgeois tastes and wallet, tend to wax poetic.

I am exasperated and worried about the people of Louisiana. How much more can they take? Do I continue to order oysters out of season in hopes of contributing to the demand for them, so that prices will go higher and help the Gulf Coast seafood industry if and when it is able to return to business? Do I continue to write purplish prose about my favorite seafood dishes while fishermen are out of work?

This tragedy should present us all with moral dilemmas. I think we must demand change, but change begins at home. As President Obama noted in his June 15 speech about the disaster, "we can't afford not to change how we produce and use energy." Boycotting BP will only hurt your local gas station owner. Instead, slow down, use public transportation, and carpool. Set your air conditioning a few degrees higher. Turn off your computer and cellphone when they're not in use. And this weekend, forgo those bottles of Champagne and imported wine and instead write a check to one of the nonprofit groups that are prepared to employ trained volunteers to help clean up the mess and restore the fisheries.

Grandma's
Sugar Cookies

I always like to shop first, then peruse my culinary library for ideas. And it was in so doing that I ran across a book that I honestly never remember looking through before. I must have gotten it from my father the last time I saw him, a couple of years ago, shortly before he died. There is no front cover, and the frontispiece is missing as well, but on the last page

The rear cover of my grandmother's copy of a 1926 cookbook.

there is my maternal grandmother's signature, Mrs. E. D. Martin. The back cover is dated 1926 and shows the book to be a Bee Brand publication of the McCormick spice company of Baltimore. At the time, my grandfather owned a drugstore in Bemis, Tennessee. His family also had an old-fashioned mercantile store that carried everything under the sun in Crump, Tennessee, just north of Shiloh Battlefield, on a large oxbow of the Tennessee River. I'm sure they sold Bee Brand products in both locations.

As I thumbed through the index of the fragile, yellowed pages, I saw Grandma's writing several places, including "Tea Cakes" written by the cookie entries. Grandma's tea cakes were legend. There was always a cookie jar full of them next to the kitchen sink; the "jar" was a wonderful item that I had for years until it finally broke in one of my many moves when I was in my twenties. A clear glass sphere with a metal lid balanced on top of a wire platform. The tea cakes inside were lightly perfumed with either mace or nutmeg—to this day when I smell either of those spices, Grandma's kitchen all but materializes before me—and they were plump, and ever-so-slightly chewy. The same cookie dough got rolled thin for Christmas cookies that we would decorate with colored glazes, sprinkles, and silver dragées.

In Mama's recipe collection, a recipe for "Mother's Tea Cakes" was obviously written during World War II when there was rationing. It is all but identical to Grandma's, except she substitutes "oleo" for butter, calls for the nutmeg that distinguishes them, and replaces Grandma's "hot oven" with 450°. Later in the book, among the four dozen cookie recipes, is "Old Fashioned Southern Tea Cakes," with the butter restored, the nutmeg missing, and the oven turned down to 375° (probably to more easily work with four kids rolling and decorating the cookies).

How odd to find the original, in Grandma's hand, after all these years. Stuck in the book on the same page as Grandma's recipe was a newspaper clipping from the Jackson, Tennessee, newspaper. The photo on the back makes me think it's from the sixties. The article claims that "Mrs. Jere Crook of Jackson makes the best sugar cookies, no doubt. . . . So, throw out all your old recipes for sugar cookies and try this one, doing each step as listed. . . ."

I have no evidence that Grandma ever tried Mrs. Crook's recipe, or that Mama did. Grandma made her own "baking powder" with equal parts cream of tartar and soda. Her cookie has more sugar, fewer eggs, and a bit of milk. I've been making them since I was a child, and I'm not about to change recipes, either.

Mrs. Fisher's Cigarettes

❯ SOFIA, BULGARIA, 2012 ···

While researching a book devoted to the oft-maligned but secretly adored subject of fried foods, I was drawn to *What Mrs. Fisher Knows About Old Southern Cooking*. Abby Fisher was an Black cook of wide renown in Victorian San Francisco. Remarkably, the city's Women's Co-operative Printing Office published the collection of her recipes in 1881. The book remained a rare and esoteric piece of American history until it was republished in 1995, with historical notes by the scholar Karen Hess. It was thought to be the first published cookbook by a Black author until the tireless culinary historian and archivist Jan Longone made public her lone copy of Malinda Russell's *Domestic Cookbook* (1866).

Though we know little of either of the authors, their recipes, now published for all to see, highlight the culinary skills of these nineteenth-century Black cooking legends. Among Mrs. Fisher's recipes, which are, as Hess points out, "all perfectly lovely, and all perfectly feasible in today's kitchens," elegant breads, perfectly turned roasts, broiled chops, delicate cakes, and hearty stews share the bill with the preserves for which Mrs. Fisher was well-known.[1] The title page of her book declares her twice the winner of medals at the San Francisco Mechanics' Institute Fair for best "Pickles and Sauces and best assortment of Jellies and Preserves."[2]

She was also an artful fryer, as is evidenced by her "carolas" (crullers), her fried chicken, and her entire chapter of croquettes. "You can make croquettes from any kind of meat you like," she tells us. "You need not use onions unless you like, but always salt and pepper." Her lamb croquettes

This article appeared in the Fall 2012 issue of *Gastronomica* (Volume 12, Issue 3).

include a little sour pickle, a brightening flavor for strong-tasting lamb. For her liver croquettes, she instructs to "season high." With a croquette of veal and calves' brains, she suggests serving an elegant sauce of parsleyed cream. What Mrs. Fisher knew was that with a little leftover meat, you can make a meal in minutes.

Veal or Lamb Vigareets [Croquettes]

To be made the same way [as preceding recipes], to wit: Boil meat rare done, pick all gristle out, grate as much onion in the chopped meat as you like. Take half the quantity of brains that comes in one head (calf or lamb), scald them, pick all the skin from them; mix them with the meat, one-half of a nutmeg, grated, pepper and salt; season high and fry the same as other croquettes. ["Have fat very hot . . . fry quick till brown."] Make a gravy of cream and pour on vigareets just as going to table. Making gravy: Put sweet cream into a clean vessel, put over steam until hot, add a very little pepper and salt, then chop some fresh parsley fine and sprinkle it over vigareets while on dish. *Make oblong cakes.*[3]
[Italics mine]

Mrs. Fisher also called for her lamb, chicken, and oyster croquettes to be oblong in shape, but she added her elegant cream sauce only to the viga-reets, whose name Hess was "unable to account for."[4]

Hess was also unable to find out much about Mrs. Fisher's life beyond the remarkable achievements of the formerly enslaved woman who somehow managed to rear eleven children, find her way across the country to San Francisco, and become so renowned a cook that the nine prominent women who championed her work would not only record her recipes from dictation, but also allow their names and addresses to appear after Fisher's Preface. All, as Hess points out, "about 40 years before women won the right to vote."[5]

I propose that that dictation and the Printing Office are the keys to the word vigareets, which is simply a typo. It should read cigareets, a common pronunciation of "cigarettes" at a time when chewing tobacco and cigars were far more common, and when the hand-rolled smokes of the wild west were oblong, dark, and about the size of, well, croquettes.[6] "Cigareets, Whusky, and Wild, Wild Women" was a popular song by the American cowboy group, The Sons of Pioneers, founded in the 1930s by Roy Rogers when Hollywood westerns were at their height of popularity.[7] The films romanticized the Wild West of the late nineteenth century, where—and when—Mrs. Fisher's book was produced.

Women's Cooperative Printing
Office advertisement, 1868.

More to the point, perhaps, is that the "c" key is next to the "v" key on QWERTY keyboards. Rotary press was invented in 1843. The first type-writers with QWERTY keyboards came along in 1867 and were put into production by Remington and others in 1873. Linotype and other typeset-ting machines weren't marketed until three years after the publication of Mrs. Fisher, but the QWERTY keyboard was well-established by the time Mrs. Fisher dictated her recipes, which were surely typed up before going to the typesetter.[8] The Women's Co-Operative Printing Office, which pub-lished Mrs. Fisher, was a successful business, housed in a huge building with an elevator.

The catalog of the 1998 exhibition "Women in Printing and Publishing in California, 1850–1940" explains that the Civil War had so decimated the male work force that women began to enter trades traditionally practiced only by men. "In San Francisco, which was becoming a center for printing and publishing in the West, women-run printing offices appeared in the 1870s and 1880s. . . . The most prominent and prolific was The Women's Co-Operative Printing Union, established in 1868."[9]

I imagine that as Mrs. Fisher spoke, in what certainly must have been an accent unfamiliar to those progressive California women, they wrote down what they thought she must be saying. "Not being able to read or write myself," she admitted in her Preface and Apology, Mrs. Fisher's crullers became "carolas," her jambalaya became "jumberlie," and her succotash, "circuit hash." Hess wrote, "Considering that the recipes were dictated, I suppose that [vigareets] could represent the transcription of Mrs. Fisher's pronunciation of some other word. But what it would have been I cannot say, nor were any of my Southern colleagues able to help me."[10]

Hess and I often shared our culinary conundrums and epiphanies with each other. I was one of those southerners who could offer her no help then. I doubt that anyone could, using the classic historical, etymological, and sociological research methodology that Hess was known for. It took text-messaging on a smartphone for me to realize wherein the meaning of vigareets lay. "Does he still smoke," I wrote to a friend whose husband was deathly ill. "No more vigarettes," she replied.

I'm only sorry Karen's not here for me to let her know.

NOTES

1. Karen Hess, Historical Notes in *What Mrs. Fisher Knows About Old Southern Cooking*, by Abby Fisher (San Francisco: 1881, fac. Bedford, MA: Applewood Books, 1995), 91.
2. Fisher, 1.
3. Fisher, 16–19.
4. Hess, 83.
5. Hess, 75.
6. See tobacco.org's Tobacco Timeline.
7. Bobnolan-sop.net includes biographies and discographies of cowboy song-writers, including Tim Spencer, who wrote "Cigareets, Whusky, and Wild, Wild Women."
8. Wikipedia has accurate histories of both the rotary press and QWERTY.
9. California Historical Society, *Women in Printing & Publishing in California, 1850-1940*. Introduction by Patricia L. Keats (San Francisco: California Historical Society, 2001).
10. Fisher and Hess, 3, 67, 119, 69, 83.

Tough Cuts,
Long Stewed

In 1975, some of my photos were chosen to be included in a University of New Mexico exhibition entitled "December 5, 1974." All of the photos in the show were taken in the United States on that date. I was working on my master's in film at the time at the University of Georgia, but I had found my true love to be still photography, which I taught as a graduate assistant. Of my photos chosen, this one was taken on a typical cool winter's day in north Georgia. As I drove through the foothills north of Athens, there was the pervasive, beguiling smell of wood fires throughout the rolling landscape, Georgia red clay peeking through the fields of harvested corn and cotton. I knew that it was the traditional hog killin' weekend, and I hoped that I would find some roadside butchering going on. I scored not far from home.

I was thrilled to return to Sofia from out of town (and a nasty drive through freezing rain) to find my winemaker/farmer/publisher friend Philip Harmandjiev bearing gifts of pickled carrots, a freshly killed rooster, and pork cheeks, from his farm at Damianitza Winery. The deep-red cheeks of hogs, imbedded in the fatty jowls, are stronger-tasting and tougher than other cuts of pork, as is the rooster when compared to young hens. They require long, gentle cooking in order for the flesh to be tender.

....

Braised Pork Cheeks

I removed the silver skin and any fat still connected to the cheeks. Though the fat (and meat) of a hog's head is more strongly flavored than the fat from elsewhere on the body (leaf lard, rendered from the soft fat around the kidneys and loin, is the most delicate), I wanted to accent the very pigginess of the cheeks. Why eat this obscure cut if you're not going to let it be what it is? I discarded the silver skin, cut the fat into small pieces, and began rendering it in a big enamel-lined Dutch oven. When all the fat had rendered out, I removed the browned cracklings and discarded them.

I cut the meat into smaller, basically uniform pieces, then put a very small amount of flour on my work surface and pounded it into the meat with a knife. On cutlets I would use the dull side of the knife, but with the cheeks I used the "sharp" side of a fairly dull knife, because I wanted to tenderize the meat as well.

I then browned the meat well in the fat in the Dutch oven, carefully cooking it on all sides. I removed the morsels to a plate, then added chopped onions, celery, and bell peppers, tossing them well and wilting them evenly. When they were totally wilted and the onions were becoming transparent, I deglazed the pan with a splash of red wine vinegar. I then added tomato puree and, after about five minutes, my own secret weapon: an herbal mix. This combination of fresh herbs, several cloves of garlic, dried herbs (I used *herbes de Provence*) and salt is chopped at the last minute then added after all other flavors have blended well.

I then returned the browned cheeks to the pot, added a dozen or more grinds of black pepper, covered the pot, and popped it into the oven that was preheated to a very low temperature (about 225°F). At the same time, I put a skillet with the pureed fat from the rest of the head in the oven to render. I figured that if I played my cards right, I could set the rendered lard outside in the snow so that it would be well chilled in time for me to make the biscuit topping for the chicken pie that I would make with the rooster.

The cheeks stayed in the oven for several hours—about 4. I checked the pot occasionally to make sure that the tomato sauce was just barely simmering, and each time, I poked the meat to see if it were yet tender. Finally, it gave to the touch of the spoon, and I pulled a morsel out of the pot to taste . . . HEAVEN! Pork cheeks are similar to slow-braised beef ribs in texture, but the powerful taste of the pork—especially from Philip's naturally raised, heritage breeds (I think one of the hogs was a cross with a feral pig)—in no way resembles beef. I served the cheeks with grits and made biscuits for the chicken pie with the lard.

Transylvania

My husband was going to a conference in Sibiu, Romania, for a week late last summer. Would I care to join him, even though he would be in meetings most of the time? Could I keep myself entertained there, alone, in the heart of Transylvania? We had been living in Bulgaria for three months at the time, and though I had traveled to many nooks and crannies of the Balkans, from the Black Sea to Macedonia, I had not crossed the Danube into the land of Dracula.

I've read none of the Twilight series, nor a single word of an Anne Rice novel—though a friend did convince me to go see the film version of *Interview with the Vampire* when it was released in 1994. (It seemed awfully silly to me; all I recall are the sumptuous wardrobes.) Bela Lugosi was the only other vampire I've known. But, as a culinary historian, I've been intrigued by Transylvania since the 1985 release of the unusual cookbook *Paul Kovi's Transylvanian Cuisine*, by the former owner and director of The Four Seasons in New York. Kovi's book is unusual not only for its combination of history, folklore, poetry, and sociology, but also for its gastronomy of this Middle Europe melting pot where Hungarians, Armenians, Saxon Germans, Romanians, and Rroma make their home. ("Gypsy" is considered pejorative.) Inspired by the 1971 classic *The Cuisine of Hungary*, Kovi combed through seventeenth-, eighteenth-, and nineteenth-century treatises and called on ten of Transylvania's best writers to help him evoke the bountiful table of this corner of Eastern Europe that for outsiders has

A version of this appeared in the Travel Section of the *Washington Post.*

always been shrouded in mystery and superstition. What I really wanted to do was to taste its legendary soups.

Once part of Hungary for over one thousand years, Transylvania is now a largely isolated portion of north central Romania, with no international borders. The surrounding regions—Moldavia, Mamures, Wallachia, and the Banat—were even more unknown and mystifying to me, but I planned to explore, in my rental car, as much of this fabled land of mountains and castles as I could in those seven days. Sibiu (called *Hermannstadt* in German, *Nagyszeben* in Hungarian) is in the south of the region, bordered by the Carpathian Mountains. It has an international airport that is linked to many European cities. We flew from Sofia to Munich, then back down to Sibiu. It was easier and faster than the drive through the mighty Fagaras range, with its summits over eight thousand feet.

The first Eastern European city to be declared a European Capital of Culture, Sibiu seemed made for visitors, with modern accommodations and restaurants and an abundance of UNESCO World Heritage Sites. The Romanian economy was said to be booming, at least partly due to the film industry, and Sibiu's architecturally fascinating old town, situated on two levels, seemed self-possessed, as though it were still the capital of the Transylvanian nation.

In Piata Mare—the "large plaza"—the presence of the Habsburgs was obvious (I'd seen nothing this grand in Bulgaria), but the medieval Saxon buildings sported eye-shaped dormer windows that seemed to follow me everywhere.

There are plenty of shops, museums, churches, and cafes to duck into, as well as other squares, each lined with structures from different eras. A narrow passageway under the arcade of the Council Tower, originally built as part of the city's second ring of forts in the thirteenth century, leads to Piata Mica, the handsome "small plaza," where the so-called Liar's Bridge abuts the elegant, arcaded Hall of the Butcher's Guild housing an ethnographic museum and superb gift shop of traditional handmade masks, carvings, fabrics, and tableware. The cast-iron bridge, the first of its kind in Romania, replaces an earlier rickety wooden one said to collapse if you told a lie while standing on it. The name stuck.

From the bridge, I was drawn down to the Lower Town, wandering through the medieval streets where everything isn't as spruced up, past at least a dozen stores called Second Hand, to the covered open-air market at Piata Cibin on the river, where I spent a few hours using Italian to communicate with the delightful Magyar, Rroma, and Romanian vendors.

Saxon home in Sibiu, Romania, 2011.

Street scene, Sibiu, Romania, 2011.

As in Bulgaria, I saw plenty of turnips and beets, but spinach was the only leafy green vegetable other than lettuce and cabbage. One Rroma vendor, his hands black from shelling walnuts, wanted to sell me not only nuts, but parsley root, bright orange catina berries (seabuckthorn), and Cornelian cherries (the fruit of a dogwood tree). I had no idea how to use them.

Since Romania became part of the EU, the butchers and cheesemakers have been moved indoors to a sterile building fitted with refrigerated cases to store their wares. Large hunks of each type of cheese, however, sat atop those coolers, for samples. A young woman from the neighboring Saxon village of Rasinari sold me some of her parents' lovely fresh sheep's milk cheese (her father, the shepherd; her mother, the cheesemaker). She spoke English.

The eighteen sheep-raising villages surrounding Sibiu—the Margini-mea Sibiului—are remarkable for their preservation of the traditional crafts of weaving, woodcarving, icon painting, egg coloring, and, naturally, cheese-making. I drove to nearby Rasinari first, where gaily painted road-side shrines adorn both country roads and the town square. Transylvanian kilims hung in the windows of the gingerbread-trimmed houses painted in pastel colors, like those of Bermuda or Charleston.

Public wells provided water for citizens to cart in buckets back to their satellite dish–adorned homes. Potatoes were being harvested in the sur-rounding fields, the hay was already stacked, and donkey carts were as common as automobiles, but the ethnographic museum was closed, and on more than one occasion I turned around because the road turned to dirt and, without a cell phone and unable to speak the language, I didn't feel comfortable. Not that that has ever stopped me before.

I probably should have joined some of the other spouses, who, through the massive, newly refurbished Continental Forum Hotel where we were staying, had hired a driver to take them on tours of the area. Especially up the treacherous, awe-inspiring Transfagarasan Highway—at seven thou-sand feet, the second highest in Europe. Somehow forgetting my fear of heights, I managed to reach the summit, passing Caspar David Friedrich landscapes at every bend, white-knuckled all the way.

A soaring monument to the mad Ceaușescu's desire to prove his might over nature's, the "highway," which took five years to build, is a two-lane blacktop hugging mile-high canyons. It is considered by many to be the best route in the world for motorcyclists; I was passed by dozens. I was for-tunate to have bright sun on the climb, but as soon as I reached the peak, chilling clouds moved in. I walked into one of the restaurants and ordered a restorative *ciorba ardeleneasca*, a traditional Transylvanian "sour" soup chock full of pork and potatoes. Chorbas are made sour by the addition of buttermilk, sour cream, lemon juice, vinegar, or, as in this case, sauerkraut juice. It was delicious.

The hilltop Saxon villages are famous for their fortified churches, several of which have been restored. In Cisnadioara, I climbed to the summit overlooking the apple orchards, then ordered the homemade lard spread and the apple soup from the German menu at the pension overlooking the town square, at the foot of the citadel. I could have been in Bavaria, or in Adams County, Pennsylvania.

Doors were closed, and several of the villages I visited appeared empty, but people were there, and working. In the valley towns, houses were built adjacent to each other, flanking the roads, with high walls; their back yards border rivers and streams. The weaving, cheese making, and embroidery is carried on behind those doors, while the shepherds tend their flocks in the neighboring hills and vales. In spite of the presence of Hungarians, Saxons, and Turks, Romanians have managed to preserve their Romance language, often described as the closest living language to classical Latin.

En route to Sighisoara, the iconic, castle-topped twelfth-century citadel, I sped through the Tarnave River Valley on the well-maintained, walnut-lined Highway 14. Outside Brateiu, an odd collection of unfinished Rroma homes flanked the road, with striking displays of copper cauldrons, stills, and trays for sale. I spent several hours with the Nicolae Caldarar family, who, when it became obvious that I was not going to buy anything, invited me into their home for coffee.

Often mistakenly identified as "Gabor gypsies" because of similar clothing, these non-traveling Rroma have been living in the same area for over three hundred years, they told me in Italian. Their name— Caldarar—means coppersmith; Gabori are tinsmiths. I asked why they didn't take their stunning copperware—all pounded by hand, with hammers on anvils—to cities where they might better be exposed to potential customers, and they told me that they, indeed, go to Budapest twice a year.

"You mean Bucharest," I said.

"No, Budapest," they insisted. "We consider ourselves Hungarian."

They have probably been in the area a lot longer than three centuries, but it is hard to trace their history since the fifteenth century, when Vlad the Impaler, the inspiration for Bram Stoker's Dracula, annihilated untold thousands of members of the lower classes, including the Rroma.

The Old Town of Sighisoara rose up over the newer sections hugging the Tarnave in an astonishing display of Saxon architectural styles clinging to the rocky massif. I was mesmerized. Perhaps there is something to this Dracula tale, I thought, as I climbed narrow stairs banked here and there with covered walkways—protections, I would learn, from heavy snowfalls.

I saw fine restored homes and churches, castles, and torture chambers. Nine of the citadel's original fourteen towers, maintained by the craftsmen guilds that built them, were still standing. The stunning rustic baroque Clock Tower had moving wooden figures that would emerge at 6 am and 6 pm; on the Citadel side, Peace, Justice, and Law appeared with angels representing day and night; on the Lower Town side, seven pagan gods representing the days of the week were cranked out automatically, keeping time the way a clock has done in this tower for over five hundred years. The tower housed an interesting museum that was overshadowed by the marvelous views from an upper wrap-around balcony. Back down on the square, once a site for beheadings, Vlad's home was marked with a plaque, and the plaza was lined with terrace cafés and shops hawking tacky Dracula souvenirs. There was a film crew working with some vintage cars, and I could see why the tour buses would line up in the summer.

I had unwittingly saved the best for last. My husband tacked an extra night onto our stay, and we spent the entire last day at the appealing Museum of Traditional Folk Civilization, known as ASTRA. Just outside Sibiu on the edge of the Dumbrava Forest, ASTRA is a 250-acre open-air museum that makes Colonial Williamsburg look like a tiny theme park. Begun in the early 1960s, the museum is a recreation of Romanian rural life, featuring 150 historical structures that have been moved to the museum and restored. It offered us a peek into the world of hunters, fishermen, shepherds, blacksmiths, wheelwrights, weavers, and potters. We saw two churches, both still in use, and a field of windmills. There was an early industrial complex for finishing textiles, a gold mine, and a water-powered sawmill. I felt like a kid again as I peered into the candle maker's workshop and the goatherd's mountain hut.

There was a restaurant on the grounds of the museum, a village tavern from a region between Transylvania and Muntenia, famous for its plum brandy ("tzuica"). The inn was built in 1850 by a family who used it until 1952 as their shop, pub, and lodge. I had been told by some of the other spouses to be sure to eat there. I thought of Paul Kovi when I ordered the cabbage cooked in bacon with the homemade sausages. They were grilled over an open fire by a zaftig cook who grimaced when I took her photo. After we ate, spicing our meals with fresh hot peppers we had been served as garnish, I went back, without my camera, and gave her the thumbs up symbol. She beamed.

A Lowcountry
Calendar

When the 20ᵗʰ Anniversary Edition of my Lowcountry Cooking was
released, I was invited to Charleston to speak at the first annual Charles-
ton Heritage Symposium. The theme was "Inside Neoclassical Charles-
ton." I shared the dais with The Hon. Simon Howard of Castle Howard,
Tom Savage of the Winterthur Museum, Elizabeth Kornhauser of the
Metropolitan Museum, and Andrew Brunk, the exuberant auctioneer.
I planned an eighteenth-century menu for the reception, which was
held at the William Gibbes House (ca. 1772). My lecture, illustrated with
dozens of slides, traced Charleston's culinary heritage. I ended it on this
note:

One of my favorite finds in my Lowcountry research was a pie chart by
Henry William Ravenel, who, incidentally, published the first treatise on
mushrooms in America in the 1850s. The chart was the frontispiece to
Francis Holmes's book, *The Southern Farmer and Market Gardener*, published in 1842. It's called *Vegetables all the Year Round*, showing when to
plant and when to harvest dozens of types of plants, including ground artichokes, drumhead cabbage, guinea squash, salsify, rutabaga, and kohl rabi.

It inspired me to put together a little calendar of my own. I no longer
live in the Lowcountry, but, for a few moments, let's pretend that I do. We'll
begin now, in October, and go through my Lowcountry year. I think this
will give you a better taste of what Lowcountry cooking is all about than all
the history and folklore and gardening techniques and photos combined.
It's very personal, and it's what Charleston's culinary heritage is to me, and
to many others, today.

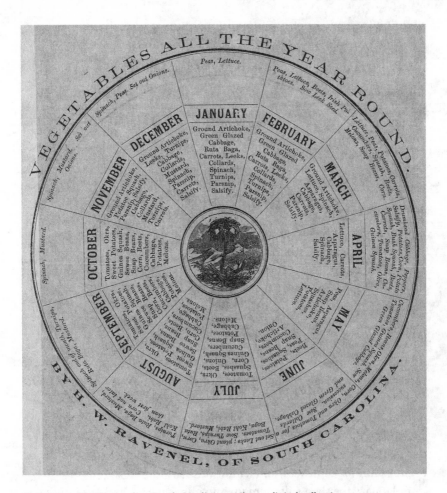

University of South Carolina South Caroliniana Library digital collection.

October is my favorite month, with its cool nights and warm days. The water temperature in Charleston is often warmer than the air, especially after the sun sets, so nighttime swimming, one of my favorite Lowcountry activities, is a real joy, especially after a day of fall planting. And I get to shoot squirrels, the bane of my existence. They are delicious as long as they don't live in pine trees. And real bobwhite quail, not those European ones they raise in captivity. And God! For the sweet potatoes! And wild persimmons, whose flowery bouquet is like a fine muscat grape.

When Karen Hess's book on the Carolina rice kitchen was released, I had a party for her at my bookstore. It was one of the freakish early frosts, and when I picked her up at the airport, freshly shot quail were hanging in the back of my pickup. I let them hang there for several days in the cool and then served them to her with spiced muscadines and rice bread. I can't for the life of me figure out why folks don't make rice bread anymore. It's so delicious and moist and stays so for days. It was once the daily bread of Charleston, but by the time the Junior League published *Charleston Receipts* in 1950, none of the thirty recipes for it that had appeared in *The Carolina Housewife* a hundred years earlier were included.

November's a funny time. You never know if it's going to be seventy degrees or fifty—it's sort of the reverse of March—and each weekend we cast the same style shrimp nets that they've been using in West Africa for over a thousand years, and each weekend the shrimp get bigger and bigger and more plentiful, it seems, until snap! It turns cold and they disappear.

December is often sunny. I've spent many Christmases in shirtsleeves outside. In my family we start with coffee and homemade pastries inside, then go outdoors to drink Champagne and eat raw oysters—and it's every man, woman, and child for themselves. We then move back indoors for ham biscuits, really twice-leavened tiny yeast rolls stuffed with salty county ham spread with fiery mustard and a sweet and spicy pear chutney. Our meal is always pan-fried quail and gravy over stone-ground grits, maybe some venison sausage, regular lard biscuits, and ambrosia, of course, made with grapefruit, oranges, fresh coconuts, and pineapple. Throughout December and into the new year, we enjoy the sweet potatoes and greens of fall, and all those holiday treats, from old-fashioned whiskey-soaked Scottish fruitcakes, black with dried fruit and rife with spices, to charlottes and eggnog, Shrewsbury cakes, and lemon curd.

In January the shad will swim up into our estuaries, and our inimitable wild oysters will be at their finest. Now that you're here in the Lowcountry during an R month, be sure to sample some if you can find them. They taste like no others.

In February we plant the last of the cool weather vegetables, like onions and broccoli, so they'll produce before the summer heat sets in, and we pull many of our meals from the freezer. But those foods worth freezing were local and at the height of their seasons—shrimp, shrimp stock, shrimp butter, duck stock, sieva beans, peaches, corn, and berries. We spice up those frozen foods with our myriad condiments that have defined our cooking for centuries: piccalilli, corn relish, peach chutney, pickled okra, and *ats jaar*, a mixed pickle that is one of the oldest recorded recipes on earth and which I traced to Java, and which, when I was growing up, was set on restaurant tables as a matter of course.

In March, the arugula—or "rocket," as the old books called it—is up, there are new potatoes and carrots and spring onions, and the coconuts are really good in the early spring. I use tried and true Lowcountry cooking techniques on the first of the English peas and the last of the shad. Wild turkey season opens on April 1, and, from the woods, I bring home fresh green grape leaves to brine.

May is just about too much to behold in the Lowcountry, shrimp and corn and all those wonderful butterbeans and field peas—the whippoor-wills and lady peas and crowders and the little red cowpeas that are the real thing for hoppin' john. And the freshwater fish finally start biting again—the bream and bass and catfish . . . and maybe one of my friends will take me out again this year to go after the pelagic ocean fish, those powerful swimmers like wahoo or the elusive cobia, locally known as crab-eaters. The first fruits appear, cantaloupes and huckleberries and blueberries, and loquats, and I'll make wine with the messy mulberries that fall and put it aside for a few years until it tastes like a decent port.

In June I'll fish along the pilings for sheepshead and make a fish stew that rivals bouillabaisse. And I'll fry hundreds of whiting and grill some porgies with guinea squash and tomatoes. When I visit my sisters in Charleston in July, I can almost forget that I don't live here anymore until I sober up, and the heat and humidity hit me, and my allergies set in. By then the gardens are already petering out and folks are planting a second crop for fall. The big, fat, freestone peaches start to arrive, and my sister takes venison out of her freezer and replaces it with summer fruits. When the smaller, deep red clingstones are ripe, I make spiced peaches, which no holiday meal is without. There are a lot of outdoor food-gathering tasks in mid-summer, such as looking for Jerusalem artichoke flowers along road-sides and flagging them so I can find the tubers to dig up in the fall. I like to go frog-gigging at least once each summer, and I'll bring back a head or two of elderberry flowers to fry for dessert, served with a simple berry sauce. When it's as hot as it's been the past couple of summers, I know a few pompano will wander this far north, and my sister's crab pot will get a heat-crazed eel or flounder.

About every third year, she and I go through the arduous process of making watermelon rind preserves, a recipe which probably came to Charleston with the Greeks in the nineteenth century. It's a real pain to remove all the white and all the red from the melons, but it's a neces-sary ingredient for the fruitcakes we'll make for the holidays, dense with dried fruits, but none of those dayglo things. The preserved melon rind is actually traditional in fruitcakes, for the citron that is called for in the old recipes is actually a melon, not the Mediterranean citrus.

If you get up early enough in the morning in late July, you can beat the birds to the figs. Southern figs, naturally hybridized, are a far cry from the brown turkey fig that is its ancestor, delicately flavored, the skin as soft as its raspberry-like flesh. We eat most out of hand, but preserves, nuts-and-citrus-filled conserves, cake fillings, and ice creams are made with them as well. And then there are the dozen varieties of wild and cultivated blackberries and dewberries, for cobblers, vinegars, wines, and dumplings.

Come August it's really too hot to garden, but deer season opens, and my hunter friends bring me tenderloins, haunches, and scraps for sausage. You can plant winter greens in August, but mostly you just wipe the sweat and swat the mosquitoes and try to find a shady spot to move your herbs. Rain is welcomed, and mushrooms pop up by the thousands under the stately live oaks. When I was growing up, my mother would cook the wild mushrooms that grew in fairy rings in our back yard, but after living in France and Italy, I became something of a wild mushroom fan. When I was researching the culinary history of the Lowcountry, I came upon the aforementioned Henry William Ravenel's treatise, and I became acutely attuned to the ephemeral but prolific season of Lowcountry chanterelles, forty pounds of which I picked one afternoon out at Middleburg Plantation, where the oldest wooden house in South Carolina stands as the precursor to Charleston's classic single house.

My sister's lemon tree nestled up next to her house and the banana hovering over her patio are covered with fruit, but it's always a toss-up of whether they'll fully ripen before the unpredictable frost. Some years it comes early—say, before Thanksgiving—and lasts a couple of weeks, but some years it doesn't come at all, and we pick citrus for two months.

August also sees the first of the local green peanuts, which when boiled are, bar-none, my favorite snack, and a real Lowcountry tradition. Our delicious native grapes, scuppernongs and muscadines, ripen, and I make jellies and preserves and sorbets with them and with our hard local Kieffer pears, which will bear fruit right up to ocean's edge.

September brings the first hint of cool weather to the Lowcountry, and while it's rarely more than a hint, oyster and clam seasons open, which see those bivalves on my table more often than you can imagine. I'm invariably asked to go on dove shoots, though I am the worst shot I know. Doves are delicious, but they're so small. I'm surprised more folks don't eat pigeons. I guess you know that all of the pigeons in this country are offspring of

European rock doves, brought here as foodstuffs by the early settlers. In Sumter, South Carolina, the nation's oldest squab farm has been raising pigeons on whole grains and spring water since the 1920s. Most of the old Lowcountry plantations had a dovecote among their outbuildings.

And in September we're most likely to catch Spanish mackerel, kings, and bluefish. Pecans aren't native to the east coast, but they have thrived here since they were planted. Although almost none of their nuts are grown in the state, Young's Pecans in Florence, South Carolina—in the Pee Dee region of the state, which is the upper coastal plain—is the world's largest seller of the nuts. When Mr. Young was asked by my mother-in-law, who lives nearby, whether he called them peecans or pecahns, he said, "Well, Dixie," (and, yes, that's her real name), "I buy peecans but I sell pecahns."

And that brings us to now. Eight years ago I moved to Washington, DC, where I witnessed first-hand the fact that climate change is making the Chesapeake share the Lowcountry's climate, if not its humidity. Gardener's calendars now place Washington in a semi-tropical zone. I have friends with a farm on the eastern shore of Maryland where I spent the past seven summers canning figs, making cherry bounce out of wild cherries, pickling green beans, and freezing blueberries. We made pear chutney and relish every year and stuffed trombetta blossoms with crab meat. Last year I moved to Bulgaria, and the first friend I made is a winemaker with hundreds of acres of farmland. He grew cowpeas and collards and crookneck squash for me this year, and when I get back, we'll prune his grapevines, and we'll wrap quail in preserved leaves and grill them over those vines and serve them with spiced grapes like those I served Karen Hess, and we'll have rice topped with crowders cooked with the salt pork he made from his prize heritage hogs, and I'll serve them with a dollop of pear relish.

Like the plantation cook, I'm always planning my next meal.

Belltowerism and Other Musings on Life in the Provinces

You can't live happily in a foreign country by comparing it to other places you've lived. And you can't judge the East by Western criteria. Though I eat everything, and with a smile on my face, there are some foods I've never been a fan of. And I don't mind saying so. It would be an awfully dull world if we all liked the same foods, the same music, or the same designs. I don't dislike tofu, but, like pasta, who eats it by itself? I've had some elegant versions of Chengdu's famous *Ma Po Dou Fu* here, but I find most versions simply too oily for my taste, and the one we had at lunch yesterday tasted sweet to me. A teaspoon of sugar is traditional for two or three servings; I'm sure there was at least a tablespoon in yesterday's. A typical recipe calls for a one-pound block of bean curd in ½ cup of red chili oil—peanut oil seasoned with about ⅓ cup of Sichuanese chili bean paste, a tablespoon of fermented black beans, 2 teaspoons of ground Sichuanese chilies (deep red, medium hot, very fragrant), and ½ teaspoon of ground roasted Sichuan peppercorns (the numbing seeds from the prickly ash tree), plus soy sauce, salt, cornstarch, leeks, a cup of stock, and a scattering of ground pork (though beef is sometimes used) . One of the finest renditions of the dish I've had was at the fancy nearby Shangri-La Hotel, where they serve many traditional Cantonese dim sum dishes.

Many foods here swim in even more oil. I've seen handfuls of both chili peppers and Sichuan peppercorns in the traditional *huǒguō* (hot pot) cauldrons, into which you dunk the foods you choose from carts wheeled through the restaurants, from mushrooms and green vegetables to pig brains and skewered meats. Everything ends up tasting like the overwhelmingly spicy oil. I always order whatever green vegetables are offered on the à la carte menu, no matter how small or large the restaurant or noodle shop; they're usually simply prepared. And rice as well. I can always find something I like to eat.

I'm loving much of the street food—much simpler fare, prepared before your eyes: super thin omelets filled with all manner of vegetables, meats, nuts, and fried doughs; *lāmiàn* (hand-pulled noodles) from a local Muslim restaurant (two dollars for a hearty bowl); *dan dan* noodles, topped with peanuts, ground pork, and scallions (street vendors sell for about a dollar, but the best I've had were, again, at Shangri-La); *guo kei*—flatbreads—of all sorts, grilled, fried, and baked (my favorite so far, sold near the entrance to the pricey middle school near my apartment, is a ball of dough filled with ground pork and spices, flattened and then fried); and myriad starch jellies.

Because Sichuan is one of the subtropical breadbaskets of the country, there is fresh and local food daily, much of it organically grown. Of course, organic means night soil, so everything must be washed in this special soap that is supposed to kill any microorganisms. People just don't eat raw foods here. And if you want salad greens, you have to go to one of the big German or French grocery chains and buy them in clamshell packages— even though they are often fresh and local. I've ordered seeds to grow the things I miss on my balcony, the way I did in Bulgaria, and I saved several varieties of the incomparable Bulgarian tomato seeds. I've got pots of mesclun and arugula outside and Mediterranean herb seedlings sprouting indoors. Most of the local produce is beautiful; even warmer climes are not far away, and I've enjoyed lots of citrus this winter. The tiny, often seedless, so-called Mandarin oranges are my favorites, but I'm afraid their season is about to end: all the ones I've had this past week were larger, and full of seeds. Blood oranges have appeared now, and I recently paired them with the insanely delicious red Sichuan carrots. They really are a rosy-red, a deep, slightly purple-pink. And so sweet. I served them with the oranges, scallions, fresh green chili peppers, cilantro, extra virgin olive oil, salt and pepper, and a hint of cinnamon for a Moroccan flavor. I added a few slivered leaves of celery, because I take advantage of any salad green that I can!

In Italy they have a word that I love—*campanilismo*. Literally, it translates as "bell tower-ism," which it is in a manner of speaking. It means excessive pride in one's hometown or region—or parochialism. You could say that I have had it for Charleston. Or Athens, Georgia. Or Genoa. The word is derived from *campanile* (bell tower), which is often the most prominent

Il Campanile di Santa Maria in Passione in Genoa, 1989.

building in Italian towns and villages. You could also say that some southerners have it for their statues of Confederate generals.

Campanilismo is all about the much-ballyhooed sense of place that we tend to look for in art—especially in books and movies, and on our plates. It is beyond fresh and local: it is a feeling of pride, of belonging, of identity. If you ask an Italian where he is from, he will invariably say "*sono genovese*" (I'm from Genoa) or "*sono siciliano*" (I'm Sicilian) before he will say he's *italiano*. Until the Risorgimento in the 1860s, there was no United States of Italy, so to speak. There were many separate states, with their own languages and dialects, their own culinary traditions, and their own histories. I use Italy as an example, because even though the country has been united for nearly 150 years, there are still many distinct regional differences—and differences within the regions. Focaccia in Genoa is not like the focaccia of Recco, a few miles to the east. Even neighborhoods within cities are rivals.

In Charleston, South Carolina, it is said that the only true Charlestonians are the ones who were there before The War. That would be the Revolutionary War. They are the true "bo'n ye'uh" (born here) Charlestonians. Everyone else is "from off." I know Lowcountry cooks who are so persnickety about the use of pig parts that they insist that collards be cooked with smoked neck bones except on New Year's, when they must be cooked with "butt's meat" (smoked hog jowl); turnips, with "side meat" (salt pork); and dried field peas or butterbeans, with a smoked ham hock (while in summer, you can use any cured meat with the freshly shelled peas and beans, though you must "fry it out" and pour off some of the fat before adding water).

This is also campanilismo.

However, the term also describes a sort of myopia and unwillingness or inability to see beyond one's borders or comfort zones. As someone who has always eaten everything—and been willing to try anything—I am always amazed when people's culinary horizons seem to be so near and confining. I cannot tell you how many times I have heard "We don't eat that." In Paris. In Genoa. In nearly every American's home I've been in. In Bulgaria. And, perhaps most surprisingly, here in China.

Me: "So you will eat the rubbery throat of a pig doused in boiling oil so spicy it both burns and numbs your mouth, but you won't eat lettuce?"

Chinese friend: "We eat all sorts of lettuce. Cooked."

The Sichuanese I have come to know are fond of saying that Western food is too sweet, but they have a profoundly sweet tooth here. Grocery stores stock huge bins of candies—front and center—and many of their baked goods and snacks are sweeter than *pain au chocolat* or Snickers—both of which are also popular here. The fillings may not be familiar to Westerners—bean paste or salted duck egg or guava, for example, and the textures can be downright bizarre (lots of sticky rice concoctions), but I'd venture to say that they have more sweets than we do, for modern China has embraced our Western confections as well, so that custards and tarts and cakes share the dessert table with sweet soups, puddings, and jellies. Some sweets are steamed, then fried. Western-style dairy products have also taken a foothold here. Ice cream shops are common, especially in the malls, and yogurt (more often sweetened than not) commands an entire aisle in supermarkets now.

A couple of years ago some friends of mine from Genoa came to visit us in Washington—during the infamous "Snowmageddon" that all but shut the city down. I shopped for hours the day the storm began, standing in lines at five different supermarkets, stocking up for our inevitable shut-in. On the fifth or sixth day, we finally ventured out, and Gianni, for whom I had cooked lamb chops and oysters and Mexican fare and grilled quail and fried fish and pilau and gumbo, confessed he wanted pasta. We went to Pesce, the delightful little Franco-Italian bistro opened years ago in Dupont Circle by Jean-Louis Palladin and Roberto Donna. While his girlfriend and I ordered fish (their specialty) and seafood salads, Gianni ordered a simple pasta dish. Basically, he was homesick. Another facet of campanilismo.

I totally understood. When I roomed with Gianni in Genoa back in the early eighties, I horribly missed long-grain rice and butterbeans and okra and grits. In French and Italian, you don't say you miss something; you say it is lacking to you: you are incomplete without whatever it is you miss. When I lived in Bulgaria, it was greens. In Paris, it was the sun. Here in Chengdu, it's both the sun and salad that I miss. I realize that I can be as provincial as the next guy.

Fresh Chinese Water Chestnuts

There are several species of the genus *Trapa* that are called water chestnuts, but I refer to *Eleocharis dulcis*, the crunchy, slightly sweet corms that we all know from Chinese restaurants in America, where canned ones are often paired with snow pea pods, and from cocktail parties, where they appear wrapped in bacon (a mock Polynesian appetizer called "rumaki," probably invented by Trader Vic). I was shocked to pick up the second edition of the *Oxford Companion to Food* (2006), a nearly 1000-page encyclopedia that is generally regarded as definitive, and to find no mention of *Eleocharis* under the entry for water chestnut (which is neither a nut nor a chestnut). I jumped to conclusions and did some sloppy reading and writing before Anne Mendelson pointed out to me that I had missed their entry, "Chinese water chestnut," that distinguishes it from the *Trapa* varieties. Common names are always problematic. *Eleocharis* is a type of water grass that emerges from these corms.

Here in Chengdu, women sit on stools at their pop-up stands, peeling them with a Chinese chef's knife, which, though similar in looks to a cleaver, is actually a razor-sharp tool that they use with uncommon dexterity to accomplish everything from chopping to delicate splitting of scallions. Their stands, such as they are, might be equipped with an electronic scale, or they might simply have a primitive balance beam scale made with sticks and string. They quickly shave the fresh, moist chestnuts of their brown outer skin and place them in plastic bags before weighing. I pay about 20 *kuai*—$3.50—for a *jin*, 500 grams (a little more than a pound).

If you have only had canned water chestnuts—pleasant enough, more crunch than taste—then you will be amazed at the depth of flavor of fresh ones. They taste a bit like apples or Jerusalem artichokes. Surprisingly sweet (hence the Latin, *dulcis*), they remind me of sugarcane and fresh coconut as well. Interestingly, though I often see them on the streets, I have not encountered them in restaurants here (perhaps they are too expensive or too time-consuming to prepare?). Fuchsia Dunlop does not mention them in her book of Sichuan cooking, but I see them being sold not only by street vendors, but also in supermarkets, so home cooks are certainly using them. As in English, they have several common names in China, but locally they are called *ma-ti* ("horse hoof"—*ma tai* in Cantonese), which perhaps refers to their shape but could also refer to the fact that they are often covered in mud.

Because of their sweetness, water chestnuts often find their way into desserts and sweet drinks. Bruce Cost includes them in a recipe for "Coconut 'Crème Brulée'" in his *Asian Ingredients*. They are also dried and ground into a flour that can be used as a thickener, like cornstarch. Made into a paste, the water chestnut has many uses in traditional Chinese medicine; it is fed to children who have swallowed coins. Amazingly, they can be enjoyed, as Elizabeth Schneider notes in her remarkable *Vegetables from Amaranth to Zucchini*, "at any stage from raw to long cooked. Boil, steam, braise, sauté, or chop and add to ground seafood or meat to bake, fry, or use as stuffing." Don't be concerned about overcooking.

Available in Asian markets occasionally throughout the year, Chinese water chestnuts will keep, unpeeled, for up to two weeks in a bowl of water in the refrigerator. Because of how they are grown, they are often coated in mud. You can scrub them gently, or you can soak them overnight, as Elizabeth notes, "and they'll clean themselves." But you will have to peel them and remove any discolored spots.

Sometimes they ferment, but the smell and taste are not horrible. Buy more than you think you will need. Shiu-Ying Hu, in her incomparable *Food Plants of China*, writes, "It is worthy of note that Chinese farmers . . . often eat the fresh products by rinsing off the mud and peeling the skin with their front teeth. From such an unhealthy practice, they are often infected by the liver fluke because the free-swimming stage of the parasite may be attached to the scales of the corms." Thoroughly washed and skinned, freshwater chestnuts pose no threat.

Dr. Hu describes their fascinating cultivation, which is intertwined with that of fish, mulberries, and silkworms. During the wet season, which begins in March, water chestnuts and fish are raised simultaneously, the plants providing shelter to the fish whose waste in turn fertilizes the plants.

In November when the dry season begins, the fish are harvested, the water is drained, the chestnuts are gathered, and the mud of the fishpond is added to the banks of mulberries, which are pruned to the ground for the winter. The new mulberry growth in the spring is the favored food of silkworms, whose pupae are then used to feed the new crop of fish.

In Southeast Asia, water chestnuts appear in all manner of salads. I like to boil them for just a minute or two, cool them, and pair them with asparagus or roasted peppers. Some street vendors skewer them raw, keep them wet, and sell them as both appetizers and after-dinner refreshments. Dr. Hu suggests simply serving them raw with toothpicks at parties. Boiled, they are sometimes offered as snacks at tea houses, either hot or cool. Boiling actually helps keep them crisp.

When used in broths seasoned with lemongrass or chili, they enliven soups with their crunch. Add coconut milk, lime, and scallops or shrimp. Wrap poached, chilled water chestnuts in prosciutto or smoked salmon slices. Stir-fry them with green beans. Add them to any kind of salad. They are so much better than the canned.

Cooking Nok Style in Ko Lanta

▶ CHENGDU, 2014 ···

Chef Nok Noi on Ko Lanta, Thailand.

Mikel and I rented a house on sandy Klong Nin Beach on Ko Lanta in southern Thailand for the first two weeks of the year. I asked the homeowner if he knew of someone who might cook for us—or someone who might at least accompany me to a market. Though I wasn't really interested in taking a formal cooking class, I was keen on watching a real Thai in the kitchen. He suggested I contact Nok Noi ("Little Bird"), who had recently opened her own restaurant on the main road of the laid-back beach village. "She's a ladyboy," he wrote. "I trust that's alright."

"Ladyboys," or *kathoeys*, as they are called in Thai (though don't try pronouncing that as if it were an English word!) are probably best known as either beautiful cabaret dancers or prostitutes in Bangkok. However, although Thailand is a generally extremely conservative country, many kathoeys are well integrated into society and are not frowned upon. You find them working as flight attendants, at cosmetic counters, and as movie stars. At least one is a boxing legend. Some, though not all, are trans-gender.

I did not delve deeply into Nok's personal life, not that she wouldn't have shared her life story with me, but simply because we had limited time together (her new spot, with only a handful of tables, was open for breakfast, lunch, and dinner) and, frankly, I didn't think it was of much importance. She grew up in Bangkok and had "always cooked." She Skyped with her family back home daily. Her former fiancé had been killed in an automobile accident, but she was by this time married to a very nice fellow. They lived above the restaurant, Nok Style, but hoped to build living quarters behind the current octagonal building and move the customer dining upstairs, away from the road. [The restaurant has since closed.] She was gracious with her time, and she was an excellent teacher (her English was very good; more importantly, she knew her stuff!), but when I told her that she should open a cooking school, she said that she wasn't interested. She just wanted to cook for people. She had cooked at a beachfront resort across the street for five years, so when she opened her own place late last year, the locals and her regulars were thrilled. Animated about food, she expressed to me the importance of respecting the ingredients and treating them properly to get the best flavors.

We began with a trip (in a tuktuk) to the Wednesday afternoon market (I had been earlier in the day, but the fishmongers and butchers weren't there yet). "You have to go after three o'clock," she told me. "That's when the chefs and home cooks are free between lunch and dinner." Most of the vendors were Muslim fishermen's and farmers' wives. They all knew Nok and vied for her business. Afterwards we went to her simple, tiny (but immaculate) kitchen, which she and her husband had built themselves, and she cooked several dishes for me with the ingredients we had purchased at the market. Afterwards, she drove me back to our beach house on her scooter, with to-go bags full of the incredibly tasty treats.

....

Tung Thong (Golden Pouches)

I had already eaten these beggar's pouches at Nok Style, so I asked that she show me how they were made. Amazingly, all of the dishes that "we" made—including these fried dumplings—tasted fine even an hour or so later at room temperature. The food of Thailand really is a hot-weather cuisine. Nok used packaged wrappers that were large squares that she cut into smaller ones, about 4 inches each. They looked a lot thinner than regular wonton wrappers to me, but she said that wonton wrappers would do fine, just be sure to cut off any ragged edge so that it both fries up right and looks nice. I think what you really need are spring roll wrappers that have no egg. You can probably find frozen ones in the States. We made ten or twelve dumplings and had a little leftover filling, which she assured me you can freeze and use later. Like many chefs who have worked in hotel kitchens, she used a "secret ingredient," which happened to be stock powder made by Knorr, the German giant that is catering to serious chefs all over the world with all-natural ingredients. They individualize ingredients for each country. The Knorr chicken stock powder that Nok used contained no MSG, though it was decidedly salty. She didn't use fish sauce or salt in these pouches because she used the powder.

She tied the bundles up with strips of pandan leaves (*Pandanus amaryllifolius*) from her yard but said you can use scallion greens instead. Pandan is used widely in Thai cooking, and it imparts a delicate breadlike flavor to many dishes. For a dipping sauce, Nok mixed a sweet and sour sauce with a spicy plum sauce. Serve with the sweet and hot sauce of your choice. This recipe is a general one. You may use pork instead of chicken, or all pork, or all chicken. Water chestnuts, scallions, onions, and/or ginger can be added to the filling if you like, but if you want it Nok Style, stick to the coriander root.

Wonton or spring roll
    wrappers
3 or 4 peeled large
    shrimp
3 ounces raw chicken
    meat
Coriander root, about
    4 inches long and
    ¼-inch thick, with
    2 inches of stem
½ teaspoon sesame oil
1 teaspoon stock powder
    (or ½ teaspoon fish
    sauce)
Pandan leaves or scallion
    greens
Oil for frying
Sweet hot sauce for
    serving

Trim the wonton wrappers of any rough edges and cut them into 3- or 4-inch squares. It's probably best to cover them with plastic wrap or a damp towel so that they don't dry out, especially if you are new at this.

Using a cleaver, mince the shrimp and chicken together, then add the coriander root and mince it into the meats. Add the seasonings and mix well. Place a heaping teaspoon of the filling on the center of wonton wrapper, and, working quickly but methodically, gather the four corners of the wrapper together to form a pouch, tucking in any errant folds. Tie with pandan or scallion leaves and set aside. Repeat with the remaining wrappers and filling.

Heat enough oil in a wok to cover the dumplings. Though I usually recommend frying most things at 365°F, Nok warned that you should fry these at a lower temperature, so that the wrappers don't burn before the fillings cook. Move the dumplings around so that they fry evenly on all sides, using the inner walls of the wok to push the ones that are cooking more quickly up out of the oil so that they are all cooked at the same time. Remove the "golden bags" from the oil with a strainer and allow all the oil to drain back into the pot before placing them on a serving platter. Serve hot, warm, or at room temperature with a sweet chili sauce.

. . . .

With limited time between lunch and dinner, Nok had asked me to let her know in advance what I wanted her to cook for me so that she was sure to have on hand any ingredients we couldn't find at the market. I really wanted to go with what inspired me at the market, but I understood her limitations. Her kitchen was not a teaching kitchen. It was very basic. So as well as the *Tung Thang** I thought perhaps I should go for the basics—Pad Thai and Green Papaya Salad.

"Chicken, prawn, or pork?" she asked. Even though I knew there were shrimp in the fried dumplings, I wanted them with the noodles and salad as well. I could buy fresh seafood—mostly farm-raised—in Chengdu, but I wanted to take advantage of the fresh local bounty. We hand-picked the plumpest ones from the vendor, whose husband had probably caught them right in front of our rented house earlier that day or the night before.

I was so excited about watching a real Thai cook cooking real Thai food. I call Nok a "cook" even though she is an accomplished chef because her food is fresh, local, and traditional. I remember my first exposure to Southeast Asian recipes was in Charmaine Solomon's incredible *Complete Asian Cookbook* (1976). Believe it or not, it's one of the handful of cookbooks I brought with me (from my thousands) overseas. She was so ahead of her time. Interestingly, the book doesn't include recipes for any of these now classic dishes. Perhaps they weren't as popular then, or perhaps she simply wanted to include the most representative dishes from each of the fifteen Asian countries represented in the massive tome. There have been several revised editions since it was originally published. In the thirty-page section on Thailand, she writes, "Thai cooking . . . is very much a taste-and-add affair. While the recipes are splendid, it is very difficult to obtain exact recipes because most Thai cooks don't use them. It is best to watch the cook closely, noting every move and taking careful and copious notes."

Describing the cook with whom she "seldom spent so edifying an afternoon," Solomon noted that "like every country, Thailand has a classic cuisine and a peasant cuisine. She uses both, depending on the occasion."

At the market I couldn't resist buying some greens and seaweed, which one of the shrimpers' wives was selling. Of the seaweed, which was the best I've ever eaten (surely because of its freshness), Nok said, "You can add it to the papaya salad." Mikel noted that the little globules burst on the tongue like caviar. It tasted the way the ocean smells. Also known as "sea grapes" or "umibudo green algae," this particular seaweed, *Caulerpa lentillifera*, is now widely available.

The greens, which Nok called *Phak Kwang Tung* (literally, Guangdong Greens), were what I would call Chinese Mustard Greens. But common names of the thousands of varieties of greens are mind-boggling. And deciphering the different species of the genus *Brassica* really doesn't matter to most home cooks, or gardeners, for that matter. Often referred to as *choi* or *choy sum*, it is more correctly called *Yau choy* or *yu choy* or *yu choy sum*. What we found were the mature, foot-long, dark green, yellow-flowering stems. It's similar to Chinese broccoli, which you can treat in the same manner. In his *Asian Ingredients* (1988), Bruce Cost wrote, "*Yow choy* means 'oil vegetable.' . . . It's the ubiquitous green of Hong Kong, where it's called simply *choy sum*, or 'flowering green.'" By the time Ken Hom wrote his own book of Asian ingredients in 1996, the green had become familiar enough to the American cook that he simply advised it "is delicious stir-fried with olive oil and garlic and used in fillings and with pasta. The cabbage leaves require little cooking to bring out their delicate, sweet, mustard flavors." That was the only recipe he offered. I was thrilled to watch Nok cooking the greens for me, using the same flavors (if not the same ingredients) that I normally use and a very similar technique. You can use Chinese broccoli, rapini, or other sturdy greens in this recipe just as well.

. . . .

Phak Kwand Tung Jeen (Stir-Fried Greens)

The main difference between the way I would normally cook greens and Nok's is that she used a touch a of sweetness, from both the oyster sauce and sugar. Her *coup de grâce* (for me, because it is a brilliant touch) was a garnish of deep-fried garlic, which she happened to have on hand. The garlic is thinly sliced and fried quickly until it is golden and sweet, but not browned, at which point it becomes bitter. You can add shrimp or chicken or tofu to this dish, adding it to the pan before the seasonings.

a bunch of Chinese flowering cabbage, Chinese broccoli, rapini, or turnip or mustard greens

a tablespoon of oil (I use olive oil)

3 cloves fresh garlic, to taste

fresh chili peppers, to taste

3 tablespoons water or chicken stock, more or less

Oyster sauce, to taste

1 teaspoon sugar (optional)

1 teaspoon fish sauce or ½ teaspoon stock powder

Soy sauce, to taste

Deep-fried garlic (see headnote)

Wash the greens and chop the stems into pieces; slice the greens as well into bite-size pieces. Don't shake off the water; you will want it clinging to the greens. Mince the garlic and chilies together. Nok did this by putting them into a plastic bag and pounding them with a pestle, to contain the pungent fumes.

Heat a wok or large deep skillet over a high flame, add the oil, then stir in the garlic and chilies. At this point Nok added the water, producing dramatic flames, but I prefer to add the greens (stems first if they are thick) and the water that clings to them, plus more water or stock if necessary. Immediately add the seasonings to taste, stirring and tossing the vegetables around until they are wilted and tender. It will take about 4 minutes.

Serve immediately garnished with the fried garlic.

About these names. Nancie McDermott tells me that she would render *Tung Thang* "as 'tong.' "Or 'thong.' 'Th' because it is a hard T, not a soft T sound at the beginning. It involves aspiration of the T sound. But the vowel is key here, and 'a' should be 'o' either way. Rhymes with 'song' as in 'sing a song,' but with a bit more of an 'oe' as in 'toe' . . . The spelling is such a challenge—no consistent way to go. I go with pronunciation, an attempt to give people a head start on pronouncing or understanding, and that is just my personal preference. Hence I despise 'larb' and use 'lahp' for the minced meat 'salad' of Northeastern origin." She should know. Google Translate gave "T̄hung thxng." I'd love to hear an American (or anyone, for that matter), try to pronounce *that*!

....

Tom Sum, or Green Papaya Salad

This tangy salad made with shredded unripe papaya is served throughout Southeast Asia. In the 1990s there was an award-winning French-Vietnamese film called *The Scent of Green Papaya*; by then, the dish was known the world over. There are dozens of variations. Nok's version included carrots, tomato, garlic, hot chilies, a yard-long bean (cut into pieces), limes, palm sugar, prawns (per my request), fish sauce, and roasted nuts. She assured me that "you can make it with any fruit—apples, pineapples, or any unripe soft fruit or ripe hard ones." Her pomelo version was a very popular dish at her restaurant.

Tom Sum in Thailand (*Som Tam* in Laos) often includes peanuts (*Tom Sum Thai*), which is the internationally renowned rendition, but similar salads, infinitely varied, are found throughout the region. The popularity of the dish lies in its medley of five major flavors—salty, sour, sweet, spicy hot, and savory, with sour being predominant (*tom sum*—Ŝmtå—means "pounded sour"). Nok's ingredients were typical, but dried shrimp, crab, pork, chicken, and other local vegetables and herbs might be added to the mortar as well. The pounding, such as it is, is crucial to the success of the dish. This is not so much a recipe as a technique. Nok highly recommended a simple hand-held grater to julienne the green papaya and carrots.

Palm sugar in Thailand is made from the sugar palm, but any of the palm or coconut sugars from the region can be used in the dish; if you can't find palm sugar or jaggery (a crystalized sugar made from a palm molasses), use brown sugar.

In Nok's very warm kitchen, her palm sugar was a thick liquid. It gave a caramel-like sweetness to the dish. Some cookbook authors recommend honey as a substitute, but I think a light brown sugar is closer in taste.

Assemble your ingredients (see text above). Nok first grates ½ of a green papaya and ½ of a very large carrot. She then makes a paste of the garlic and chilies in her Thai mortar, using a big metal spoon to divert the fumes from her nose and eyes. The long beans are then added and pounded a little—just enough to bruise them, but not crush them. A tablespoon of palm sugar, 3 tablespoons of fish sauce, and the juice of ½ of a lime are added and mixed in well. The tomatoes and all the vegetables are added, tossing while running the pestle down the inside walls of the mortar, firmly but without crushing the vegetables.

In the meantime, put a tiny amount of water into a pan, bring it to a boil, and add the peeled prawns, cooking them for about 3 minutes, until just done.

A handful of roasted nuts and the prawns are added, and the salad is tossed one last time and served. We added our seaweed to it at home.

Pad Thai Nok Style

Nok's restaurant and her kitchen were both minuscule, but they were spotlessly clean and very well organized. Though southern Thailand is heavily Muslim, Nok is Buddhist; she had a spirit house behind the bar where they prepared delicious, fresh-squeezed fruit juices, smoothies, and shakes. Like most chefs, she had her *mise-en-place* indeed in place before she began.

Nok explained to me that she prepared two basic types of Pad Thai and that we would be making both—stuffed and stir-fried. The stuffed one is simply the stir-fried one served in a thin omelet. Full disclosure: I seem to have lost the second two pages of my notes from my Pad Thai lessons. Fortunately, I have the ingredient list and my photos (which are my major note-takings anyway). I do have a few things written down that Nok told me: "Don't cook any of the ingredients too long" and "You can use rice noodles or glass [cellophane or bean curd] noodles. And many vegetables." She became animated as she rattled off possible ingredients: "Almost every vegetable! Sprouts—but from green [mung] beans, not soybeans; cabbage, purple cabbage; carrots—for color. Color is very important on the plate. Scallions. And pickled turnip! Or is it radish? [It is.] Pressed tofu, not the silky one. And tamarind sauce. Can you get it in the States?" Fish sauce. Sugar. And, for garnish, fried onions, deep-fried Thai chilies, and ground nuts.

To make the omelet, Nok beat one very large egg very well and poured just enough oil into a nonstick skillet to coat the bottom of the pan placed over medium-low heat. She poured the egg into the skillet and swirled it around until it was a thin film coating the entire bottom of the pan. At one point, she drizzled the tiniest amount of extra oil around the edges of the omelet, then when it was completely set, she lifted it up and lined our to-go box with it. For the stuffing, she stir-fried the vegetables, then pushed them up onto the back side of her spatula and up the side of the wok and added the noodles and a bit of water to the bottom of the wok, where there was direct heat.

She then began stir-frying the tofu and pickled radish in a little oil, to which she added the shrimp, and then one more egg, which she broke into the pan but did not beat, explaining that there should be both cooked white and yolk for texture and flavor.

"Look," she said, "can you see? Everything is perfectly cooked. Taste it. All it needs is something spicy and something crunchy."

When the noodles were cooked, she added the vegetables and seasonings and tossed it all together, stir-frying for just a little to warm everything through.

She spooned it into the omelet and garnished it with fried onions (a friend's mother makes them. I told Nok that we can buy cans of them in the States, and she looked at me as though I were crazy), nuts, chilies, and lime wedges.

"Sweet. Sour. Spicy. Savory. Salty. But you must have textures, too," Nok said, as we gathered my goodies. I hopped on the back of her scooter, and she drove me back to the house. Like Charmaine Solomon forty years ago, "All in all, I have seldom spent so edifying an afternoon." Thanks a million, Nok!

Baking with Olive Oil

In the 1990s, I was one of several dozen food writers whom the International Olive Oil Council (IOOC), based in Madrid, treated once or twice a year to marvelous tours of the olive-producing regions of the Mediterranean—from North Africa up the Atlantic coast of Portugal and into Spain and Italy and France, Greece, and the Middle East. We visited groves and mills, stayed in some amazing *pousadas* in Portugal and *masserie* in Italy, and dined in a Greek convent, Michelin-starred temples of gastronomy, famous wineries, and barns and mills throughout the region. We attended conferences, some of them co-sponsored by Oldways, and tasted traditional regional fare wherever we were. The idea was that, as food writers, we would spread the word about olive oil. Prior to these elaborate press junkets, where we learned about every phase of olive oil production, from seed to table, olive oil was, to most of the world, just another necessary ingredient that added regional authenticity to Mediterranean recipes.

Italians, Spaniards, and people from North Africa, Greece, southern France, Portugal, and the Middle East, as well as their descendants, many of whom had opened restaurants throughout the world, well knew that necessity. I remember Greek friends in Charleston, South Carolina, who would go to visit family in the "Old Country" and return with cases of oil, primarily from family groves. But many of us outside the major metropolitan areas simply didn't have access to the fresh, minimally processed oils that now abound throughout the world. I'm pretty sure that these tours— as costly as they were to produce—paid off. Here in China, even the supermarkets that normally do not stock other imported foods are filled with shelf after shelf of extra virgin olive oils.

Cakes at my mother-in-law's house near Pamplico, South Carolina.

Last year I was visiting my in-laws, who live on a farm in the middle of nowhere in the Pee Dee region of South Carolina. In the nearest town (2012 population was 1,235), the local grocery store (I hesitate to call it a "supermarket") stocked some two dozen extra virgin oils! There were church women out front selling cakes. You can bet several of them were "chiffon cakes." It's a good thing I didn't buy one; when I got to my mother-in-law's, there were already three cakes being offered at lunch: a nine-layer caramel cake, a seven-layer lemon cake, and an orange chiffon cake.

If you Google "chiffon cakes," you'll find all sorts of information, including history, about them. Said to be the 1927 invention of a California insurance salesman named Henry Baker, the exceptionally light cakes were considered revolutionary because his formula called for beating the egg whites separately and using vegetable oil instead of butter. He even sold his recipe to General Mills, who aggressively promoted the light-textured cake. Magazines and newspapers wrote about it endlessly for twenty years until it became an American classic, particularly in the South, where lighter flour made the cakes even airier than the California original. Angel food cakes, using only the whites of eggs, are another American invention of the early twentieth century. (Take that, *pâtissiers!*) It seems that there may be some truth to the Baker story; the recipe is indeed a brilliant combination of angel food and sponge cake techniques, with oil replacing butter. What's particularly wonderful about chiffon cakes is that they can take just about any sort of flavoring, from liqueurs and chocolate to citrus, as in the one at my mother-in-law's house.

Of course, people in the Mediterranean had been using olive oil in their cakes for no telling how long. The internet is filled with the history of carrot cakes as well—another American favorite that uses oil in lieu of butter. But it, too, did not appear in its present form until fairly recently. I love the not-quite-as-sweet (and not-quite-as-light) orange- and lemon-flavored cakes of the Mediterranean. Many of them are made with olive oil. I have had them in Provence, throughout Italy, and in North Africa. A classic one is made with ground almonds; one of my favorites is made with cornmeal. (The recipe is basically the same as a typical southern skillet cornbread baked at a lower temperature, with sugar and citrus added.)

Desserts made with olive oil are all the rage now. Gelato is common, as are brownies and chocolate mousse. Numerous claims are made about the better health benefits of olive oil sweets, but honestly, I find most health claims sort of silly if refined flours and sugars are going into the cakes and cookies. I stick to my mantra: moderation in everything, and if you're really concerned about your heart, your cholesterol, and your insulin, perhaps you should choose your grandparents! However, it is true that the vitamin E in olive oil acts as an emulsifier, helping produce a finer, smoother, tenderer crumb. More stable than butter, olive oil cakes stay fresh longer and taste lighter. Though I love butter, I also find that I can taste the other flavors more in sweets made with oil.

Always buy olive oils labelled as Extra Virgin. Further, you should try to buy single-source oils (estate bottled, like wine), which should indicate that the olives were crushed shortly after picking. Foremost, however, is the date the oil was processed and how it has been stored since the oil was pressed. I buy only oils that have harvest dates on them and are sold in dark containers. If you see an oil sitting in the sun in the window of a "gourmet" shop, avoid both the oil and the shop. If you live in a large western city, you should be able to find a reliable seller of fine foods who is knowledgeable about oil. The better shops will let you taste their oils.

There are more varieties of olives than there are of wine grapes, but, unlike many wines, no olive oil improves with time. Heat and light are also its enemies. Though few oils are varietals (that is, made from a single variety of olive), as many wines are, there are many regional styles of oils. For baking, you may want to look for some of the sweeter oils that include some of the more delicately flavored varieties, such as Cellina de Nardò from Puglia, Taggiasca from Liguria, or Casaliva from Lake Garda. Fruitier varieties include the Sicilian Biancolilla, the Spanish Arbequina, and the Tunisian Chetoui. Everyone's taste is different; I urge you to cultivate your own olive oil palate. As with wine, the only way to do so is by tasting, and by remembering the ones you like.

I developed a recipe for the IOOC when they were assembling a cookbook of traditional American recipes that either already used olive oil as an ingredient or were adapted to include it; used with sweet potatoes, it makes a variation on carrot cake that is a real crowd-pleaser. I also make some cookies with olive oil that I adapted from *Popular Greek Recipes*, published by the Greek Ladies Philoptochos Society in Charleston in 1957. They are orange-flavored, have a delicate crumb, and are not too sweet.

· ·

Sweet Potato Cake

This chiffon cake is light and moist and keeps well. Make sure all of your ingredients are at room temperature before you begin. If your mixer has only one bowl, beat the egg whites first, then turn them out into another bowl—preferably copper—while you continue with the dish. Use a 10-inch tube pan for this cake, but don't grease it: you want the batter to cling to the sides and rise high. Non-stick pans with removable inserts work particularly well with this recipe.

I have found that sweet potatoes, because they keep so well, vary widely in how moist they are. If yours seem watery, you can dry the grated flesh in the oven for a while.

1 cup fruity extra virgin olive oil

2 cups sugar

4 eggs, separated

½ cup hot water

2¼ cups soft southern flour or cake flour

1 large or 2 to 3 medium sweet potatoes, peeled and grated to yield 2½ to 3 cups

(CONTINUED)

Preheat the oven to 350°F.

In the large bowl of an electric mixer, beat the oil with the sugar until it is well mixed. Use the paddle attachment if your mixer has one. Add the egg yolks one at a time, beating well after each. Slowly pour in the hot water and continue to beat until the mixture is light.

Sift ¼ cup of the flour over the sweet potato in a large bowl and toss so that it is lightly

1 teaspoon baking
powder
1 teaspoon baking soda
½ teaspoon salt
1 teaspoon ground
ginger
1 teaspoon ground
freshly grated nutmeg
1 teaspoon vanilla
extract

coated. This will keep the potato from sinking to the bottom of the cake.

Sift the remaining flour with the baking powder, soda, salt, ginger, and nutmeg. Add the dry to the wet ingredients and mix well, then add the vanilla and the sweet potatoes.

Beat the egg whites until they hold medium-firm peaks, then fold them gently but thoroughly into the batter. Pour the batter into a 10-inch tube pan and bake for 1 hour, or until the cake is lightly browned and a long wooden skewer poked into the cake comes out clean. If the top of your cake is browning, and a wooden skewer poked deep into the cake does not come out clean, float a piece of aluminum foil on top of the cake and let it cook until it does.

Remove from the oven, invert the pan, and allow to cool completely.

Serves 12.

. . . .

Greek Cookies

Serve these irresistible cookies with a glass of port. The dough can be refrigerated for several weeks in an air-tight plastic bag and baked at a later date. You can mix this dough by hand, using a wooden spoon.

1 orange
1 cup fruity extra virgin
olive oil
2 cups sugar, plus 3
tablespoons
2 eggs
½ teaspoon baking soda
2 teaspoons baking
powder
3½ to 4 cups sifted
all-purpose flour
2 cups water
1 teaspoon ground
cinnamon

Preheat the oven to 350°F and grease 2 baking sheets.

Grate the zest of the orange and set aside in a small bowl or pitcher. Juice the orange, adding the juice to the zest.

Beat the oil and 1 cup of the sugar together well, then add the eggs, one at a time, beating constantly. Dissolve the baking soda in the orange juice and add to the creamed mixture. Add the baking powder, then enough of the flour to make a soft, manageable dough.

Take small pieces of dough, about the size of a walnut, and shape each into a ball. Place the balls on a cookie sheet, and flatten each one into a 2- to 3-inch cookie, ¼- to ⅜-inch thick. Bake for 20 to 25 minutes, or until they just begin to blush with color.

While the cookies are baking, combine 1 cup of sugar with the water in a small saucepan. Bring to a boil, then reduce the heat to low to keep the syrup warm. Mix the remaining 3 tablespoons of sugar with the cinnamon in a shallow bowl. Place in a sugar shaker if you have one.

When the cookies are done, remove them from the baking sheet to cool. Place wire racks over a baking sheet and, as the cookies cool, use tongs to dip each cookie quickly into the syrup. Place on the racks and sprinkle with cinnamon sugar.

Makes about 50 soft, delicate cookies.

Black Walnuts

I've always loved the gamey taste of black walnuts (*Juglans nigra*), but I can't say that I've always loved dealing with the nuts themselves. My maternal grandmother had a tree in her immense, magical yard, surrounded by a privet hedge, creating an outdoor room. I always thought the "room" itself was pretty cool, but years later when I became professionally interested in natural history (I was the staff artist at a wildlife preserve for a while), I found out lots more about this native American nut besides the fact that they are very hard to hull; picking the tasty kernels from the shell is almost as hard as getting into hickories (*Cayra alba*). All ten species of the *Juglans* genus are noble trees, producing both wood and nuts. I can think of no other tree genus that is as valuable to both man and fauna.

All walnuts—and hickories and pecans—are members of the *Juglandaceae* family of trees—large, aromatic, usually handsome trees that produce some of the prettiest wood and most delicious foodstuffs on the planet. *Juglans regia* L., the so-called "Persian walnut," is one of the most valuable nut crops in the world. They are wildly popular in Europe, where, in several languages, they share the word for "nut." Americans tend to call them "English walnuts," but in England they are simply called "common walnuts." Their native range has traditionally been said to have stretched from the Balkans eastward to the Himalayas, and they are consumed with abandon in Southwest China, where I lived and where they are considered to be a *bupin* (a restorative health food), often included in medicinal "teas." But the encyclopedic *Food Plants of China* notes that "there is no indigenous species of *Juglans regia* L. in Europe and Iran," citing recent floristic studies. "The common walnut is of hybrid origin. . . . Its first cultivation in Nanjing was between ad 222 and 277." In northern China, the walnut was traditionally fried then mixed with white chicken meat, but it has now been replaced by cashews.

Origins aside, walnuts have been cultivated in Europe for millennia: Romans made both hair dye and a wine (called *carynium*) from the nuts. They used unripe walnut shells to color cloth. Though they planted the trees throughout northern Europe prior to the rise of Christianity, walnuts were popularized by Middle Age monks who cultivated the trees for their nutritious nuts and medicinal leaves. In the Balkans, where I have also lived, walnuts fill not only pastries, but also sauces, dumplings, and folk customs. In America, walnuts are mostly used in cakes and breads, but in southern and eastern Europe, north Africa, Turkey, and the Middle East, they appear in sauces to accompany pasta, meats, and vegetables. Tarator is a Bulgarian soup that I often enjoyed in Sofia. The word is from the Ottomans, who ruled in Bulgaria for five hundred years, but the soup, with yogurt, is decidedly Bulgarian. Just north of the border, in Transylvania, a favored dish in Jewish homes is pike stuffed with a filling of walnuts, bread, eggs, and marjoram.

Walnuts are used as a meat substitute in some cuisines. In an Indian restaurant in Washington, DC, I had *Akhrot Kofta*—walnut "meatballs" that were a sort of dumpling of goat cheese and walnuts swimming in a creamy sauce. They weren't that good.

Black walnuts are about as American as you can get. They were once the majestic kings of the eastern forests, but they were cut down indiscriminately for their superior wood, which made not only durable fence posts and rails, but also the finest gun stocks. Even old and worn furniture made of black walnut is "bought and sawed thin for the same purpose," Julia Rogers lamented in her famous 1912 *Tree Book*. "Do we realize yet the usefulness and the beauty of black walnut wood? The silvery grain, the rich, violet-purple tones in the brown heart wood, the exquisite shading of its curly veinings, and the lasting qualities of the wood? If we did, we would plant groves of it." While she admitted the limitations of the nuts, because the oil in the kernel goes quickly rancid, thereby limiting the range of its market (in 1912), she failed to point out the single most peculiar trait of *Juglans*: like all walnuts, the roots, husks, and leaves secrete *juglone* into the soil. Though used as a dye in clothing, cosmetics, inks, and foods, juglone is a growth inhibitor to some plants and is toxic to others. Rarely will you see weeds growing under a black walnut tree, even in the wild. Hence, my grandmother's outdoor "room" around her black walnut tree, separating it from her gardens. Juglone is a common ingredient in natural herbicides. It kills apple and birch trees, and tomato plants. The use of black walnut wood in horse bedding can cripple the animals. Strong stuff.

Culinarily, however, the nuts are divine, and taste unlike any other food I can think of. I call them "gamey" for lack of a better word to describe their unique flavor. The flavor is deep, of the woods, with a lingering, slightly metallic aftertaste. They taste more like some smells that come to mind rather than flavors—my grandmother's house, sorghum syrup being boiled down, or autumn leaves. But perhaps that's just nostalgia on my part, as they evoke childhood memories. Composed of sixty percent fat, which carries flavor better than any other food element, it's no wonder they are so powerfully flavored. That fat is why they are favored in baked goods. They are so famously paired with chocolate that Euell Gibbons, the grandfather of the foraging movement (he died in the 1970s) stated, simply, "this is the nut to use in fudge." My favorite brownie recipe is a dense one made with black walnuts.

Nearly all black walnuts are hand-gathered from the wild; most of the commercial harvest is done in Missouri, where Hammons has a virtual monopoly on the business. Forty percent of the nuts harvested go into commercially produced Black Walnut Ice Cream, the third best-selling flavor! I order one-pound tins of the nuts, and they last me through two or three recipes. But I tend to entertain, and the following tart that I recently made (I didn't have a recipe, but I wrote down what I did) served 8. It is delicious and not too sweet, like pecan pie. I don't use corn syrup but rather light brown sugar thinned with a little sorghum and bourbon (for flavor).

....

Black Walnut Tart

For the dough:
1½ cups all-purpose flour,
  plus more for dusting
  (I use soft southern
  flour such as
  White Lily)
1 teaspoon sugar
A good pinch of salt
4 ounces (1 stick) cold
  unsalted butter, diced,

(CONTINUED)

For the dough: Grease a 10-inch tart pan and set aside. Put the flour, sugar, salt, and butter in a food processor and pulse until the mixture is fairly uniform. Add the egg, turn on the processor, and begin dribbling in the water a little at a time until the dough forms a ball. You may only need a couple of tablespoons of water. Turn the dough out onto a floured counter and form it into a flattened disk. Without overhandling the dough, try to make the disk as perfectly round as you can.

plus a little room-temperature butter for greasing the tart pan
1 large egg, beaten
¼ cup, more or less, ice water

For the filling:
5 large eggs
1¼ cup light brown sugar
¼ cup liquid such as sorghum syrup, honey, and/or bourbon
2 ounces (½ stick) unsalted butter, melted
2 cups chopped black walnuts

Wrap the dough in parchment or wax paper or, if you must, plastic, and put it in the refrigerator for 30 minutes or in the freezer for 10 minutes.

Preheat the oven to 375°F.

Roll the dough on the floured surface out into a round that is an inch or so wider than the tart pan. Roll it up onto the rolling pin and lay it down in the pan, pressing it lightly into place. Run the rolling pin over the edge to cut off any extra dough, then gently squeeze all along the inside of the rim of the pan, pushing the dough up slightly over the top of the tart pan. If there are any places in the dough that look thin or uneven, you can use the trimmed dough to make repairs.

Line the tart shell with parchment paper and enough pie weights (or beans or rice) to cover the bottom of the dough so that it does not rise up while baking. Bake for 15 minutes, remove the parchment and weights, and poke holes in several places in the dough with the tines of a fork. Return the pan to the oven and bake for another 10 to 15 minutes or until it is lightly brown. Transfer to a rack and allow to cool completely.

For the filling: Separate 1 of the eggs and put the white aside. Mix the yolk with the other 4 eggs, the sugar, the liquids (I used 2 tablespoons of sorghum syrup and 2 tablespoons of bourbon), and the butter until the mixture is smooth. Add the black walnuts and mix well.

Place the tart shell in its pan on a baking sheet. Beat the reserved egg white until slightly foamy, then paint the inside of the tart shell with it. Pour the filling into the shell and bake until the center is set, 30 to 40 minutes. If the edges are browning too rapidly, you can cover them with aluminum foil or with a pie crust edge cover made for the purpose. Allow the tart to cool completely on a rack before serving.

I like to serve this tart with a dollop of crème fraîche, but whipped cream or vanilla ice cream would do as well.

On Pepper

In 2007, I had the great fortune to spend a couple of weeks in Sri Lanka as a guest of USAID (United States Agency for International Development), which had brought a handful of spice importers, food writers, and chefs to the Isle of Smiles, as it's called, to discover the remarkable culinary heritage there. We visited cinnamon and nutmeg plantations, pepper farms, and rice fields. I tasted twelve of the fifteen major varieties of rice grown there. We tasted sambols, mallums, and curries enlivened with local cardamom, ginger, mace, and cloves. Perhaps most enlightening to me was the taste of pepper. *Piper nigrum*, that is.

The word "pepper" in English covers a lot of territory, including the Capsicums—both the fiery hot chilies, such as the local bird's-eye pepper here in Cambodia, and the mild bells and bananas. There is also Melegueta pepper, from an entirely different plant family; Sichuan pepper, from the prickly ash tree; Guinea pepper, also known as Grains of Selim (also not related); and *Piper longum*, which is related to black pepper and similarly spicy.

But it's Piper nigrum that Ferdinand and Isabella sent Columbus to find. You could say that it was taste that inspired the great discoverer's voyages.

For years, like most recipe writers even today, I recommended seasoning nearly every savory dish with salt and pepper. It was almost by rote. But after tasting fresh black pepper in Sri Lanka and realizing that the volatile oils dissipate as soon as the peppercorns are ground, I stopped nearly all use of black pepper in cooking until just before serving. A few whole peppercorns can go in stocks, but grinding pepper onto a piece of fish or chicken before frying is a waste of good peppercorns.

You've probably heard of the famous Tellicherry and Kerala peppers. They are justly renowned. But the bright, intense flavors of the fresh Ceylon pepper blew me away. I stopped grinding pepper on anything until it was ready to be eaten. My cooking changed.

Some twelve years later, I have come to understand pepper even more, for here in Cambodia, Kampot pepper is coming into its own. During the French occupation of Indochina, it was known as *poivre indochine*, but now Kampot's two varieties of *Piper nigrum* are protected with an appellation of origin. Grown in the foothills of the quartz-rich Elephant Mountains, the pepper smells and tastes of its distinctive terroir.

Kampot pepper is organically produced, and the same plant gives us green, white, red, and black peppercorns. The vines are grown on poles perpendicular to the ground. Harvested green, the tendrils are clustered with berries, which are used fresh in many Khmer dishes, especially stir-fries. I like to muddle them in gin cocktails. They are also "pickled" in salt and are then used in salads or sautés like capers or simply as a snack (see instructions, below). The stems of the pepper plant are also stir-fried, most famously with Kep crab (from a neighboring village).

Most of the green berries are placed on mats in the sun until they become dried and wrinkled: black pepper.

The berries are red when fully ripe. The red ones are picked just before they rot. They, too, are dried on mats in the sun. More intensely flavored than the black, they are also more expensive.

For white pepper, the mildest of all, orange and red berries are soaked in water, which loosens the outer husk, so it can be removed before drying. Much milder, white pepper should also be ground at the last moment.

Piper longum is also grown in Kampot. It is hotter than black pepper, but similar in taste. It grows on conical spikes which also must be ground before using to appreciate their full potential.

Look at the harvest dates on any spice you buy. It should be as fresh as possible.

. . . .

Pickled Green Peppercorns

If you are lucky enough to find clusters of fresh green peppercorns, you will need to use them immediately or preserve them. The process is the same as for Moroccan preserved lemons.

Clean the peppercorn clusters by soaking them in water. Place them on a towel and pat them completely dry. You will need ¼ cup of fine sea salt and 6 to 12 limes for every pound of peppercorns. You can remove the berries from the stems or leave them on. Pack the dried peppercorns into sterilized jars. Add salt and fill the jar with freshly squeezed lime juice. Cap the jar and shake well. Continue to shake the jar once a day for a week, at which point you can begin using the pickled peppercorns. I can't resist munching on a few as a snack as I cook, but I always use a clean spoon to remove them from the jar to prevent spoilage. Like preserved lemons, they keep well—locals tell me up to two years. I use them the way I would capers—in salads and sauces.

Chef Sopheavy Cheaneng owns two of Phnom Penh's most popular restaurants. She taught me another method that produces a crunchy version: Soak the peppercorns in freshly squeezed lime juice for a week or more, until they taste very citrusy. Pour off the lime juice and place the peppercorns on a bed of rock salt in the sun to dry. When they are completely dry, mix the peppercorns and the salt together and spread onto a baking sheet and roast in a low oven until they are crisp. Use in soups, salads, or stir-fries, or put them out with drinks as snacks. They're addictive.

Time for a Drink!

··

Though I'm fond of saying that I lived on beer and eggs in college (and it's not far from the truth—the whole truth), as soon as I was able to afford decent wine, I never looked back. I don't think I've had even five beers in the last twenty-five years. And I never much cared for most cocktails because so many of them are just too sweet for me. Yes, I've had my share of celebratory drinks—punches and eggnog during the holidays, Cosmopolitans at Gilson's, Negronis with Richard, Martinis with Tom, Mojitos with Betsey, and the required Sazerac or Ramos Gin Fizz when in New Orleans. But they are the exception, not the rule: I'd much rather celebrate with Champagne, and when it comes to dessert, just pour me another glass of red wine, please. I like to cook with bourbon, but brown liquors just aren't my cup of tea. I was always told no brown liquor until after Labor Day. In Cambodia, it's just too hot.

Somewhere along the line, however, I started drinking margaritas. I think Fran McCullough, the editor of my first two books, started me on them. In Charleston, Mikel and I used to go boating on Sunday afternoons with our friends Dana and Ella Grace and Ted and Clay, and we invariably had margaritas when we got back on shore. I'm not offering any history here about the drink, except to say that it seems to have been concocted in the 1930s or 1940s. The ingredients were traditionally fresh-squeezed lime juice, tequila, triple sec, and salt. Today there are dozens of variations, some folks calling for the finest top-shelf tequila (and even condescendingly suggesting that nothing less will do, when, in fact, there were no top-shelf tequilas then). Diana Kennedy, the ninety-seven-year-old "Empress of Mexican Cuisine," who has been awarded Mexico's highest honors, calls simply for "white tequila" in her ground-breaking and seminal *The Cuisines of Mexico*, first published in 1972 and edited by Fran. "The ordinary whites [are] best for mixed drinks," she writes. (It was Diana who pointed out to me the lack of top-shelf tequila when the drink was invented.) Her recipe for "New York's lustiest margarita" came from Carlos Jacott and calls for 1 part triple sec, 2 parts lime juice, and 3 parts tequila. There are dozens of other ratios, and folks not only freeze them, but also use Cointreau and all sorts of additions.

I make my margaritas a little differently from Diana. First of all, I buy the plumpest, thinnest-skinned limes I can find. Look for limes that are very smooth-skinned and fat, with almost none of the hard pebbly skin you often see on the limes in supermarkets. It's a good idea, in fact, to seek out limes in Latin American or Southeast Asian markets, where they know from limes, as they say. I wash citrus with soap and water before I put it in the vegetable drawer of my refrigerator. If there's room, I put them in a bowl so that they are not touching anything else. Since they are already cleaned, I can pull them out for zesting or for slicing to put in drinks or as garnish/condiment on plates. I try to buy citrus on the day that I am going to use it, so that it doesn't have to go in the fridge anyway. You get more juice from a warm lemon or lime. Before you juice them, roll them around on the counter, pushing down with your palm. When you slice them for juicing, poke the flesh in numerous places with a sharp knife to help release even more juice. (I have even been known to microwave limes to coax more juice from them!)

....

My Margaritas

Squeeze the juice from a bunch of limes. I used to use an electric juicer, and it used to be my favored hostess gift when I would visit friends: I liked to walk in with a juicer, a bottle of tequila, a bottle of triple sec, and a bag of limes. But for years now I have relied on the simple hand squeezers. I don't strain out the pulp, but not much goes through the squeezer anyway, and seldom do these modern Persian limes have seeds. Measure the lime juice and pour it into a pitcher. Add an equal portion of white tequila. Add half a portion of triple sec. Add lots of ice and stir very hard until the mixture is well-blended and beginning to foam.

Now, about those salted rims: Encourage folks to let you salt the rims of their glasses. They don't have to lick it all off, the way I do, but it is an important element of a perfect margarita. With the saltiness of the glass rim, the sweetness of the triple sec, the sour bang of the healthy dose of lime juice, and the bitterness of the lime peel, you will get all of the basic flavors as well as an incredible mouthfeel that is all and none of the above at once.

To salt the rims, cut a lime lengthwise into 4 to 8 slices (depending on the size of the lime), and then cut each slice in half crosswise down through the flesh to the rind. Slip the lime slit down onto the rim of a glass and run it around the edge of the glass, using a new slice for each glass and saving each slice for garnish. If your limes aren't pretty, simply use one of already-squeezed lime halves to rim the glass before salting. Dip the glass rims in pure salt that you've poured onto a plate. Kosher salt is too coarse. Most sea salts are either too coarse or too fine. Diana recommends table salt or finely ground rock salt, but I actually buy margarita salt: the best brands are pure salt, with no additional ingredients such as the stuff they put in table salt. It comes in its own tub with a cover and even the widest margarita glass will fit down in it. Stored with the rest of the barware, it is there when you need it. Repeat the process for each glass. I do not use a margarita glass, but I do like to use stemmed water glasses so that hands don't freeze; otherwise, provide cocktail napkins. Now, add a few ice cubes to each glass and pour in the margarita, and slip the reserved lime slice over the edge of the glass as garnish, or simply go ahead and squeeze it and dump it into the glass.

The first thing your folks will say is, "Wow! That's tart!" But watch what happens. They will drink it up. They will ask for another. And another. Two of my nieces once came to visit us in Washington (yes, they were of age!) and we had five pitchers one night, but not one of us had a hangover the next day. I say it's the lime juice. And none of us has scurvy, either! Margaritas have become such a tradition associated with Mikel and me that when we visit with his family, I know to take a case of limes. Here in Phnom Penh with no family around, isolated from our stateside friends, but with an abundance of limes, we drink them far more often than I ever would have imagined.

Pasta alla Checca

Working on a self-portrait; Monterosso al Mare, Italy, 1983. Photo by Gianni Martini.

This is a simple dish that I learned to make when I lived in Genoa in the early eighties, where we called it simply *"pasta dell'estate"* (summer pasta) or *"pasta alla salsa cruda"* (pasta with raw sauce). It's a dish that both of my friends, Gianni (who had grown up in a peasant family up in the Apennines) and Alberto (who was a "city boy" from Santa Margherita), knew from childhood, so I was surprised to see that a famous Roman restaurant critic and historian credits the dish to a chef in Rome in 1972! In David

Downie's excellent *Cooking the Roman Way* (HarperCollins, 2002), he says that the dish disappeared along with the chef in the mid-1980s. I had lunch with the eminent art historian John Pope-Hennessy in Rome in 1983 and was shocked to see the dish offered on a menu as "*pasta alla checca*." Downie explains that "Romans love making off-color remarks." They even name some of their favorite dishes after body parts and functions. Actually, this is true throughout southern Europe: There are French cheese *crottins*, or turds; *merda de can* (dog shit gnocchi) in Nice, and all sorts of puffy foods called nun's farts throughout the region. But the Genoese are very proper folks, and I never heard any foods called by such vulgar names there.

So I was surprised to see the dish called *pasta all checca*—faggot's pasta. Downie quotes the historian Livio Jannattoni, who says that the name of the dish comes from the inclusion of fennel seeds—*semi di finocchio* in Italian—in the recipe, explaining that "finocchio is also an old-fashioned and inoffensive way to say homosexual, and so is the term checca." I think that Jannattoni, now deceased (his work on the culinary history of Rome and Lazio was published posthumously), is wrong on several points. Surely the dish evolved in kitchens throughout Italy on hot days long before 1972. Further, if you call a man—certainly a Genoese—a checca or a finocchio, he will definitely be offended, even if he is gay. And while other writers have translated checca as the perhaps less insulting "fairy" or "pansy," I think that "faggot" is a more appropriate translation, particularly if you are to believe that fennel seeds are a necessary ingredient. According to the OED, a faggot in English originally referred to a stick, or bundle of sticks, specifically as for fuel—more like "kindling." By the fifteenth century, it had come to refer to the practice of burning heretics alive: "to fry a fagot" meant to burn someone alive. It then came to be used as a general term for the heretic. Later, it was applied as a term of abuse or contempt to a woman. But today it means but one thing: a perjorative term for homosexuals, who were once burned at the stake, fired by burning twigs of fennel.

. . . .

Summer Pasta

Downie's version may be the original pasta alla checca, with its fennel seeds, olives, parsley, basil, capers, and an insistence on plum or cherry tomatoes, but my version, with tomatoes, oil, garlic, and basil, we'll just call "summer pasta" and leave it at that.

Raw tomatoes and basil are chopped and added to cooked pasta; hot, garlic-flavored olive oil is poured over the dish to warm it all through. It is essential that you use firm, ripe tomatoes for this dish. The recipe feeds two, but you can multiply it without fear.

½ pound dried pasta of your choice
¼ cup extra virgin olive oil
4 or 5 garlic cloves, peeled, the tough bottom and any green shoots removed
1 firm, ripe tomato
fresh lemon juice (optional)
½ cup firmly packed basil leaves
salt and freshly ground black pepper
parmesan (optional)

While you cook the pasta, put the olive oil in a small saucepan over medium-high heat, and add the garlic cloves. They will begin to sizzle in the oil after a moment or two. Continue to fry them in the oil while you prepare the tomatoes and basil. You want the oil to stay very hot, but you do not want to burn the garlic, or it will impart a bitter flavor. Turn down the heat when they turn golden or move the pot off—or partially off—the heat.

Core the tomato and cut it up into large dice. You should have about a cup of chopped tomato. Taste it for acidity, and if it's not the perfect summer tomato, squeeze a little lemon juice over the pieces. Sprinkle the basil with a small pinch of salt, and coarsely chop it. You should have 3 to 4 tablespoons.

Just before the pasta finishes cooking, put the oil back over high heat to get it very hot again. When the pasta is cooked, quickly drain, then transfer it either into a large bowl or back into the empty pot in which it was cooked. Distribute the tomato and basil over the pasta, then pour the sizzling oil over the pasta through a sieve so as to catch the garlic, which you then discard.

Toss quickly together and divide among two pasta bowls. Let each diner season to taste with salt, pepper, and, if desired, freshly grated parmesan.

Serves 2.

Anchovies
and Pasta

One of my favorite ingredients is salted anchovies. If you have lived or travelled in Italy, you have probably often wondered what some of the "secret ingredients" were that imbued the traditional dishes with an indescribable depth of character. Many Italian cooks, particularly in the South, rely on *acciughe salate*, salted anchovies. In Italy, they are sold in 1-kilo tins. Agostino Recca, from the Sicilian port of Sciacca, is a reliable producer whose product is now widely available in the States.

The headless, gutted anchovies are packed in salt and brine. After opening the tin, I remove them to a jar, cover them with more sea salt (I use salt from the Sicilian flats near Mózia), and store them in the refrigerator. Italian grocers carry them; you can also find them online. I used to buy mine at Vace, a venerable Italian deli in Cleveland Park, in Washington, where they told me that if stored properly, "they'll last forever." You don't have to refrigerate them, but I do.

Those little tins of anchovies in oil can be substituted, but they are my fourth choice after the salted ones, the ones in jars, and the tubes of anchovy paste. I rarely use an entire tin since I am mostly cooking for one or two people at a time, so what's left over in the jars and squeeze tubes simply goes into the refrigerator.

A typical quick stove-top meal for me often begins with some rinsed and boned salted anchovy filets warmed in olive oil. A pasta sauce that might include garlic, sage leaves, hot pepper flakes, and perhaps some capers evolves as the pasta cooks. I sometimes blanch broccoli in the pasta water, cook the pasta al dente, then toss the broccoli and pasta together in the hot, seasoned oil. I sometimes add raisins, and sometimes I add pine nuts. I have been known to add breadcrumbs (which is a great trick to extend a meal when you are low on ingredients, and someone decides to stay for dinner); nearly always I freshly grate some parmesan over the dish. I serve the meal with crusty bread and follow the pasta with a salad.

Slowly cooked ragus begin with the anchovies as well. Like the garum of ancient Rome, the fish sauces of Asia, the dried shrimp of Africa, and the prahok of Cambodia, a little dab of anchovies adds an amazing amount of umami and depth of flavor. They literally melt in the oil and disappear into sauces, drawing no attention to themselves. I've never had anyone say that they taste the fish, even sworn anchovy-haters.

Salted anchovies are neither oily nor fishy. They must be soaked for a brief while in water or held under running water to desalinate them and to remove the backbone, but after the salt is removed, they are used in dishes with lamb, rabbit, broccoli, beef, eggplant, tomatoes, and cheese. They provide salt while accenting other flavors, the way a wine can point to certain elements in a complementary meal. They are puréed into salad dressings and tossed with butter for a perfect topping for steak or egg noodles. Needless to say, they dress a pizza with pizazz as well, and I have been known to put them in cracker doughs, such as for cheese straws.

You will note that I am just giving guidelines here. Some folks don't like a full ¼ pound of pasta. The amount of garlic and the amount of oil is personal as well. Several of the ingredients are optional. This makes a delightful lunch. Have it with a glass of Roussane from the Pays d'Oc.

. . . .

Pasta with Broccoli

The flowerets from two medium heads of broccoli

Salt

12 ounces to 1 pound of the pasta of your choice

⅓ cup extra virgin olive oil, more or less

3 anchovy filets, more or less, rinsed and boned if salted

(CONTINUED)

Add the broccoli to a large pot of heavily salted boiling water and cook it for a few minutes. You want it to be still bright green, but not quite done. If you are afraid you have overcooked it, put it in ice water to stop the cooking. Remove it from the water and set aside, return the water to a boil, and add the pasta.

You can make the sauce in a large pan big enough to hold the finished dish, or you can use a smaller pan, then use the pot in which the pasta is cooked for the final assembly.

2 ounces or ¼ cup of
    raisins, optional
1 ounce of pine nuts,
    optional
1 or 2 cloves of garlic,
    more or less, peeled,
    any green shoots
    removed, sliced
Hot pepper flakes to
    taste, optional
Butter, optional
Grating cheese of your
    choice, optional

Heat the oil and the anchovies over medium heat, stirring the anchovies until they melt into the oil. Add the raisins and pine nuts, if desired, and the garlic. Don't let the garlic brown. Add hot pepper flakes, if desired. When the pasta is al dente, drain it, and add it and the broccoli to the oil and toss all together so that everything is evenly coated with the oil. You can swirl in a knob of butter if you like. Depending on how much broccoli and pasta you have, you may want to add a little more oil, but ⅓ cup should be plenty for four people. Divide among pasta bowls and let everyone grate their own cheese, if desired, to taste.

Serves 4.

Mostarda

▶ PHNOM PENH, 2020 ••

Mostarda is an odd Italian word for a condiment that can be jam-like, chutney-like, or relish-like. It can mean "mustard," but only in the sense of a prepared condiment. *Senape* is the Italian word for the mustard plant and/or seed, though it can refer to several different members of the *Brassica* (mustard) plant family. "Mostarda" is based on the Latin *musto*, or must. Many *mostarde* do contain the fiery oil from mustard seeds. They are rarely made by home cooks in Italy today, no more so than chutneys are made at home in America. In the best-known version, from Cremona, tiny whole fruits or fruit pieces are candied in a sugar syrup until they are clear. They are traditionally served with bollito, a classic meal of boiled meats. Of the traditional southern condiments that I make, the one that most closely physically resembles mostarda di Cremona is watermelon rind preserves; taste-wise, it resembles my chutneys. Like my chutneys, mostarda recipes might contain any of a number of peeled and pitted fruits such as apricots, figs, cherries, melons, peaches, apples, plums, and quince. Old recipes call for making a must of unripe grapes (hence the word), which few people make today.

Some of the popular versions of mostarda are simply jams or marmalades made from figs, tangerines, pears, or plums, though they, too, may be seasoned with mustard or other spices, vinegars, or herbs. Mostarda di fichi, for example, is made with ripe green figs and balsamic vinegar from Modena, though I frankly prefer my mother's fig conserve made with pineapple, black peppercorns, and walnuts. Both are excellent with cheese and cured meats.

Some mostarde are made with vegetables instead of fruits, like our sweet relishes and bread and butter pickles. As in America, in Italy they seem to be most prevalent in the South. In 2007, I visited my friend Anna Tasca Lanza at her cooking school and family winery in Sicily. She made a very sweet one with zucchini. I've seen green tomato mostarda, horseradish mostarda, and this surprisingly delicious celery mostarda. Not surprising, I guess, to folks who grew up drinking Dr. Brown's Cel-Ray soda, but I think I can say that sweet celery concoctions are rare. Serve it with fresh, soft cheeses before or after dinner, or even on ice cream!

Mostarda di Sedano (Celery Relish)

If you would like this relish to be spicy, add ½ teaspoon of mustard seeds.

2 hearts of celery, 1½ to 2 pounds total
¾ cup sugar
Pinch of salt
3 ounces freshly squeezed lemon juice, from 2 to 3 lemons

Wash the celery and separate the stalks. Using a sharp knife at an oblique angle, cut down through the base of each stalk from the inside just to the outer edge. Carefully break the base away, pulling any tough strings on the outer peel down and away from the stalk. Turn the stalk around and cut off the tip in a similar manner, pulling any stringy outer peel away. (If you prefer, you can peel off tough strings with a vegetable peeler, but I prefer my method.) Repeat with the remaining stalks, then cut the stalks into several strips lengthwise, and then cut the slivers into tiny dice of uniform size.

Put the minced celery and the remaining ingredients in a heavy stockpot, stir well, and simmer, covered, for about 15 minutes. Uncover the pot and continue to simmer until nearly all of the liquid has evaporated and the mostarda has become very thick.

Pour into a sterilized pint jar with lid, and process in a boiling water bath if you want to keep the preserves for any length of time, or simply store in the refrigerator indefinitely.

I like to serve this atop a mound of a creamy blue cheese. If you add the mustard seeds, combine it with an unripened soft chèvre. I've never been an admirer of factory-produced cream cheese, but I see it all the time at parties, topped with chutney or pepper jelly. This really isn't that much different from that, is it?

Rockfish and Callaloo

▶ PHNOM PENH, 2020 ··

There are at least a dozen different "rockfish," a common name often given to any fish that lurks among rocks. The striped bass (*Morone saxatilis*), called rockfish on the Chesapeake, is also called Atlantic striped bass, line-sider, striper, or just "rock." It's an anadromous fish, like salmon and shad, that lives in the open ocean but swims up into rivers to spawn. It is native to the eastern coast of North America but has been introduced into inland bodies of water throughout the US. There is another strain in the Gulf of Mexico. The rockfish is the state fish of Maryland, as well as South Carolina, where it's called striped bass. It is the saltwater state fish of several other states of the eastern seaboard.

When I lived in Washington, DC, I often went to the Wharf down near the Jefferson Memorial and bought beautiful four-pounders. The most popular gamefish of the Chesapeake, they were fished to near extinction until rigorous stocking programs, pollution controls, and, most importantly, fishing limits were put in place to help restore their populations. The fish rebounded, but in 2004 their numbers declined again, and in 2006 they succumbed to a devastating disease that affected half of the Chesapeake stripers. Though they are anadromous, they have thrived in inland water bodies, such as the huge manmade Lake Murray in South Carolina, near where I grew up.

Traditional mid-Atlantic recipes for rockfish always surprise me, because they rarely differ. I do believe that the best cooking of fish is always the simplest, and that the rules are the same no matter what species or cooking method you're using. Most important is not to overcook the fish. That said, with the current interest in culinary history and "fresh and local," I'm surprised that I am not seeing more recipes for rockfish soups and stews. Perhaps chefs are frightened off by some of the nineteenth-century writers who instructed their readers to "boil steadily for three quarters of an hour" (a recipe attributed to Miss Fannie Nelson of Yorktown, Virginia, in *Housekeeping in Old Virginia*, written in Lynchburg in 1877). Worse, another contributor advises, "It takes two hours to boil." At the time, "boiling" was not the precise term we know it to be today. Many recipes instructed the cook to "boil" when simmering was clearly meant. Mary Randolph's excellent *The Virginia House-Wife* (1824), for example, declared rockfish "almost equal to stewed crab." Her recipe "To Boil Rock Fish" instructs to "put it into the fish kettle with cold water and salt, boil it gently and skim it well." But neither *Maryland's Way*, published by the Hammon-Harwood House Association in Annapolis in 1963, nor John Shields's *Chesapeake Bay Cooking*, published in 1998 as the companion to his television series, offer any fish soups or stews!

The fishing season for rocks varies widely and frequently. In Maryland this year, the season is open May 16 through August 15, and September 1 through December 10. Anglers will be able to keep one striped bass per person, per day, with a minimum size of nineteen inches. 2018 populations declined again, so the Atlantic States Fisheries Commission determined that conservation measures were needed for the 2020 fishing season to reduce the amount of striped bass being removed. This included dead discards, which are fish that die after being caught and returned to the water. Trophy rockfishing (that is, capturing large specimens) has been eliminated on the Chesapeake.

The season in South Carolina is very different. Each inland lake and open body of water has a different season and size limit. In most of the Lowcountry rivers that flow into the ocean, the season is October to June 15. But in the Santee River System, for example, only three fish may be taken per day during that time. They must be between twenty-three and thirty-five inches, though only one fish may be greater than twenty-six inches. On Lake Murray, licensed fishermen can take five fish, but they must be at least twenty-one inches.

The rules for both recreational and commercial rockfishermen change frequently. What I usually saw at the Wharf in DC were three- to eight-pounders. They are always tagged if they are legal. In South Carolina, it is illegal to sell any freshwater fish from the wild. Fortunately, when I lived there, either I caught my own or my fishermen friends shared their catch. I've always liked to pair them with greens.

I have been around boats for much of my life and have travelled extensively, and I've lived in parts of the Caribbean where soups filled with greens reflect the African heritage of the islanders. Throughout the region, you find variations on an eponymous soup called callaloo (also spelled calaloo, callilu, calalou, and callau), after the principal ingredient, which are the leaves of two different plants that are used interchangeably. One is Chinese spinach (*Amaranthus gangeticus*), also known as yin-choi, hon toi choi or bhaji; the other is the leaves of elephant ear (*Colocasia esculenta*) or taro (also known in the Caribbean as dasheen or eddo). Taro leaves must be cooked to be edible, and they marry well with coconut milk; they are served throughout much of the tropical world. (I see taro root in every market here in Cambodia, but I have yet to see the leaves. The plants are hard to come by as well, even though it is a major food crop. The elephant ears I have in pots on our patio I have grown from bulbs purchased in food markets.)

The simplest forms of callaloo—the soup, that is—contain only some seasoned pork as flavoring. Martinique, Guadeloupe, St. Lucia, Haiti, and Jamaica all have similar recipes. Trinidad is often credited as its birthplace; that island's version often includes crab. In the Virgin Islands, where I lived in 1979, their Kallaloo contains fish as well as crab. A recipe from *Famous Native Recipes of the Virgin Islands* by Dea Murray, published when I lived there, says that you can substitute 1½ pounds of spinach plus ½ pound of turnip greens for the 3 pounds of kallaloo greens called for in the recipe. In my version, I've used all turnip greens, which are more in keeping with my own heritage, the West African countries whence came the enslaved in the Caribbean, and the soups of the Portuguese—who, as major traffickers in the Columbian Exchange, carried those verdant dishes with them back to the Iberian Peninsula, where they have thrived, and to Brazil, where they are mainstays.

In the Virgin Islands, the soup is served with "fungi" (pronounced "FOONghee," like the Italian "funghi") which has nothing to do with mushrooms! It is what Italians would call polenta and Americans would call cornmeal mush. Other islanders serve the dish with dumplings (which can be made from flour, cornmeal, or alternative flours made from root vegetables), or coo-coo, a side dish made variously from breadfruit, cassava meal, or plantain flour. I serve mine with cornbread.

I use two pots. This is not strictly the classic one-pot cookery of West Africa, Brazil, the Caribbean, or the Lowcountry, but the two pots are necessary to get the clean, bright flavors that I'm going for in this callaloo. I also have included carrots in my fish stockpot, along with unpeeled onions, celery, and a handful of herbs from the garden (parsley, thyme, oregano, and one leaf each of basil, sage, and bay). Carrots are generally considered too sweet to be included in *fumet* (classic French fish stock), but this Caribbean stew is usually served with a sweet hot sauce such as Jamaica's Pickapeppa. I prefer to have the slight sweetness of carrots in the background of the broth rather than the cloying sweetness of Pickapeppa right up front. I have also used turnip greens, which need to be cooked longer than spinach or taro leaves, and which welcome the "pinch of sugar" that carrots provide.

Salt pork is cubed and cooked in a large heavy pot until it turns clear and begins to give off its fat, at which point washed turnips and garlic are added to the pot.

My friend Al Schaaf is a chef who has cooked at fine restaurants and aboard the Windjammer schooner *Fantome* (which sank in Hurricane Mitch in 1998). He now owns a restaurant in Phnom Penh, and we have been exchanging ideas about Caribbean soups. A recent Pepper Pot he made with "the most unorthodox stock . . . started with chicken feet as opposed to the bull hoof we used when I worked in the Caribbean. After the chicken feet cooked for 3 hours, I just added prawn shells and chicken thighs and aromatics to gently simmer for 45 minutes . . . I'll remove the thighs and debone . . . strain, and chill. Then finish with rest of ingredients . . . okra, chili, onion, more fresh thyme . . . Instead of the spinner dumplings we made in the Caribbean, I'm going to make a choux dumpling (à la Thomas Keller but with chicken schmaltz instead of butter) . . . my plan is to blanch spinach in stock. Remove, shock it, then purée with a portion of chilled stock and keep separate . . . I'll add the purée with a touch of coconut milk and prawns to the soup per order . . . Hopefully it will retain a nice green color . . . trying to refine it to a real restaurant-style dish." I think he succeeded.

You may find my homier version not so daunting. I haven't found turnip greens here in Cambodia, but I have seen amaranth, which is often used in the Caribbean, and I have used spinach as well.

Callaloo (Fish Stew with Turnip Greens)

For the greens:
2 pounds turnip greens
¼ pound salt pork, diced
3 cloves garlic, peeled,
  green shoots removed,
  sliced

For the fish:
a 4-pound rockfish
  (striped bass) or
  similar white-fleshed
  fish, scaled, gutted,
  and gills removed
2 carrots, broken into
  pieces
2 stalks celery, cut up
1 large yellow onion,
  quartered
A handful of herbs,
  including a bay leaf
2½ quarts cold water
1 pint dry white wine

**For final assembly and
  serving:**
1 pound fresh or frozen
  okra, cut into ½-inch
  pieces
1 can coconut milk
Salt and freshly ground
  pepper to taste
Hot sauce, preferably not
  a sweet one

Rinse the greens, remove any tough stems (a few pieces can stay if they aren't too big; they'll cook down fine), cut them up, and put them in a sink full of cold water, shaking them around to loosen any recalcitrant bits of dirt or sand clinging to them.

In a large, heavy 4-quart pot, over medium-high heat, cook the salt pork until it turns clear and begins to give off its fat. Turn the heat to high and add handfuls of the greens with the water that clings to them, stirring to distribute them evenly in the pot. As the greens wilt, add another handful, stirring well. Repeat until all the greens are in the pot and wilted. Add the garlic, stir, turn the heat down to medium-low, and cover the pot. Continue cooking until they are done to your liking (about 15 minutes more), remembering that they will cook a little more in the soup.

In a separate pot, cover the fish and aromatic vegetables with cold water and wine. (Mary Randolph knew what she was talking about when she said cold water. Fish stock can become bitter if allowed to boil rapidly or for too long.) Bring slowly to a low boil and allow to simmer for 20 minutes, or until the fish barely flakes from the bone.

Remove the fish to a platter to cool and allow the stock to simmer for another 20 to 30 minutes, or until the vegetables are soft.

While the stock is cooking, and as soon as the fish is cool enough to handle, pull the skin from the flesh, and pick the meat from the bones. Be sure to get the tasty cheeks from the head. You should have 3 to 4 cups of fish. Discard the skin and bones. Set the fish aside on a plate while you finish assembling the soup.

Strain the stock and add it to the greens pot, along with the okra and coconut milk. Stir well and bring to a simmer, skimming the soup of anything unsightly on the surface. Cook for about 5 minutes, until the okra is soft, and add the fish. Correct the seasoning with salt and pepper, and serve the soup piping hot with cornbread and your favorite bottled hot sauce.

Makes 8 servings.

Galletto
alla Piastra

Vintage photo courtesy Ostaia do Richetto dal 1890.

The venerable old Ligurian restaurant Ostaia du Richettu is a magical place, more like an old-fashioned country tavern. You drive through a massive old archway to a parking area set in the verdant Peralto Park, due north of Genoa on the Righi hill. The setting is a vertiginous one on the eastern hillside of the Fosso del Lagaccio, where the manmade lake is ringed by ancient fortresses. You won't find tourists there, but there are hordes of Genoese escaping the heat of summer. The last time I went, it could not have been busier, but there was a magnificent breeze, a hint of autumn in the air. Families were celebrating one last night out as the two weeks that culminate in the Ferragosto holiday (August 15) came to a close. There was as much dialect being spoken as Italian.

The first time I went, in 1982, their chicken was a sort of epiphany for me. *Galletto alla piastra* (young rooster on a slab)—often called *pollo al mattone* (chicken under a brick) or *pollo alla pietra* (chicken under a stone)—is one of the signature dishes of du Richettu, and it was the best grilled chicken I'd ever had. In the States, I had for several years been disgusted with the flabby, yellow, cottony, big-breasted chickens available in supermarkets, and had simply stopped eating them. But in England I ate my weight in local Sussex chickens and found them to be remarkably tasty. The butcher told me he thought all the falderal surrounding "free-range" was silly, that if you feed chickens, they won't wander far, and that in order to call them "free-range," you simply had to give them a twelve-foot-long outdoor pen. Rules have tightened in both the EU and the States now, but I have learned that it's the breed and the feed of the chicken more than anything that determine taste and texture. I find most discussions of humane treatment of animals raised for food peculiar at best.

Nearly all chickens in America have been bred to have big breasts. They're big, all right, but they are nearly flavorless. In Genoa the merchants who sold me chickens had raised them themselves. The *pollivendola* in Genoa, from a village near Gavi, had been selling her galleti (and occasionally an old hen) in Via dei Macelli at the time for over thirty years. I asked her about the breed, and she told me that they simply called it *Cabannina*, after the rare local breed of dairy cattle whose milk they fed to the chickens.

At du Richettu, the chicken was marinated in oil and herbs and placed over a roaring wood fire. Several feet over the fire was positioned a heavy, flat grill—the "slab." The bird—always a plump young rooster, never a hen (in the States, you're looking for a real fryer, about ten weeks old and no more than four pounds. Better yet, no more than three. Good luck!)—is spatchcocked, or split and made to lie flat.

An aside, *con permesso*: There's no getting around the word "cock" when you're talking about roosters, unless you want to use the generic, though asexual, "chicken." The word for rooster and the word for penis have been the same in many cultures since time immemorial, and it wasn't until prudish nineteenth-century Americans dispatched "cock" for "rooster," a word previously unknown in English. As though hens don't roost! In Sanskrit the word is *kukkuṭa*; in Old Slavic, *kokotŭ*; in Old Teutonic, *kok*; and in African Senga, as in Kaffir, it's *kuku*; in Wisa, *koko*; and, most telling, perhaps, in Latin, it was *cucurio*, meaning, "I crow." I've not lost my love of linguistics, however seldom I get to do the research these days!

"Spatchcock" has a cloudy etymology, but it probably evolved from dispatch + cock. It's a fairly new term, but the technique is ancient. Many cookbook authors will tell you to remove the backbone, but that is butterflying, not spatchcocking. The bones are wonderful to crunch on. Simply cut straight through the backbone with heavy poultry shears, then flip the bird over, splay it, and press firmly down on the center of the breastbone with the heels of your hands (or with the help of a heavy pan, such as a cast-iron skillet) to get the bird to lie as flat as possible. Some chefs remove the ribs so that diners don't crunch down on the tiny bones, but the moist little morsels of flesh surrounding them are delicious, so I say give everyone bibs and hand towels and let them go at the bird in medieval fashion!

I like to brine the bird (using ½ pound salt—about ¾ cup—to every 3 quarts of water) for about 2 hours. I pat it dry then marinate the bird in olive oil seasoned with fresh herbs—your choice—and garlic as well, if you desire. Overnight in the refrigerator is good. The next day, remove the bird and bring to room temperature about an hour before grilling. While you're preparing your grill fire, you'll need to gather your weights. I have several common bricks that I wrap in heavy aluminum foil and oil well, but a cast-iron skillet with other weights in it will do. I've used rocks from a driveway at a friend's house. It needs to weigh a lot, about 10 pounds.

Your fire should be medium-low, so that you can hold your hand over it for 5 or 6 seconds. Remove the chicken from the marinade and let it drain for a moment, then place it skin side down onto the grill. Immediately place the bricks on top and allow it to cook undisturbed for 15 to 20 minutes. The skin should be golden brown. If it's not golden brown, let it go another 5 minutes. You can cook this bird in a skillet set over medium-low heat as well. Pour a little of the marinade into the pan before you begin, and let it heat up until it's just beginning to sputter a bit before you add the chicken and weights. When golden brown, turn the bird, being careful not to pierce the crackling skin. You may have to scrape under the chicken a little at a time with an overturned metal spatula to get it up. When the bird is turned, replace the weights and cook for another 15 to 20 minutes, or until the juices run clear and the internal temperature is at least 160°F. Remove the weights, remove from the grill or pan, and allow to rest on a plate for a good 10 minutes. I like to squeeze lots of fresh lemon juice all over the bird, then plop it down in the middle of a platter of arugula that I bring to the table, allowing guests to carve off what they will. I might add quartered boiled potatoes and eggs to the greens and drizzle them with a mixture of olive oil, salt, and pepper. For a meal like this, I give everyone a hand towel in lieu of a napkin, and I serve a bright wine from the south of France—red, white, or rosé.

Coconuts
and Fish Amok

Me up the mast of the Sandlapper.
Hilton Head, 1970. Photo by my father.

I've always loved coconut. When I was young, we would celebrate October birthdays with my mother's brother's family and our family's friends the McGees and the Robinsons, up in the mountains of North Carolina when the autumn leaves peaked. Mama would make a red velvet cake, and Mrs. McGee would make a German chocolate cake, which remains my favorite. I don't have the typical southerner's sweet tooth, but I'll eat just about anything made with coconuts. My first taste of fresh coconut was in the summer of 1958 in Panama; sailing as a teenager with my parents in the Bahamas and the Caribbean, we found coconut in all manner of dishes from breakfast to fish soups to sweet tarts.

After grad school, I freelanced as a photographer in the Virgin Islands, where I would stumble down the hill in the morning to buy coconut patties hot from a local woman's home oven, then over to the waterfront for a fresh coconut right off a boat from down island. I would drink the soothing juice, then have the boatman whack open the coconut for me to scoop out the unripe, gelatinous flesh. Ten years later, living in Italy, I came to love the similar pulp of unripe almonds, which, like coconuts, are classified as drupes—fleshy fruits that generally have a single seed. Here in Southeast Asia, we are blessed with an abundance of delicious drupes— cashews, rambutans, mangoes, sapotes, lychees, and sopadillas, as well as coconuts.

Coconuts—*Cocos nucifera*—now flourish around the world in tropical climates. They are grown in nearly a hundred countries and are a major food source for a third of the world's population. No one is sure of the plant's exact origin because of maritime migration of both plant and people from its probable origins in the Southeast Asian islands, but it was already cultivated by Austronesian voyagers on Madagascar as early as 1,500 years ago. Charleston led the way for coconut cookery in America. Custards, ice cream, and macaroons were popular in the eighteenth century; recipes appear in Lowcountry plantation journals.

On a press junket to Sri Lanka in 2007, I learned new ways with coconut. *Mallums* are mixtures of shredded green leaves that are used as condiments. They usually contain shredded coconut. *Mallum*, or *mallung*, means "mix-up" in Sinhalese. *Kolakenda* is a soup of brown rice and coconut cream that is flavored with several green herbs and is often served at breakfast in one of the small, sweet local coconuts. Revered as the "tree of life," coconuts are ubiquitous in Sri Lanka and are used not only as food, but to provide shelter and medicine as well. In the nineteenth century, coconuts were at the center of the nation's economy. Ropes, drinking cups, serving ladles, beads, rafts, furniture, doormats, brushes, canvas, and mattress filling are among the many products made from coconuts. The sap, known as toddy, is tapped by daredevil toddy tappers who climb the trees, wearing nothing but loincloths, and cross on tightropes from one tree to another, bleeding the sap of the flowers into pots. Fresh toddy, full of yeast, quickly ferments and is drunk as a light, fruity, beer-like beverage, but when distilled the toddy becomes coconut arrack, the national drink.

I became inordinately fond of an arrack cocktail upon my first taste. Coconut arrack is not unlike rum, but it has a unique, sweet hint of coconut to it. It is generally served in an ice-cold drink not unlike a margarita, with lots of fresh lime juice.

Here in Cambodia, coconuts find their way into sweets, soups, rice dishes, and the national dish, *Trey Amok*. (Trey means fish, but it does not mean fish gone crazy!) There are as many ways to make fish amok—sometimes translated on menus as Khmer Fish Stew—as there are cooks. The ingredients are often the same, but the dish might appear as an elegant soup, a hearty stew, or a flan-like dish. It is invariably served with white rice. Chunks of firm white fish fillets are cooked in curried coconut milk. It is often steamed in banana leaves. It is traditionally bolstered with *nonni* leaves (a type of moringa tree), but you can use Swiss chard or bok choy. You will need to make a Khmer curry paste (*kroeung*), which might involve a trip to an Asian grocer, and you may have to substitute some ingredients, but the paste will keep in the freezer for several months.

At the base of this "curry" and many other Khmer dishes is a reprehensible-smelling fish paste called *prahok*. There is a family that makes it on the other side of the river from our house, and when the wind blows from the East, the odor is like that of the stinkiest cheese you have ever encountered. Cambodians laugh at our repulsion and say, "It's Khmer cheese!" It's made from fermented fish. Like salted anchovies and Asian fish sauce, prahok brings a remarkable umami to many dishes. I cannot eat it on its own, but a tiny amount—say, a half-teaspoon—added to composed rice dishes can be illuminating. Fish sauce, known as *teuk trey*, is thin, like soy. It is made with the juice that drains from the prahok paste. You will probably more easily find *nuoc mam,* the Vietnamese version, or *nam pla,* the Thai version. Same difference. If you can't find a fish paste, you might find a shrimp paste. Use it. Or use a salted anchovy mashed with fish sauce.

....

Makrut Limes

Makrut lime leaves—*kroy saoch* in Khmer—provide a unique flavor to Southeast Asian cuisine. The fruit has been called kaffir limes for decades, but the term kaffir is an Arabic word meaning infidel or unbeliever, and it is used in South Africa the same way that the "n" word is used against Black people in the United States. There has been a movement—#KaffirNo More—to ban its use, especially now that the bumpy green fruit—*Citrus hystrix*—is becoming a favored ingredient of brewers, chefs, and bartenders. Hangarı, the distillery in California, even makes a Makrut Lime Vodka.

A 2014 *National Geographic* article cited the work of David Karp and my friend Cara de Silva:

In 1998, [Karp] and writer Cara De Silva proposed in the journal *Petits Propos Culinaires* that the lime gained its name from Indian Muslims, who borrowed the Arabic word *kafara* ("infidel" or "disbeliever") to describe products coming from Buddhist Southeast Asia. In 2004, they wrote an update, reporting that they had found the name (in a Portuguese spelling, *caffre*) in a reference published in England in 1888, describing a fruit that a botanist had found in Sri Lanka. In their thinking, the fruit—with name already attached—came with those traders to Africa, where "Kaffir" had separately been introduced as a term of abuse by Arab slavers. To finesse potential offense, Karp and De Silva described the fruit in their articles as "infidel lime."

Dr. Julia Morton, author of the brilliant *Folk Remedies of the Low Country* (1974), went on to do extensive research in Asia. Her *Fruits of Warm Climates* (1987) describes the fruit as "porcupine orange," but "makrut" is the Thai word, offensive to no one. The fruits are much more acrid and pungent than Persian limes. They are put on door sills to discourage critters from entering. You see an occasional slice in a cocktail, but it's the aromatic leaves—the very essence of the tropics—that flavor Southeast Asian dishes. I like to make a chiffonade of fresh, tender ones to finish off salads and stir-fries. You can freeze them for months. If all you can find are dried ones, use twice as many dried as recipes call for, and remove them before serving the dish. In soups and stews, they are used the way we would use bay leaves.

Both makrut limes and lemongrass grow well in the subtropics. My lemongrass grew to eight feet tall every year in Savannah, even if we had a frost and I cut it back to the ground, and a friend's garden provided makrut limes leaves for a Khmer feast we had at our house last spring—mostly for me to become acquainted with the cuisine. It was scrumptious! I made the following curry paste, adapted from *Cambodian Cooking*, by Joannès Rivière, in Savannah. Don't hesitate to make substitutions (I used ginger instead of galangal, for example, and made my own "fish paste" with anchovies and fish sauce, as above).

Bananas do well in the coastal American South as well. If you have clean banana leaves, you can scald them or hold them over heat to make them pliable, and then steam the amok (using thick coconut cream instead of milk, with an egg added) and serve it in bowls fashioned from banana leaves held together with wooden skewers or toothpicks. But that's tricky.

If you want to sample these flavors, and you don't have a Cambodian restaurant nearby, you might try asking for the Laotian dish *Sousi Pa* or Burma's *Nga Baung Doke*—they're similar.

· ·

Khmer Curry Paste

¼ cup oil such as peanut, canola, or sunflower

2 inches fresh ginger root, about 2 ounces, peeled and shredded

2 inches turmeric root, about 1½ ounces, peeled and shredded

6 cloves garlic, peeled and chopped

4 stalks lemongrass, the tender inner part of the bottom third of the stalk, minced

5 shallots, peeled and chopped

12 makrut lime leaves, thinly sliced in chiffonade, tough ribs removed if any

2 teaspoons fish or shrimp paste or a salted anchovy, rinsed and mashed with fish sauce (see above)

Heat a wok over medium-high heat, pour in the oil from around the inner rim, swirl it around, and add all the ingredients and stir-fry until golden brown. Transfer to a food processor or blender and purée. Store in a jar in the refrigerator or freezer.

Fish Amok

This soupy version is sometimes served in coconut shell halves.

¼ cup oil such as peanut, canola, or sunflower

2 tablespoons Khmer curry paste, above

1 pound firm white thick fish fillet such as snapper, sea bass, or cod, cut into bitesize chunks

3½ cups nonni, Swiss chard, or bok choy leaves, thinly sliced

1-14oz can of Coconut milk, preferably Southeast Asian (see note)

1 teaspoon brown sugar

¼ cup fish sauce

Heat a wok over medium-high heat, pour in the oil from around the inner rim, swirl it around, and add the curry paste, stir-frying until it is browned. Add the fish and the greens, stir-frying until the leaves wilt. Add the coconut milk, the sugar, and the fish sauce. Heat the mixture through, but do not let it come to a boil. Serve immediately in bowls or in coconut shells.

Makes 4 servings.

Note. Cans of coconut milk might say "Coconut Cream." Shake the can to see if it is, indeed, liquid. That's the one you want.

On Cast Iron,
Lard, and Frying

··

Since I first began writing about cooking in cast iron in the 1980s, southern cooking has taken on a new life. Now there are as many southern food experts as there are Italian, which is no wonder, since the South has more than twice the population of Italy. Many culinarians argue that they have always washed their cast iron with soap and water, as did their grandmothers. My friend the Georgia cookbook author Virginia Willis, whom I have known for more than thirty years, admitted in *Garden & Gun* that she does, adding, "But if someone else's grandmother taught them otherwise, who am I to tell them their grandmother was wrong?"

My hand-me-down cast-iron skillets from my mother and grandmothers have never seen soap. Both of my grandmothers, from either end of Tennessee—McNairy County on the Tennessee River and Sevier County in Appalachia—cooked every day in cast iron, and they both made the same cornbread in their skillets: truly southern, with no sugar or wheat flour. Granny, my father's mother, made biscuits in hers as well. Mind you, these women could not have been more different. The South is a *big* place, and there are hundreds of miles and hundreds of years of diverging histories between folks in the Mississippi Delta and those in the Smokies. Tennessee is L-O-N-G. But cast iron—for sautés and stews and frying and cornbread and upside-down cakes—is one common denominator. It's long-lasting, it's non-stick, and, when used in an oven, it holds the heat well. Cast iron is not the most even conductor of heat, but I can think of no pan I own that has as many uses as my well-seasoned cast-iron skillets, griddles, and Dutch ovens. Yes, I wash them, and, if necessary to remove the rare recalcitrant piece of food stuck to the pan, I might use hot water, but I use only natural bristle brushes and, more often, cold water. After each use, I rub the dried pan with a bit of bacon grease and wipe it clean with a paper towel.

Some authors say that the fat in never-washed cast iron goes rancid. I have never smelled or tasted anything off in my pans, and in fact they lend their own umami to dishes. I use bacon grease to keep my pans seasoned. I think that both the salt and the smoke in the fat preserves the cast iron. I also never wash with soap my grandmother's wooden rolling pin, which I inherited. It has pressed countless pie crusts, cookies, cheese straws, and pasta without flavoring the doughs.

It used to be fairly easy to find well-seasoned cast-iron pans in antique and junk stores. Now not only are they collectible, but they're also cherished and used by master chefs and home cooks around the country. Besides my hand-me-downs, I have several others that I have acquired over the years for specific tasks. If you're buying vintage cast iron, it should have a clean, smooth, shiny black interior. If you're buying new cast iron, I don't suggest following instructions that would have you season the pan with vegetable oil. I tried it once and ended up with a sticky mess. If you're a vegetarian, I'm sorry, but I can't help you on this.

Instead, wash the pan once with soap and water, then render some lard in it. Ask your butcher to save some clean pork fat for you. If he'll run it through the meat grinder for you, that will save you a step. Put a thin film of water in the pan. Add the ground or diced fat to the pan and place it over very low heat or in an oven preheated to 225°F. You want to melt the fat very slowly, until any solids—the cracklings—turn brown and sink to the bottom of the pan. It can take an hour or more. Strain the lard through several layers of cheesecloth, or through a very fine mesh stainless steel strainer, into sterilized jars. Cover the jars with cheesecloth to keep out dust and insects, but leave them at room temperature, and do not cap them for two days. Covered, the lard will last several months in the refrigerator.

After you have rendered the lard, wipe out the pan, which you will never wash again with soap—unless that's what your grandmother did. After each use, paint the inside of the cast iron pan with lard or bacon grease, and wipe it out. If you must wash it, use cold water and a natural bristle brush. Always wipe the greased pan dry, and admire the shiny black patina.

For frying, I prefer to use large cast-iron pots—the bigger, the better. The larger the quantity of oil, the easier it is to maintain its temperature. For deep-frying, the pot should be wider than the heat source and deep enough to hold 2 inches of oil in which foods can bubble freely without overcrowding. Dutch ovens are fine, but I have one big rectangular cast iron pot that is 4 inches deep, 12 inches wide, and 20 inches long. It fits perfectly over two burners of a standard stove. A gallon of oil fills it an inch and a half deep.

Mama's Cornbread

▶ PHNOM PENH, 2020 ···

April 30 would have been my mother's one-hundredth birthday. She was four days older than my father. I have written so much about them over the years, but I am always remembering special things that make me realize just how lucky we were to grow up in a house of adventurous intellectuals. I can't remember if Mama's cornbread recipe is in her manuscript cookbook, Purdue, or not. Remarkably, I did not bring my copy with me to Cambodia. And I don't really know if the recipe originated in her family, from western Tennessee, or in my father's, from the hills of eastern Tennessee. It's the classic Appalachian skillet cornbread—the same recipe used by Ronni Lundy, an expert on the music and foods of the Mountain South, and who hails from Corbin, Kentucky (where we have relatives), and by celebrity chef Sean Brock, from coal country in Southwest Virginia.

It is easily the most popular recipe in my cookbooks. It has been published and republished so many times that it seems redundant to offer it yet again, but it really is the best and therefore bears repeating. Mama made it several times a week, even after she became a "gourmet" cook. Mama and my grandmothers loved to dip leftover cornbread in buttermilk—a taste I never acquired. Actually, I don't really care for this cornbread left over, though I have been known to split the pie-like slices horizontally, paint them with a little olive oil, and grill them to make them crisp to have with soups. Mikel and I rarely finish even a small skillet of cornbread, so I just tuck the leftovers in a plastic bag and freeze them for use in cornbread dressing later. Dressing is one of our favorite foods, and I have never understood why it's relegated to the fall holidays only. We have it once a month. A simple recipe follows.

Skillet Cornbread

My sophomore year in college was my first experience living in an apartment on my own. When I got to school that year, I realized that I didn't even know how to make cornbread, so I wrote my mother and asked her to send me the recipe. She replied on a postcard: "To two cups of buttermilk, add an egg and leavened meal to thicken. Bake in a hot skillet till golden brown." I got her to give me more precise instructions and have been making it myself now for over fifty years.

I sold stone-ground, whole-grain, heirloom corn grits and cornmeal for over thirty years. I highly recommend that you use good meal in this recipe. Find a miller close to you who grinds heirloom corn that has been grown, harvested, and milled properly, with nothing added to the corn or taken away from it. Because it's whole grain, store it in your freezer.

This is the best cornbread you'll ever eat—truly southern, with no wheat flour or sugar, baked in a sizzling-hot cast-iron skillet seasoned with a little bacon fat for that golden brown crust. You will need a 9- or 10-inch well-seasoned cast-iron skillet for this recipe.

1½ to 2 teaspoons strained bacon grease
1 large egg
2 cups buttermilk at room temperature
1¾ cups cornmeal, preferably whole-grain, stone-ground
1 scant teaspoon salt
1 scant teaspoon baking powder
1 scant teaspoon baking soda

Add enough bacon grease to the skillet to coat the bottom of the pan, then put it in a cold oven and preheat to 450°F. In the meantime, mix the egg into the buttermilk, then add the cornmeal and mix well.

When the oven has reached 450°, after about 10 minutes, the grease should be just to the smoking point. Quickly stir the salt, baking powder, and soda into the batter, and add the batter all at once to the hot pan. Bake for 15 to 20 minutes, or until the top just begins to brown. Turn the bread out onto a platter and serve hot with lots of butter.

Makes 8 to 10 slices to serve 6.

CORNBREAD DRESSING

This isn't much of a recipe, but it's what I do: fill a baking dish with crumbled cornbread, then dump it into a mixing bowl and add onion and celery sautéed in lots of butter. Sometimes I add nuts; sometimes, oysters. I add a beaten egg and some herbs (both fresh and dried, always including some sage), mix it all together, and dump it back into the dish, now greased. I add turkey or chicken stock until it's thoroughly soaked, as much as it will hold, and bake it in a medium oven until browned, about a half-hour, and serve with giblet gravy.

Daddy and Paella

Daddy wasn't one to talk on the phone, but after he got a computer and taught himself to type, he became an assiduous proofreader of my manuscripts. A typical email might go like this one:

Hey Bub,

Just a quick note to tell you that I made the potato croquettes, but you didn't specify what kind of potatoes. I used russets, because that's all they had at the supermarket in Palatka, which is a half-hour drive that I try to make only once/week. You say "boiled and peeled" but in an earlier recipe you said steaming was better. I also remember you telling me that they don't have russets in Italy, but you are calling these Italian. You say to "form little tubes of the mixture about the size of 2 fingers," but tubes are hollow. Why don't you just say form croquettes?

I divided the recipe by three because it was just Lila and me, and your yield is dead-on. I was hoping to get 6 croquettes—3 apiece—but I made 4 bigger ones instead. (You say the full recipe makes 16.)

Just wanted to give you a heads-up on the above. They were delicious. I didn't have a shallot, so I used onion, and I didn't have fresh herbs except mint. We were having lamb, so that worked out!

Have you made the paella? I'm not giving up your mother's paella pan any time soon.

Love
Daddy

When my mother became ill, Daddy took to the kitchen as though born to it. He had learned from Mother, as I had, to shop first, buy the prettiest, freshest foods you could find, then go home and relax with a glass of wine while perusing her vast culinary library. None of her cookbooks, which I inherited (Dad keeping a few precious gems for himself), are stained or tattered. Say my father had caught some grouper or shot some quail, or Mother had found beautiful veal in a local market. She would go sit with her favorite authors, reading what the experts had to say first, planning her meal to best show off what she had to work with. If she indeed decided to follow a recipe, she would read it through first, understanding the methods and techniques involved, then scribble some notes about proportions and timing on a card that she would then stick to the hood of the stove to follow while she conjured her magic in the kitchen.

I was living in Genoa, Italy, when the doctors told my family that my mother would not last but a few more days. My sisters called me to tell me to come home if I wanted to see her. When I got home, she hadn't eaten in days, and I asked to be left alone with her. I poached her an egg and made her a piece of plain toast, with the crusts cut off. I knew that if she could eat anything, that would be the dish. Miraculously, she not only ate, but rallied and lived for several more months. My father and I were able to keep her at home the entire time, so that she could spend her final days watching the river go by, as she wanted.

He and I never once discussed the meals, or who would shop, or who would cook, or who would clean. We were, in our own way, like the dolphins in the creek, perfectly synchronized. He had always been the grill cook at home, and he had always chosen the wines for dinner, but he had never cooked before. Though his style was much heavier than mine or Mother's, his sauces richer, his spices hotter, he knew how to temper his taste and his presentation to make the little bites that she wanted both attractive and palatable to her.

He was a typical scientist in the kitchen, measuring out all his ingredients beforehand—preparing his *mise-en-place*—and taking notes on what worked and what didn't. Later, when I became a food writer, we began a new and lively correspondence based around our own meals and experiences in the kitchen. He read, and re-read, and re-read my manuscripts, checking my recipes, and my grammar, syntax, and style. His corrections were vital to the overall success of my first book, and to say that I took his suggestions to heart is an understatement.

He glowed when he was the host to a dinner that he had prepared well, when all the courses tasted good and came out of the oven at the right time, and he knew that others appreciated his effort. I think it was a special feeling of accomplishment for him, since that was a role that he hadn't taken over until he was in his sixties. He often told me, "Never say 'never,' Bubba; it's never too late to *learn*."

Once on his sailboat in the Grenadines, we were able to sail on one tack through a sixty-mile stretch of open ocean. It was such a rush that he actually let me take the ship's wheel for a while, something he reluctantly gave up to others. He beamed the entire day.

About a month after Mother died, he pulled out the last bottle of 1949 Chambolle Musigny that he had cellared since buying two cases of it, as futures, before it was released. Mother was saving a bottle for "John's wedding." Daddy knew better. I ordered natural, grass-fed beef from Brae Beef in Connecticut, which I think was probably the only company in America that was selling it then, and we opened the thirty-three-year-old wine. Daddy told me how the 1949s were harvested on the day I was born and that, as luck would have it, he had bought two cases of what turned out to be one of the greatest vintages of all time. I joked with Daddy that some Christians believe that you get your soul when you're thirty-three, which was how old Christ was when he died. And we agreed that the wine not only had soul, but that it was an old one. It was a bittersweet meal, but we chewed on that wine and closed our eyes and described each mouthful. We would describe, in clichés, what we tasted: black cherries, plums, leather. But the wine triggered memories as well, its smokiness somehow making me think of my grandmother's attic. Daddy just cried and said, "It reminds me of your mother." I don't remember a finer meal in my entire life. Of course it was the company. We were both very sad over the loss of Mother, but we were in the moment, as Buddhists like to say.

Six months before Daddy died, I went to spend a weekend with him and his wife, Lila, in Welaka, Florida. I am always pleasantly surprised by the landscape in north-central Florida, where rolling pastures of horses and cattle are punctuated by stately live oaks, evoking England more than stereotypical palm-fringed Florida beaches.

It's definitely "cracker" territory, where wooden boats and cotton shrimp nets are still made by hand, and grocery stores are thirty miles apart. Welaka lies in a verdant bend in the beautiful St. Johns River, which flows north through cypress bottoms dripping with Spanish moss. I saw gallinules and coots, herons and egrets, hawks and eagles, and an otter. I also found boiled peanuts and sampled the delectable local satsumas and calamondins at a roadside stand. My father is a great cook, and he managed to replace on me the weight that I had lost the week before by walking on the beach! My first night there, he prepared my mother's version of Paella Valenciana. The recipe, from her personal journal of recipes, follows. For breakfast the next morning, we had his version of Eggs Benedict, with thin-sliced country ham, eggs, and hollandaise atop an authentic rusk. I don't know where my father got the rusk, but I saw his old copy of the Brennan's cookbook pulled out over on the sideboard, so I imagine he rekindled his recipe recall with a quick look in that book. The country ham is so much better than the traditional Canadian bacon! For dinner my last night, he made old-fashioned Italian American spaghetti with meat sauce. Who *doesn't* love that?!

Here's my wording of my mother's version of this old Spanish classic. Like pilau from the Lowcountry, paella has as many versions as there are cooks. In Valencia, it often includes rabbit, snails, and beans, but no shrimp; this version can be done just about anywhere, even in north-central Florida.

. . . .

Purdue Paella

Mama's recipe was recorded seventy years ago in the Deep South. A pinch of saffron, which she probably didn't have access to then, is traditional. In Spain, the tomatoes are often grated rather than chopped. You can use Spanish paella rice if you can find it, but Mama didn't. This is her version.

2 tablespoons olive oil
2 cups chopped celery
2 cups chopped onion
4 cups peeled and
    chopped ripe tomatoes,
    or one 28-ounce can
    peeled and chopped
    tomatoes
2 cloves garlic, peeled,
    green shoot removed,
    and minced

(CONTINUED)

About 2½ hours before serving, preheat the oven to 325°F. Heat the olive oil in a paella pan (or large shallow flame-proof casserole dish) over medium heat, and add the celery and onion, cooking until the onion begins to become translucent. Add the tomatoes and garlic to the pan, cover, and place in the oven until all the flavors have mingled, about 30 minutes. Season to taste with salt and pepper.

Add the chicken to the pan and return to the oven, covered, for another 30 minutes.

Salt and freshly ground
 black pepper to taste
2 skinless and boneless
 chicken breasts, cut
 into bite-size chunks
¾ cup raw white rice
1 cup chicken stock,
 boiling
1 pound peeled large
 shrimp
½ pound country ham,
 diced
½ pound green peas,
 fresh or frozen
1 cup small cooked
 artichoke hearts
½ cup sliced roasted
 pimientos or other
 mild red peppers
Fresh chopped parsley for
 garnish

About 45 minutes before serving, add the rice and the boiling stock, and cook for another 30 minutes, covered. Remove the cover and add the shrimp, the ham, the peas, and the artichokes, and return to the oven until the shrimp are cooked and the entire dish is warmed through. Just before serving, add the roasted pimientos, toss, and serve. Garnish the plates with fresh parsley.

Mother always served this with a tossed salad and cornbread. My father likes to serve a Greek salad, with feta cheese and black olives.

Makes 8 servings.

. . . .

Epilogue

Though he had cut way back on his drinking by the time this photo was taken, I knew that he would appreciate the moonshine my millers had given me to take to him. It was very special applejack, very hard to find, and sure to spark some old memories from his hillbilly upbringing. He and I hit the bottle pretty hard, and I begged him to teach me one of the old mountain jigs that his ancestors had once danced in the Tennessee hills. In the photo, I am trying to learn the complicated footwork. The next morning, hungover, I remembered nothing, and Daddy refused to admit that we had even had the experience. Thank goodness Lila took photos! It is my favorite photo of us. It sits on my desk, and I see it every day. It never ceases to amuse me. He really was special.

Dancing with my father in Florida, 1999. Photo by Lila Taylor.

Dance Lessons

❯ PHNOM PENH, 2021

Everyone in my hometown danced. There were some shy girls, but if I grabbed their hands at a sock hop, they'd join in. Dancing is infectious, but it's also tribal. If you grew up in a dancing town—like Orangeburg, South Carolina, or Memphis, Tennessee, or Athens, Georgia—you surely dance. I loved to. I had two older sisters, so I never had to buy 45s because they had stacks of them. I was six when Nancy bought *Hound Dog* by Elvis Presley. She had pictures of Fabian and Ricky Nelson pinned to her bulletin board, but it was The Diamonds' "Little Darlin'" in 1957 that really got me going. The song was originally recorded by a Black group from South Carolina, who later became Maurice Williams and the Zodiacs, whose *Stay* from 1961 propelled them to fame—and me and my junior high friends to the dance floor.

The summer of 1958, we went to visit some friends of my parents in the Panama Canal Zone, where the calypso beats were intoxicating. We were already singing Harry Belafonte's "Day-O" (the Banana Boat Song); his *Calypso* album was the first record to sell over a million copies. Lucho Azcarraga was playing the organ at the Hilton with his band. It was the liveliest, best music I had ever heard—a combination of jazz, calypso, and his own mix of local folk traditions and early rock. We bought the album, and to this day it's one of my favorites, with crazed percussion and rapid-fire timing.

The first album I bought with my own money was Booker T & the MG's *Green Onions* in 1962. I was a dancing fool. The Mashed Potato. The Bristol Stomp. The Swim. The Jerk. The Charleston. The Watusi. The Twist. Orangeburg was a typical little southern town, mostly Black but completely segregated. There were two historically Black colleges in town, but any mixing of the races was discouraged, if not all but forbidden. I never knew a Black person my age until our high school was integrated in 1964. But I certainly loved Black music. By 1961, when I was eleven, I was enamored of the songs of Carla Thomas, The Marvelettes, Ike and Tina Turner, Gene Chandler, and Chubby Checker—another South Carolinian. My father was a ham radio operator and an electronics wiz. We had the first color TV and the first transistor radios in town because he built them. I'd stay up way past my bedtime listening to the hits on WLS, a powerful radio station in Chicago whose signal somehow made it to my bedroom.

As a white southern boy, I was expected to hunt and fish, but also to take golf, tennis, horseback riding, and dance lessons. I was a bad shot at both birds and at the basketball goal, but I was a scrappy guard, and I could steal the ball from even the tallest players. It was all dance to me. Ballroom dancing was taught by Isabel Whaley Sloan, who was born in 1897, and who traveled around the state teaching dance and etiquette to generations of pubescent South Carolinians. We would meet once each month in a fellowship hall where chairs lined the walls—the boys on one side, the girls on the other. After two years of lessons, Mrs. Sloan chose someone to be her assistant in each town. It was my first "job"—albeit nonpaying—which I kept throughout high school. It was considered an honor.

I was known as a good dancer. In Augusta, Georgia (home of James Brown!), which was seventy-five miles away but to this day is a good hour and a half by car, the local television station broadcast live a Saturday show called "Top Ten Dance Party." Kids from all over South Carolina and Georgia were invited to come on. We got a busload of dance partners together and went to Augusta to appear on the show, which was modeled after any number of sixties teen dance party shows airing throughout the country. I won the contest. I think Patty Still was my winning partner because I can remember brushing her hair on the bus on the way there. I remember no prizes, but high school friends still mention it occasionally.

I wanted to dance professionally and was envious of my sisters' lessons in ballet and tap. As I recall, the male instructor told my mother that he didn't teach little boys because, you know, he might grow up to be . . . well, you know. Well, indeed, now I know! I have never been one to have regrets or to second-guess the past, but I do wonder what would have happened if I had become a professional dancer. Would I be long dead from AIDS? Years later, the summer of 1970, before my senior year in college, my father arranged for me to be a public relations intern at his company headquarters in New York City. My mother was not having it. She hated the thought that I might be gay, but she also knew that I probably was and feared what might happen to me as an impressionable twenty-year-old in Sin City. Instead, I interned at the State Development Board in the state capital and lived with my sister Sue—herself a fabulous dancer. When the "Dirty Dog" was a becoming a popular dance when we were in high school—she, a senior; me, a freshman—she and I could do it in public without the chaperones prohibiting it because we were brother and sister. I distinctly remember one night at the Riviera, a city-owned community center on the banks of the Edisto River. It was also called the Pavilion. She had been dancing with Louie Argoe. I don't remember anything about him except that he was an exceptional shagger. The Shag is the official state dance of South Carolina—a sort of slowed-down, sleazier jitterbug. Imagine my surprise years later when, outside of South Carolina and Georgia, people were appalled to hear me talking about shagging in junior high school! I was in my twenties before I heard the British use of the word.

We danced all the time. Everyone. The shy girls. The football players. The geeks. The rednecks. We chanted the lyrics as we danced, with the same spirit that fueled the cheers for our basketball players: "Louie Louie, oh no, Me gotta go!" "Bend over, let me see you shake your tail feather!" "'Cause I try and I try and I try and I try, I can't get no, I can't get no . . ." Dancing was as much a part of our rituals as swimming and barbecue and church. The Baptists weren't supposed to dance, but I swear they were always the best shaggers. In the late fifties and early sixties, the Development Board was successful in luring businesses to our mostly rural farming community. Smith-Corona, the typewriter manufacturer, came from California, and then Utica Tools moved its operations from New York to Orangeburg, bringing teenage girls with their miniskirts and record albums that went beyond the R&B and beach music we had been dancing to—the British Invasion. The Pony replaced the Slop; we Shimmied as well as Shagged. Beatlemania edged out nearly all the country music. Patty and Beverly Townsend went to Statesboro, Georgia, to see the Rolling Stones play at Georgia Southern College in 1965.

It's probably best that Mama didn't let me go to New York. Though I had grown up in a family of intellectuals, I was never challenged in high school, and I was lazy because I never had to make an effort to make good grades. I was seventeen and immature when I entered the University of Georgia. I chose it purely for a new experience. While I loved my friends back home, I didn't want to go to school with the same people I had been to high school with, which would have been the case at any college in South Carolina. At summer orientation before my freshman year, I met a girl from Memphis. We were acting silly in the bookstore, and she asked me if I liked to dance. Her high school boyfriend had been the drummer for the Box Tops, whose song "The Letter" went on to top the charts that fall. She had grown up with Alex Chilton, who sings lead on the original, and which Joe Cocker covered to great acclaim several years later. Booker T & the MGs played at her high school dances. She and I became fast friends, at least partly because we would marvel together at the bass line in a song; moreover, I could cut a rug.

I went home after my freshman year to work in a bank to earn enough money to buy a car. My friend Mary's brother had been killed in automobile accident, and I spent nearly every free moment at her house, where her mother was distraught. We spent hours practicing our shag routines. Although the basic swing-like dance steps are precise, our own variations were like jazz musicians' riffs. We were coloring outside the lines, but anyone could see that we were shagging. Not that anyone saw, because there was really no place for us to go, and Mary's mother needed us close by for comfort. Though most ballroom dances traditionally stick to the male leading and his partner following, the pattern of the shag is not so much about being in charge as it is suggestive. Mary invented some very clever dance steps that she could signal to me with a slight hand movement. I followed her suggestions as often as she did mine. It was definitely give and take, like our friendship.

I returned to school in the fall of 1968, just as popular music was becoming more expressive, more experimental, and more political. The Beatles, the Stones, Aretha, Jimi Hendrix, Van Morrison, the Kinks, Jefferson Airplane, Janis Joplin, and Simon and Garfunkel were at the top of their game. Bob Dylan had gone electric, and James Brown was singing, "Say it Loud: I'm Black and I'm Proud!" Live concerts were becoming huge dance parties. Frank Zappa was pushing musical boundaries. George Clinton was overseeing a sea change at Motown, while funk expanded the standard 4/4 beat of the Carolina Shag with new time signatures that made our dancing change as well. Big hits by Sly and the Family Stone and, in 1969, the Jackson Five, would continue to make us dance to the 4/4 beat, but they pushed the beats per minute up to 100. R&B had been 60-80 BPM. Rock was becoming even faster, about 140 BPM. By the time of the Woodstock Festival, we were all basically doing solos on the dance floor or in pastures.

"Rock Lobster," 1978, St. George Island, Florida.

In the mid-seventies, I returned to graduate school in Athens, where an alternative music scene was evolving. The members of the B-52s were friends of mine, and my apartment was occasionally the scene of wild dance parties. We would take turns manning the turntable because all our recordings were on vinyl. We'd play a British rock group followed by an American R&B number: David Bowie, then Aretha; The Stones' "Satisfaction," then Devo's version. We were dancing to New Wave and Punk bands—the Sex Pistols, the Ramones, and Blondie, but Marvin Gaye was making new music as well. We danced to all of it. John Beal was my boyfriend at the time. An impossibly handsome young man, he all but abandoned his painting studio his senior year in art school to concentrate on theatrical dance. He moved to New York and danced with Twyla Tharp and John Kelly.

I have moved around a lot: to the Caribbean, New York, France, Italy, and back to South Carolina. Amazingly, I fell in love with someone who rarely dances, though I have shagged with his mother. She had a very smooth style. Robert Waldrop, who wrote some songs for the B-52s, said she was like "air and cream." My husband and I have been together for nearly thirty years, and occasionally we'll be at a party, and I'll dance with some of our old friends. But mostly, I dance the way I have since the seventies: by myself. The kitchen is my dance hall. I have arthritis and a fake knee, but it is simply impossible for me NOT to dance to Junior Walker's

"Shotgun." My best friend Dana says that it's required to dance to it, even if you're in the checkout aisle of the grocery store and the Muzak version starts to play. I've long since forgotten most of those formal dances I taught with Mrs. Sloan: the Foxtrot, the Rumba, the Viennese Waltz. When those 4/4 beats are playing, whether it's the Temptations' "My Girl" or the Rolling Stones' "Beast of Burden," I shag. I'm not really alone, because my friend Mary, who died three years ago, and I perfected so many steps of our own that I dance with those memories.

Fennel

It was the week of my twelfth birthday when *Mastering the Art of French Cooking* was published, forever changing the way Americans thought about food. My father was in Europe with Fritz Hollings, then Governor of South Carolina, trying to attract foreign industry to the state. My mother, perhaps then more than ever, was totally immersed in her cooking; Dad was always bringing home fabulous bottles of rare vintages and stories of meals in the world's finest restaurants. We would take family trips to New York or San Francisco and stay in modest hotels, but we'd always dine in the best eateries. Friends would ask me at school what we had eaten at home the night before, then roar with laughter when I would say "squid"—which they knew I would have had to go buy at the bait shop in the "colored" neighborhood. This was Orangeburg, South Carolina, in a very different time. (Just two years before Hollings was elected, Strom Thurmond had spoken for twenty-four hours and twenty-seven minutes *against* civil rights, setting a filibuster record. Integration wasn't mandated until another two years later.) I'm pretty sure we were the only people in town eating squid. I don't even remember fried calamari on the menu of our local pizza joint.

Mother would have the local grocers bring in flats of vegetables they had never heard of, and then she would get her bridge club to buy them with her. I loved going to Mary Fanning's house for sieva beans or to Bud Moore's for fried chicken—we had to beg for "normal" food at home. But how I loved my mother's cooking! I would come home from school and find her immersed in the enormous tome *Larousse Gastronomique*, which had been published that year, or poring over the Julia Child collaboration.

But never once did I see a cookbook in the kitchen. Mother taught me early on that recipes were merely guides, and that books were to be treated with care. She was a natural in the kitchen, but she was continually expanding her culinary repertoire. When she died in 1982, I inherited her enormous collection of cookbooks, all in pristine condition. To this day I neither take recipes literally nor take my cookbooks into the kitchen. Like Mother, I might find some beautiful fennel at the farmers' market, then come home and read what Elizabeth Schneider or Richard Olney or the editors of Larousse have written about the vegetable, then go into the kitchen on my own. If I do want to follow a recipe, I make notes on little slips of paper.

I find *Mastering the Art of French Cooking* difficult to follow, misleading, and a far cry from the French food I love—cookbooks have come a long way in the past six decades, and I have lived in France and know the real thing. But Julia Child did help lift the American home cook out of the drudgery of gloppy casseroles and set her free to soar through the uncharted constellations of the *univers culinaire. Mastering the Art* does have its brilliant moments: the first recipe in the first chapter, for *potage parmentier* (leek or onion and potato soup), begins: "Leek and potato soup smells good, tastes good, and is simplicity itself to make. It is also versatile as a soup base; add watercress and you have a watercress soup, or stir in cream and chill for a vichyssoise. To change the formula a bit, add carrots, string beans, cauliflower, broccoli, or anything you think would go with it, and vary the proportions as you wish."

Fennel is something I think goes with it very well. A common plant in eighteenth-century Charleston kitchen gardens, fennel—or finocchio— had all but disappeared from the local culinary vernacular until the late 1980s, when it began appearing in supermarkets. It was once so commonly planted in the Southeast that it has naturalized locally in some areas. Old homesites along riverbanks are often dotted with the feathery, dill-like stalks of "wild" or "dog" fennel. Native to the Mediterranean and southern Asia, finocchio probably came to the Lowcountry with early Greek settlers, though by the time of Senator Thurmond's filibuster, when Charleston's Ladies of the Philoptochos Society compiled its excellent *Popular Greek Recipes*, it was no longer mentioned.

Fennel's flavor is often compared to licorice (which belongs to a completely different plant family) or to anise (only vaguely related), and many grocers have the annoying habit of marketing it as anise, adding to the confusion. Some might find fennel's sweet, celery-like crispness more to their liking than the bittersweetness of aniseed. When I lived in Italy, we would dip fresh, chilled ribs of raw fennel into salted olive oil as an appetizer, in the same way we Sandlappers might plow sticks of celery through a bowl of pimiento cheese. Perhaps *the* classic preparation is "à la Grecque," that is, poached in a seasoned court bouillon and served chilled. In southern France, fish is grilled over a fire of the dried stalks. You can stuff fresh stalks into the cavity of whole, oily fish like bluefish or Spanish mackerels for a similar effect.

Try this elegant, simple soup, which is delicious served either hot or cold.

Fennel Soup

Buy fennel bulbs with the feathery stalks attached. For every 2 servings, you will need about a cup of chopped fennel bulb, ¼ cup of loosely packed, chopped fennel leaves without stems, and 2 cups of the stock of your choice. I buy an extra fennel plant and make stock the night before with the fennel as the predominant aromatic in the stockpot.

For the soup, sauté the fennel in a little butter with sliced leek or onion, then add the stock to the pan with ½ pound of peeled and diced potatoes for every two people. Add some salt to taste (Julia says to oversalt, as "salt loses savor in a cold dish") and simmer until all the vegetables are tender, about 45 minutes. Put the fennel leaves in the bowl of a food processor and chop finely, then add the soup in batches, and purée it. Correct the seasoning and add some whipping cream, if desired. Chill, then serve in chilled bowls with a garnish of more fennel leaves, fresh dill, or chives. I sometimes garnish with a dollop of unflavored yogurt.

Fennel and Oranges

There are some flavors that pair so perfectly together, like tomatoes and basil, that it's amazing to me that the plants didn't evolve in the same plot of land. Tomatoes originated in the high Andes and were cultivated by the Incas and Aztecs by 700 AD. They didn't reach Italy for centuries. And while we also associate basil with the Mediterranean, particularly Italy, it is native to India. It is assumed that it arrived with navigators of the spice trade in the fifteenth century, like oranges, whose origins are obscured in history. Fennel is native to the Mediterranean basin, and I think it is a natural with oranges. Though no one has yet pinpointed the first combination of fennel and oranges as a salad, it is likely that it emerged in Sicily after the Arab invasions. You see fennel and orange dishes all over Italy now, especially during the winter months when both are available throughout the country.

Fennel is one of those foodstuffs, like dill, that I buy every time I see it in Phnom Penh if it is pretty. I make salads with raw slices, poach it "Greek style," and pair it with shellfish, particularly shrimp or scallops. Invariably, I include oranges in the salads.

I don't think I have ever used a measuring cup or spoon when making a salad—except when codifying a recipe for publication. I have made dozens of fennel and orange dishes through the years. In 2013, while writing about wild garlic, I wrote, "I never tire of the combination. Often, I'll use red onions for a third type of sweetness (along with the fennel and orange), but I didn't have any, so I used my mandolin to cut thin slivers of carrot instead. [This] salad also contains the wild garlic. Anointed with my favorite delicate Ligurian oil, and dusted with a little cinnamon and cayenne, and the whole balanced with the juice of a lime, this one was one of the best yet!"

At the time, I was living in Bulgaria, where several wild garlics grew. Bulgarians are famously superstitious: according to local traditions, garlic is not only thought to ward off vampires, but also to prevent miscarriages, to keep *navi* and other evil spirits from attacking newborns, to bring good luck to young married couples, to protect the dead from both being a victim of vampires and becoming one, to bring in the new year with the promise of good harvests, to welcome spring, to prevent drought, to encourage growth, and to celebrate the fall harvest. In short, garlic is used in virtually every ritual from birth to death—and before and beyond.

In Cambodia, despite the enduring cultural damage done by the Khmer Rouge, some superstitions are still believed. They believe that the dead do not know they are dead; not only are ghosts real, but they eat; and if you sing while you are cooking, you will marry a widow or widower. I haven't seen anyone here shun garlic, onions, leeks, or any other of the lilies of the table, cultivated or foraged from the wild. They are consumed in vast quantities with wild abandon.

· · · · · · · · · · · · · · · · ·

To make a fennel and orange salad, I remove the center core of fennel bulbs and slice the bulb crosswise into thin slices. I also slice some onions. I section some oranges, squeezing the juice onto the fennel and onion slices. I drizzle some good olive oil over the salad and toss it, then season with whatever I feel like—salt, pepper, cayenne, cinnamon. I taste it and adjust the seasoning, often adding a squeeze of lemon or lime to brighten it. I toss it again, garnish with some of the feathery leaves of fennel, and serve immediately.

···

Fenouil à la Grecque aux Oranges
(Fennel Cooked in the Greek Style, with Oranges)

Court-bouillon means quick stock in French, but in Louisiana, where it's pronounced 'coobeeyon,' it's a soup made by the addition of fish to the stock as it cooks. Neither the French nor French immigrants in Louisiana would dream of cooking shellfish or fennel in unseasoned water. The quick stock is made in a matter of minutes to provide an aromatic poaching liquid. Fennel is traditionally poached in a court-bouillon and served cold as an hors d'oeuvre. For some reason this very French preparation is called *à la grecque* (in the Greek style).

Traditional recipes for *fenouil à la grecque* call for fennel simmered in a mixture of water, wine, citrus juice, onions, herbs, and olive oil, though the wine is often replaced with vinegar or tomatoes. Let this mixture cool completely and serve it at room temperature, adding orange sections and garnishing it with delicate fennel leaves.

2 large fennel bulbs with
   stalks attached
1 small onion, peeled and
   chopped
½ cup extra virgin olive oil
1 cup water
1 cup fresh-squeezed
   orange juice
1 bay leaf
¼ teaspoon cayenne
5 or 6 black peppercorns
A sprig of fresh thyme
Juice of 1 lemon
1 red onion, peeled and
   sliced
Sea salt
1 or 2 oranges, peeled
   and sectioned

Trim the stalks from the fennel, reserving a few of the feathery leaves for garnish. Place the stalks in a stockpot with the onion, olive oil, water, orange juice, bay leaf, cayenne, peppercorns, thyme, and lemon juice. Bring the mixture to a boil, reduce to a simmer and cook, covered, for 20 minutes.

Strain the court-bouillon and discard the solids. Cut the base off the fennel bulbs, but do not core them. Remove any discolored or damaged outer ribs and discard. Slice the fennel into ¼- to ½-inch slices crosswise, about 6 per bulb. Place the fennel and the red onion slices in a large sauté pan with the court-bouillon, bring to a boil, reduce the heat, and simmer until the fennel and onion are cooked through but not mushy, anywhere from 15 to 45 minutes. How long is a matter of personal taste. Stir occasionally as it cooks, breaking up the fennel clusters so that they cook evenly. Remove the fennel and onions and place in a serving bowl. Add 1 teaspoon of salt to the juice and boil hard, about 5 minutes, to reduce by ⅔ to 1 cup. Pour the sauce over the fennel. At this point you can serve the dish warm, or you can let it cool and serve it at room temperature later, adding the orange sections and garnishing with the fennel leaves.

Serves 6.

. . . .

Clams or Shrimp in a Fennel-Tomato Court-Bouillon

If you use shrimp instead of clams, you will need ½ pound of shrimp (or 1 pound of head-on). They will only take about 1 to 2 minutes to cook, uncovered. Farm-raised clams should be free of grit. If you have any worries, add some fine cornmeal to a pot of cold water, and let the clams sit for an hour to purge themselves. I have used both *Meretrix* and *Donax* clams, farm-raised here in Cambodia. They appear in some local Italian restaurants as *vongole*, though *vongole veraci*—the real ones—are from a different genus. I've also used Surf clams (*Paphia undulata*), the beautifully marked, more elongated ones, which I've also been served as "vongole" in local Italian restaurants, though, they, too, aren't the real deal. I prefer the white and brown ones. I have no idea why the brown ones are more expensive. It's the same clam as the white ones. Use whatever small clams you can find.

4 dozen small clams (or ½ pound of shrimp, see above)

1 small onion, peeled and chopped

2 tablespoons olive oil

2 cups water

1 cup Vermouth or dry white wine

1 bay leaf

¼ teaspoon cayenne

(CONTINUED)

Clean the clams in cold water, then put them in the refrigerator or on ice. If using shrimp, peel and head them, cover them, and put them in the refrigerator.

Sauté the onion in the olive oil until it is transparent, about 5 minutes. Add the water, wine, bay leaf, cayenne, peppercorns, thyme, lemon juice, and garlic. If you are using shrimp, you can add the heads and shells to the broth. Trim the stalks from the fennel bulbs and add them, saving a few of the

4 or 5 black peppercorns
A sprig of fresh thyme
Juice of 1 lemon
1 garlic clove, unpeeled but crushed
2 fennel bulbs with stalks attached
2 average ripe tomatoes, peeled, seeded and diced

feathery leaves for garnish. Raise the heat, bring to a boil, reduce to a simmer, and cook slowly, covered, for 20 minutes.

Strain the court-bouillon and discard the solids. Cut the base off the fennel bulbs, but do not core them. Remove any discolored or damaged outer ribs and discard. Slice the fennel horizontally into ¼- to ½-inch slices, about 6 per bulb. Place the fennel in a large sauté pan with the court-bouillon, bring to a boil, reduce the heat, and simmer, covered, for 5 minutes.

Add the tomatoes to the pot, raise the heat to medium-high, and cook until the liquid is reduced by half, about 10 minutes. Stir occasionally as it cooks, breaking up the fennel clusters so that they cook evenly and intermingle with the tomatoes.

Add the clams, cover the pot, and cook, shaking the pan occasionally, until all of the clams open, about 5 minutes. If using shrimp, do not cover the pot. They will cook in just a couple of minutes.

Divide among pasta bowls, garnish with the reserved fennel leaves, and serve immediately with crusty bread as an appetizer, or refrigerate immediately and serve chilled as a light lunch, with a glass of a white Côtes du Rhône.

Makes 4 appetizers or 2 mains.

Fishing

First fish, Key West, 1952. Photo by my father.

I caught my first fish in Key West when I was three years old. We were getting ready to move from Baton Rouge, Louisiana, to Orangeburg, South Carolina, where the Ethyl Corporation, for whom my father did research and development, had purchased a chemical plant where he could expand and manage their experiments. Both of my parents were intellectuals, and it was a difficult move for my mother, who had been living in college towns and Washington, DC, since she had married ten years earlier. She had a nine-year-old, a six-year-old, and a three-year-old. She would be leaving easy access to the decadent, sophisticated city of New Orleans, whose population was nearly half that of the state of South Carolina at the time. Where would they buy wine?

Orangeburg lies just south of the Sandhills, which can be viewed simplistically as former dunes on the ocean shore. It's the outermost limit of the fabled Lowcountry—the coastal plain. It's about the same distance from Orangeburg to Charleston as it is from Baton Rouge to New Orleans.

Mother was fond of Grand Isle, a wisp of a barrier island in the Gulf of Mexico that has recently (once again) been battered by hurricanes. Its population is half what it was in 1953, when we moved. Much to my parents' surprise, my first memory is from Grand Isle: I am lying down, but I am falling. I see turquoise walls and louvred doors moving past me as I fall. I told my parents about this profound memory—mostly visual, the way I think—and they couldn't believe me. "There's no way you can remember that," they both said, "You were an infant." I repeated what I remembered with a few more details. "What you probably remember was me being mad," my mother sheepishly admitted from her bed, where she was dying of leukemia at the time. "We had rented a house there, and your father had put you in your bassinet on the kitchen counter." I could all but see a light bulb flash in my father's mind. "Your mother had been out of the room, and just as she walked in, the bassinet fell off the counter. She was furious. What you probably remember is her yelling at me. I don't think she's yelled at me since. But I don't see how you could possibly remember that. You were about nine months old."

I think they believed me, but they were all but in a state of shock. "Wasn't I already talking by then?" I prodded. "A few words," Daddy said. "Complete sentences," Mother corrected. "'Sue gone' was one of the first things you said." Sue was my six-year-old sister, whom I've always been close to.

Charleston had better shops and restaurants than Orangeburg, but it was no New Orleans. The state capital, Columbia, was only forty miles away, but it offered even less. What drew my parents in was Edisto Island on the coast. Among their best friends were the McGees, who had a big pink beachfront house, and the Robinsons. Page Robinson was the plant's accountant. His wife, Margaret, was the daughter of Cap'n Mac Holmes, who was the first person to live permanently on the front beach at Edisto. We spent countless weekends at the beach, where I learned inshore, offshore, and deep-sea fishing. Of course it was fishing that had lured my father to Grand Isle in the first place.

Back home in Orangeburg, we fished most often in Wannamaker's ponds. Mr. Wannamaker had owned the chemical plant, and he and Daddy became close friends. The pond was well stocked with bass and bream. (Several freshwater panfish are called "bream" in the South. It's pronounced "brim.") My older sister Nancy and I loved to fish. We would beg Daddy to take us. For several years, I was content to stand on the banks of the first iteration of Wannamaker's—a small, circular pond I imagine wasn't much more than an acre, if that. I would use worms on hooks on lines at the end of cane poles to catch bream. I remember once landing my line atop a bream bed and pulling in dozens of them, one right after the other. My father told me to stop, knowing that we had more than we would eat that night and, he knew, more than I would clean myself. At our house, we had a small porch off the back of the house that was about counter height—just the right height for cleaning fish, though I had to stand on a crate. Daddy taught me how to tie fishermen's knots and how to scale and gut the fish. What we didn't eat that night went into milk cartons filled with water and placed in the "deep freeze" for later use. We had milk delivered in glass bottles, but Mother gradually began buying milk in cardboard cartons from the grocery store.

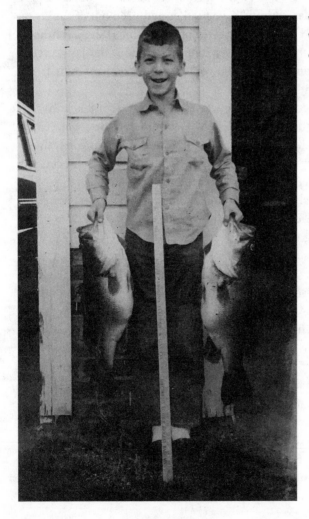

With big ones from Wannamaker's pond, ca. 1958.

Mother would fry the sweet bream—to this day, my favorite fish prepared my favorite way—and make hushpuppies. If the fish were females full of roe sacs, she would place the sacs down in water and refrigerate them, then scramble them with eggs the next morning. As her palate became more sophisticated, she branched out, cooking French, Middle Eastern, and Viennese specialties. Many families had Black cooks. I had several friends whose mothers couldn't boil the proverbial pot of water. I don't remember when Mother stopped frying, but she was already making fanciful desserts and elaborate dinners in the early sixties. By the time I was in high school, we were on our boat every weekend, sailing among the barrier islands. A bridge to Hilton Head had been built in 1959. Mother said at the time that it was "the end of paradise."

In the summer of 1958, we had gone to Panama to visit my parents' friends the Baileys. Dr. Bailey had been my father's lab mate at Purdue, where Daddy had gone to grad school after serving on the Manhattan Project. Dr. Bailey was a specialist in radioisotopes at the Gorgas Hospital in the Canal Zone, but he was perhaps best known as a marlin fisherman. His wife, Jean, was the *Time-Life* correspondent in Latin America and the author of children's books that she would read to us. Dr. Bailey had been fishing in Piñas Bay the day before we arrived and had landed a seven-hundred-pound black marlin. Their Panamanian cook fried big cubes of the fish in butter, a technique that lends itself well to other firm-fleshed pelagic species, such as cobia.

The summer after our trip to Panama, my grandparents were visiting from western Tennessee. My paternal grandfather had died when my father was a small child, and Grandpa Martin and he became best buddies. They bonded over hunting and fishing. We had been out to Wannamaker's pond, hugging the red banks, casting with artificial lures, hoping to get one of the whopper bass that lurk in the shadows under the overhanging bushes. I can hear my grandfather calling out softly, "Come on, Red Bank! Give it up for Grandpa!" I don't remember if we caught fish that day (I have to rely on photos to jar my memory, and I lost most of the family photos in Hurricane Hugo), but it didn't matter because we were headed to Edisto to go cobia fishing that weekend. Back in Orangeburg after fishing, I was preparing Gravy Train to feed our dog, pouring the hot broth Mama had made over the food. I poured it all over my stomach and had a second degree burn that covered my entire belly. That happened on a Wednesday, and Daddy let me skip school and go with him and Grandpa down to fish with his cigar-smoking buddies. Mama came later in the station wagon with my siblings and cooked big chunks of cobia just the way we had had the marlin in Panama.

When Daddy and I would go pond fishing alone together, we'd leave the house as the sun rose and head first downtown to Mutch's bakery. The Mutches lived across the street from us and ran an exceptional German American bakery. They weren't open yet, but Daddy would call them and tell them we were coming, and we'd go to the back door and get doughnuts before they were glazed.

We didn't fish much on Hilton Head. Our first sailboat was all wood and brass, which meant five weekends of brightwork (imagine putting a varnished piece of furniture in a bath of saltwater and leaving it there) and then one of sailing. But there was plenty of fish to be had on the island. Charles Claussen's charter boat captain was always bringing in fresh tuna and dolphin (the fish, not the mammal), and we'd catch eel and flounder in our crab trap. I learned to throw both a mullet net and a shrimp net. Back then, the nets were hand-tied by old-timers on the island. They were made of cotton and weighed a ton. The weights on the mullet nets are heavier than on the shrimp nets, and I could manage, even as a wiry and strong teenager, perhaps two throws before I would be exhausted. But mullet are easy to catch. There was a culvert near the marina that filled a brackish impoundment twice each day with the eight-foot high tide. I would stand on the large pipe and look for the telltale swirling motion of a school of mullet. They tend to whirl around like menhaden when they're in shallow water. One toss of the net would usually bring in the entire school—certainly enough for breakfast. Mullet are bottom feeders, and they must be cleaned immediately, or the flesh takes on a muddy appearance and taste. We usually smoked them.

The salt marsh estuaries more often than not provided us with our meals when we were on the boat for the weekend. Young creek shrimp appear in the spring in the estuaries. You catch them by casting the circular net at low tide at the entrances to small salt marsh creeks. During the R months at low tide, I might simply go gather oysters or clams from the exposed mudbanks. But in the spring, and again in the fall, more than likely I would cast the shrimp net. If the weather were foul, I might check the crab trap, where there might be the aforementioned eels and flounder as well as both blue and stone crabs. We smoked the eels as well. By the mid-sixties, monofilament nets were available. They weighed a lot less than the old cotton ones. I have been known to cast a net all night long when the creeks are full of shrimp, never tiring.

I didn't fish for years, but I did live in Charleston for a year in the mid-seventies and tried to make up for it then. I mostly surf-cast for spottail bass. In the eighties I was living in Italy, where the closest I came to fishing was trying to catch the common octopus that lives along the rocky shore of the Cinque Terre. We would buy long, thin cane poles and tie three-pronged treble hooks to the tips of the poles. A piece of white fabric would be loosely woven through the hooks. We plunged the poles down in between the rocks, close to the sandy floor of the bay. And wait. That's the real beauty of fishing. Waiting. It may sound boring, but it's relaxing. You're on the water, which is always changing. The slightest ripple can throw you off guard. A series of ripples (known as capillary waves) can be mesmerizing. I can get lost in a sort of non-thinking bliss. But you wait, paying attention, and looking for an arm to come reaching out from under a rock to explore the white fabric. And then, like crabbing, you let the creature pull the fabric, and with it the tip of the pole, under the rock. The octopus by this point is surrounding the fabric, the pole, and the hook. You jerk the pole upwards, hoping to find purchase. If you're lucky (and, yes, *all* fishing requires a certain amount of luck), you will have hooked an octopus. You then quickly pull the rod up and slam the tip on the rock, killing the creature. You continue to pound it to tenderize it. If they're small, you cook them quickly. If they're large, you let them stew.

Back in Charleston, I ran my store by myself for the first seven years and didn't fish much, but in the nineties I met my future husband, and his mother put a pond in her back yard and had it stocked with bream and bass. I was back to my childhood fishing, using cane poles off her dock for bream and casting artificial lures for bass from her jonboat. I have since caught and fried dozens of fish and served them with slaw and hushpuppies over the years. When we moved to Washington, DC, in the 2000s, I was thrilled to find that bream were being farm-raised in Maryland and were for sale at the Wharf. I continued frying. I never fished when we lived in Bulgaria or China, but I had a Greek fishmonger in Sofia who would get me anything I wanted, and in China they eat everything from the sea. I made fish fries for Mikel's Peace Corps staff in both countries.

We bought a house in Georgia in 2014, where bream are also farm-raised for sale. Mikel worked in Washington, and we would meet at his mom's. It's in the middle of nowhere in the Pee Dee region of South Carolina. The pond rarely gets fished, so I am reminded of that time as a child when my cane pole line landed on the bream bed. Except I needn't be on a bed because the pond is full of fish. The last time I went, I took a bunch of

Mikel with bass on his mother's pond.

cleaned fish (frozen in water in a milk carton) to my sister Nancy. She was beside herself.

Eighty-five percent of the protein eaten by the Khmer here in Cambodia is from dozens of species of freshwater fish. I'm trying to learn the ones I've liked. They're raising cobia, my all-time favorite saltwater fish, in the ocean off Vietnam, so I can now have a fish fry and know what it is going to taste like. Plus, I have a Khmer friend who has a fish restaurant where I can go and have snapper or sea bass any time I want. Or I can have her order fish for me; she gets shipments from down on the coast several times each week. But it's not the same as the thrill of the pull on your line. Setting the hook. Reeling it in. I've spent two hours at a time battling big ones offshore, and I've lost far more than I have caught. But fishing is in my blood, even if I almost never do it. Several of Mikel's colleagues here in Phnom Penh go fishing every chance they get. I should ask them if I can tag along.

Body Count

I wake up to pee and can't get back to sleep, so I obsess over tomorrow's shopping list and dinner party, an essay I'm working on, or, more likely, I count sheep: places I've lived, people I've slept with, teachers I've had. I can remember my teachers in grammar and high school, but junior high and college are a blur. My forgetting the former can be blamed on hormones; the latter, on beer and pot. The addresses I've had—fifty-four, at last count—come easily, but the lovers come and go from my memory. I've stayed in touch with most of the living, but some of them are dead: Keith, Mary, Kent, Bill, John, Alberto, Jeremy, Eric (cancer, cancer, suicide, fire, AIDS, cancer, cancer, AIDS). My mother died when I was thirty-three. She was sixty-two. I never slept with women again. I'm sure both Freud and Jung would have a heyday with that.

My maternal grandfather's was the first death I can recall. I was twelve. I'm now older than he was when he died. That summer, I went to spend some time with my grandmother. Her sadness permeated every conversation and meal, but she taught me domestic skills in both the garden and kitchen that would serve me well years later as a food writer. Kennedy was assassinated the following year. I can recall almost no deaths during the next seven years, through high school and college. I was unfocused and naïve; I wasn't a good learner. I remember the people who died, but I place their deaths years before they were laid to rest. I thought the neighbor across the street was killed in a boating accident when I was in high school, but the internet says it was in 1970. I also placed my mother's best friend's youngest son's skydiving death in the sixties, but he died in 1981. A girl-friend lost both of her parents, and she moved in with another family. They had a bomb shelter where I first kissed her, so I assume we were in high school then. She broke up with me the next day: that, I remember.

The accidental murder of a dear friend's grandparents—who were friends of my parents—I also misremembered as having been during those tumultuous pubescent junior high years, which saw my three best friends—all girls—moving away from town. Anne had lived with her grandparents, and I blamed their deaths on her leaving. But now I see that they didn't die until 1970, and she married in 1971. We were in college then. It's as though the chapters of my life are a manuscript whose pages have been shuffled.

I went away to college in 1967. My friend Mary's brother was killed in an automobile accident. Her mother, Sarah, barely coped. She closed off his room and told me that I had to be there for her, that she considered me her son. She drank heavily. I spent summer evenings after my freshman year playing bridge with Mary and Liboo at Mary's house, if only to be there for Sarah. My parents had forbidden me from coming home from college except on holidays, but Sarah—Mary and I called her "The Bra"—insisted I come one weekend to see the new room she had prepared for me. I hitched a ride with a guy from a neighboring town, but we were stopped at the county line by armed guards: there had been a massacre of Black college students in town, and there was a curfew. Because Sarah's husband was the City Judge, I was taken in a squad car to their home. My driver was re-routed around the county.

The assassinations of Martin Luther King Jr. and Bobby Kennedy, the Vietnam War, Richard Nixon's hateful rhetoric, and the unequal status of Black people, women, and gay people infuriated me. I never moved back home again. I had yet to find a focus in my studies, but I marched for peace and equal rights. My photography hobby turned professional, and in 1972 I returned to school to pursue a master's in film. Both of my grandmothers died when I was in grad school, in 1973 and 1974, respectively. After graduation, I freelanced as a photographer and artist, worked at a wildlife preserve, lived in the Virgin Islands, New York, France, and Italy, and then my mother got sick, and I came home to bury her, only for her to hang on for the rest of the year. My father and I became close. Mama died in our arms. I wrote in my journal at the time, "She flew from us like a moth and her body lay there, an empty cocoon." Everything I knew about my mother had left her body the moment she died. Her death was an awakening moment for me, having witnessed just how final it is.

I moved back to Europe, where it became clear to me that my boyfriend, who had lost his father when he was much younger, and who had spent years in therapy, no longer loved me—despite his having called me every day for nine months, saying otherwise. I landed a job with a French magazine and moved to New York, where AIDS was beginning to take its toll. Ricky was the first among us to go. We were blindsided by his death. In his honor, we replaced some trees in the cherry esplanade at the Brooklyn Botanic Garden. I was making a name for myself in food writing circles, but I never had enough money to truly enjoy the city. Reagan was reelected, the French franc went to hell, and the magazine folded. I moved back to South Carolina to open my culinary bookstore. I renewed friendships with much older people whom I had met there in 1975, when I took my hiatus from grad school. AIDS claimed more friends. Ed and Tommy in New York. Then John and Greg and Bobby. And then Thom in Florida. And Mike in Georgia. The body of a friend in Charleston who died was refused by a funeral home. A Black undertaker agreed to embalm him. I had two back-to-back lovers test positive. I was running the bookstore by myself, and I was past deadline for my first book. I hunkered down to work and was celibate for five years.

Hurricane Hugo put me out of my home and business for a year, from 1989 to 1990. The following year I was working on my final drafts when I got the call from some high school girlfriends: Mary Ashley was dying, and she wanted us all to gather at Edisto Beach, an hour south of Charleston. They wanted me to cook. I arrived late on Saturday evening after closing the shop. There were a half-dozen of my high school girlfriends, most of whom I had not seen more than once since our teenage years. We drank; I cooked; Mary Ashley didn't take her meds so that she could drink with us, one last time. After dinner, we skinny-dipped in the ocean. At some point we saw turtle watchers approaching us on the beach. They patrol at night not only to monitor the loggerhead nests but also to make sure that beach houses don't have lights burning. As the turtle crew approached, they flooded us with their flashlights. We startled them, and Mary Ashley cried out, "What's the matter? Turtle watchers like you never saw a single-breasted night swimmer before?!"

She died soon after. I went to my hometown for the funeral. Strom Thurmond was there. When he died, obituaries noted that he was the longest-serving US Senator in history, but Mary Ashley's father, who had died in 1995, had served longer in the South Carolina State Senate. I returned to Orangeburg twice more, first for my mother's best friend's funeral in 2003, the same year Thurmond died. I was a pallbearer. In 2012, while on tour to celebrate the publication of the twentieth anniversary of my first book, I returned with my childhood friend Nancy Jo to attend my forty-fifth high school reunion. One of the sons of my mother's deceased friend was running the old folks' home outside of town, and he invited me not only to stay there, but to give a lecture. "Bring lots of books. We can seat a hundred and sixty, and it will be a full house." There were people I hadn't seen in sixty or more years. A Sunday school teacher. My fourth-grade teacher. Four or five of my mother's bridge partners. And some of my best friends from high school, and their parents. And some of my sisters' friends. And some of my brother's. I sold a lot of books. I can name at least six of those older folks who have since died.

Over the years, I had lost many colleagues whose work I admired: Bert Greene in 1988, Richard Sax in 1995, and Camille Glenn in 2010. Some, like Bill Neal, who died in 1991, had become dear friends. In 2006, R.W. "Johnny" Apple died. I cooked his last meal. Karen Hess, the culinary historian who had mentored me, died in 2007, and I was profoundly sad. We gathered in New York to celebrate her life. Her son Peter gave me the last wooden spoon she had cooked with. She was a couple of years older than my father, who comforted me over the phone. He knew how important she had been to me.

My parents' friends and my friends' parents were dying, but Daddy lasted until 2008. I had fallen in love with Mikel in 1993; we're still together. My older friends in Charleston began dying: Robert Marks in 1993, John Henry Dick in 1995, Ethel Jane Bunting in 1997, and Alice Marks in 1999, right after I closed the store. The first three years I was open, Alice brought me lunch several times a week. Her pimiento cheese is legendary. Several old-timers who had taught me so much about Lowcountry cooking died. I wrote three more books before I closed the store. And then Ruby Pendergrass Cornwell died. She was just shy of her 101st birthday. I had visited her that day at Bishop Gadsden, where she was living. She was Charleston's Rosa Parks: just before she was arrested for attempting to desegregate the Fort Sumter Hotel's restaurant in 1963, she was told, "Miss Ruby, you know that we don't serve Negroes here," to which she replied, "I wasn't planning on ordering any." We talked about gay rights, and she encouraged me to "always fight for what is right." I had met her through Alice in 1975.

I used to place events chronologically by school year: We went to Panama the summer after third grade; we sailed in the Grenadines my senior year in college. You'd think I could remember when my friends died, but I have to check the obituaries to get the dates right. Now COVID-19 deaths haunt me as I try to sleep. The pandemic seems to have juggled everyone's sense of time. I asked one college friend when Joe Belew died. She couldn't remember, even though she had flown to Washington, where Mikel and I had moved in 2004, to attend the funeral. And so I Google and see that it was in January 2009. I don't remember it being cold. He was such a warm guy, a remarkable man who knew no enemies.

In 2010, Mikel and I were among the first to register for a license in DC, when same-gender marriage became legal. The following year his work took us overseas. A few months later, Liz Young died. She was one of the grandes dames of Charleston, with centuries-old family history in the area. Neither she nor Ruby had ever missed an event at my bookstore. I had met her in 1975 through my sister Nancy, who was a sorority sister of hers, though a generation apart. A week later, Lucille Grant died. Lucille was Black, one of the great cooks of Charleston, from whom I learned more about hospitality than I had in fifty years of living in the South. I called Lucille's daughter Lynn from Bulgaria and asked her what I could do from there. "Send food," she said. My sister Sue went to the Piggly Wiggly and took fried chicken and greens and mac and cheese for fifty. I hated not being there for her family, the way she had always been there for me with my questions and problems.

Mikel lost an uncle. Then both of our fathers died. And then his mentor, his real father figure, died. I lost a first cousin. I had a knee replacement, we moved to China, and from then on time sped up, and I lost the tiny bit of chronological perspective I once had had. There were no more school years to count by, just increasing deaths among our parents' generation and our own. Mikel's mother became frail, and she, too, had to enter a home. We returned to the States and spent the better part of five years apart, he in Washington, and me in Savannah, meeting at his mom's monthly. I lost myself in gardening; Mikel, in his work. Our friend Chuck's husband and son and I were holding Chuck when he died. His last words to me were, "Finish the book!" I rewrote and reworked that novel with recipes several times—in first person, in third person, and as a self-help book. It's still a work in progress.

In 2018, Madeleine Kamman, another of my mentors, died. Then three girlfriends from my youth within a few weeks of each other, all from cancer. I had known them since kindergarten. Though I didn't see Mary often, we did try to get together once a year while she prepared my tax returns. She had ended up caring for both of her parents before they died. Those yearly visits were the only time in the past fifty years that I got to play bridge. I sobbed uncontrollably at her funeral, a spiritless Roman Catholic affair. Her daughter didn't put an obituary in the newspaper because "it cost too much."

I got a call from Keith, my first lover. We had stayed in touch all those years. She was giddy on the phone, high on the drugs they had given her to alleviate the pressure in her brain, which was tumored. She was reminded of our first days of smoking pot in 1967. She wasn't afraid of death. We laughed, we promised to stay in touch. And then she died in December.

In January my mother-in-law died. And then her sister. And then another friend committed suicide. They "passed," they like to say in the South. I think it's meant to imply that they have passed on to another place—heaven, perhaps—but to me it simply means that they passed through this earthly realm, stardust in a different form. But I probably smoked too much pot and paid too much attention to inner voices and song lyrics when I was younger and impressionable. After a week of me sleeping but an hour or two a night, Mikel expresses his concern, and I reply with a Warren Zevon quote: "I'll sleep when I'm dead." We both are now orphans, so he took a job abroad again. There are paintings on our walls here in Phnom Penh done by artists who are no longer with us: Margaret's life-size portrait of me from 1977, its reticulated surface a wonder; a watercolor by Marian Cannon Schlesinger, given to me right after her death at age 105; and paintings by the Haitian masters Felix LaFortune, André Pierre, and Antilhomme. They live on through their art.

Before we moved overseas, I gave my library and papers to educational institutions. I can't imagine what someone could learn from my unpublished song lyrics, short stories, poems, or novels, but the College of Charleston had solicited them. They are like my offspring, and I can remember entire chapters. I sometimes rewrite them in my mind when I can't sleep. I sold my business to my niece for ten dollars. She has battled cancer for years, and a day doesn't go by that I don't worry about her. Two close friends—like me, in their seventies—have been at death's door forever, it seems, but our emails and text messages have always been joyful. Like Keith, I don't fear death. I find comfort in the unknown and in having known so many people whose lives I remember, even if I can't place their deaths chronologically. And the deaths continue: two ex-sisters-in-law died last year; Nach Waxman, who mentored me as a bookseller, died in August; and in October, my dear friend and colleague, the archaeologist and educator Daphne Derven, lost her battle with cancer.

Lately, I count off the COVID-19 victims I've known as I toss and turn. Arnold and Lorlee Tenenbaum died five days apart last March. We were

COVID-free here in Cambodia, and I couldn't imagine how Savannah royalty had succumbed. But people from all walks of life in the States were dying. A nurse. A banker. A truck driver. A politician. And then friends of friends. And then a relative. I try to think of more names as I wallow in my insomnia, but I've lost count, so I start again, this time going through the houses I've lived in. There's a limbo of time between our home in Louisiana, where I was born, and South Carolina, where we moved when I was three. I somehow remember that year, but that was long before the schoolteachers, the sexual partners, or any of the deaths. I count off the houses, dorm rooms, apartments, boats, and trailers I've lived in: places where I used to sleep.

Acknowledgments

Because most of this collection has already been published—in books, newspapers, magazines, scholarly journals, or on the internet—I am hoping that everyone was long ago thanked. I naively thought that I might list only those people who were around for the specific essays included here, but none of this would have happened if it hadn't been for Jean-Sébastien Stehli having hired me to write about food in 1983; moreover, for having me interview Karen Hess. My life changed overnight in both instances. Nach Waxman mentored me as a bookseller. I miss him. My book editors, Fran McCullough, Roy Finamore, Rux Martin, and Elaine Maisner have kept my writing relevant. Fran helped me find my voice in English; Roy inspired me to take up photography again. Elaine introduced me to Aurora Bell, my editor and collaborator on this project. Working with her has been fun. The book is as much hers as mine. I also acknowledge other helpful folks at the press who helped me to pull this book together: Pat Callahan, Jolie Hale, Kemi Ogunji, and Kerri Tolan. Thanks also to Emily Weigel for the groovy dust jacket design. The background is an embroidered story map by the Hmong ethnic minority who settled in the central highlands of Cambodia in the '90s.

The frontispiece by Margaret Katz was painted in 1977 when she was a college student. She did not have a photo to work from, and she had not seen me in several months. It remarkably captures my introspective nature at the time. The larger-than-life-size painting has traveled with me to three continents. It's a constant reminder of my friend, who died in 2015. I dedicated the book to Margaret and a handful of women who are no longer with us but who all influenced who I am. The Huguenot Torte essay that opens the book was first published by William van Hettinga, also deceased, whose cheeky publication was continued by Pete Wyrick. Mary Huguenin helped me in my research of that misbegotten Charleston classic; Joann Yaeger and I developed the recipe together. Joann was always one of my most loyal customers in the bookstore. Many other regular customers kept the wolf at bay: Richard Perry, Bill Hughes, John Bahr, Townie Krawchek, Margaret Passailaigue, and Ray Davis, to name a few. The latter two have bought dozens of copies of my books over the years. The scholars Harlan Greene, Warren Slesinger, and Alexander Moore were among the first to encourage my Lowcountry studies. Many professional farmers, chefs, butchers, and restaurateurs have supported my work or business, among them Frank Stitt in Alabama; Joe Hunt, Terry Berch, and Michael McNally in Philadelphia; Stephen Stryjewski, Donald Link, Wes Kenney, Susan Spicer, Kyle Waters, Jacques Soulas, and Ryan Hughes in Louisiana; Jeff Tunks and Chris Clime in Washington, DC; Bette Kroening in California; Todd Bricken and Neal Langerman in Maryland; James Clark in North Carolina; Bob Sparrow in Michigan; and Frank Lee, Philip Bardin, Bill Twaler, and Tank Jackson in South Carolina. Several magazine and newspaper editors fostered my career: Tina Ujlaki, Jane Daniels Lear, Zanne Early Stewart, Jan Newberry, Joe Yonan, Gale Steves, Donna Warner, Joanne McAllister Smart, Barbara Fairchild, Russ Parsons, Marion Sullivan, Mike Butler, and Eric Asimov. Nancy Harmon Jenkins at the *Journal of Gastronomy* early on championed my research, as did Darra Goldstein at *Gastronomica*, four articles from which are included in this anthology. The International Olive Oil Council, Oldways, and USAID included me on several press junkets that informed these essays. George and Cecilia Holland continue to grind the best grits and cornmeal, and Martin Yordanov in Bulgaria keeps me internet savvy.

From 350 articles, I chose 118 for this collection. We've culled it down to 42. The assembling and editing were done not only during the pandemic but also while I recuperated from surgery. I am forever moved by the loving care that my husband, Mikel Herrington, gave me for the six months of my recovery. He has been my rock for three decades. Here in Cambodia, the staff at Peace Corps has been exceptionally thoughtful and kind, and our friends here have brought me books, food, wine, and good cheer. Many thanks to Muna Haq, Massi Tropeano, Maryellen Countryman, Ben Wohlauer, Lisa Heintz, Matt Cohen, Kathleen Norman, Sopheavy Chea, Sophal Thim, Mike Gebremedhin, Caroline Blair, Véronique Laverdure, Jack Weatherford, Loïc and Caroline De Laubrière, Angie Bushnell, Jim Malster, Lisa Larson, Matt and Justina Edwardsen, Al Schaaf, and Thierry Pradelet at La Ferme de Bassac.

I am especially touched by the fossilized sharks' teeth that Henny Hall sent me from Edisto. Bud Moore confirmed my memories of Nellie Queen Young's fried chicken at his home when we were children. And for help with illustrations, I owe thanks to Michael Lachowski, Robert Reeves, Gerald Wilkie, Sarah Robinson, Kate Bennett, and Lila Taylor.

My family has always been supportive, especially my sister Susan Highfield, who ran my business for several years, and our nieces Jennifer Graham and Sarah Ferrell. My stepmother Lila continues to be generous and kind, years after my father's death. My extended family of friends never fails me, year after year: Dana and Ella Grace Downs, Mary Edna Fraser, Cathy White, Scot Hinson, Elizabeth Schneider, Ken Bullock, Debbie Marlowe, Bob and Julia Christian, Sally Perez, Ann Yow, Richard Little, Gilson Capilouto, Shari Hutchinson, Tim Carrier, Kate Pierson, Keith Strickland, Kelly Bugden, Ann Brody Cove, Sarah Ross, Bessie Hanahan, Betty Alice Fowler, and Betsey Apple. My colleagues Cara da Silva, Anne Mendelson, Andy Smith, and Nancie McDermott are due thanks for their enthusiastic endorsements of my findings. It's been 25 years since I had a book published. Anne Byrn brought me into the 21st century with invaluable advice; we have a mutual admiration society.

How can I properly acknowledge Jessica Harris, who despite her insanely busy schedule, took time to write the foreword? I am humbled. Jessica and I have shared the dais in South Carolina, Louisiana, Mississippi, and New York. We worked together on the first planning committee for the Smithsonian's African-America museum back in the 90s. And she's seen me hollerin' goat. What knowledge I have of the African diaspora is largely because she has shared so much through the years, and not just through her books, but in emails and phone calls and conversations over Champagne. If ever I have had a soul mate, it is she.

Thanks also to Philip Harmandjiev in Bulgaria, Gianni Martini and Ester de Miro in Italy, Marghertia Orsino in France, Nok Noi in Thailand, Courtenay Daniels in New York, Anne McInnis in Georgia, and the Caldarars in Romania. I am grateful for the coveted Amelia Award that Cathy Kaufman and the Culinary Historians of New York presented me. If I have omitted someone, I blame it on my advanced age. I am truly lucky to have been surrounded by joy my entire life. In her review of my first book, Anne Olsen recognized that joy. I hope that this collection is similarly seen.

Index

Recipes are listed in **boldface**. *Italicized* page numbers indicate illustration captions.